LANGUAGE *for* SPECIFIC PURPOSES

Related Titles from Georgetown University Press

Working Portuguese for Beginners
Monica Rector, Regina Santos, and Marcelo Amorim, with M. Lynne Gerber

Working Mandarin for Beginners
Yi Zhou with M. Lynne Gerber

LANGUAGE *for* SPECIFIC PURPOSES

Trends in Curriculum Development

Mary K. Long, Editor

GEORGETOWN UNIVERSITY PRESS
WASHINGTON, DC

© 2017 Georgetown University Press. All rights reserved. No part of this book may be reproduced or utilized in any form or by any means, electronic or mechanical, including photocopying and recording, or by any information storage and retrieval system, without permission in writing from the publisher.

Library of Congress Cataloging-in-Publication Data
Names: Long, Mary K., editor. | International Symposium on Languages for Specific Purposes (2nd : 2014 : University of Colorado Boulder)
Title: Language for specific purposes : trends in curriculum development / Mary K. Long, editor.
Description: Washington, DC : Georgetown University Press, 2017. | The project emerged from the Second International Symposium on Languages for Specific Purposes which was held at the University of Colorado, Boulder in spring 2014. | Includes bibliographical references and index.
Identifiers: LCCN 2016026990 (print) | LCCN 2016040658 (ebook) | ISBN 9781626164185 (hc : alk. paper) | ISBN 9781626164192 (pb : alk. paper) | ISBN 9781626164208 (eb)
Subjects: LCSH: Sublanguage—Study and teaching—United States—Congresses. | Terms and phrases—Study and teaching—United States—Congresses.
Classification: LCC P120.S9 L33 2017 (print) | LCC P120.S9 (ebook) | DDC 401/.47—dc23 LC record available at https://lccn.loc.gov/2016026990

♾ This book is printed on acid-free paper meeting the requirements of the American National Standard for Permanence in Paper for Printed Library Materials.

18 17   9 8 7 6 5 4 3 2 First printing

Printed in the United States of America

Cover design by Martha Madrid.

Dedicated to

Dr. Ellen Haynes and
our International Spanish for the Professions students

In memory of

Dr. Lilian Fernández de Robinson
Pioneer in the field of Spanish for Business
Director, 1973–97
International Spanish for the Professions Major
Department of Spanish and Portuguese
University of Colorado, Boulder

Contents

List of Figures	ix
List of Tables	xi
Acknowledgments	xiii

	Introduction: LSP Studies and the Creation of Translingual and Transcultural Competence *Mary K. Long*	1
1	New Directions in LSP Research in US Higher Education *Lourdes Sánchez-López, Mary K. Long, and Barbara A. Lafford*	13

PART I New Directions in LSP Curriculum Development

2	Developing and Implementing LSP Curricula at the K-12 Level *Mary Risner, Melissa Swarr, Cristin Bleess, and Janet Graham*	37
3	Preparing Students for the Workplace: Heritage Learners' Experiences in Professional Community Internships *Carmen King de Ramírez*	55
4	Developing Intercultural Competence and Leadership through LSP Curricula *LeAnn Derby, Jean W. LeLoup, James Rasmussen, and Ismênia Sales de Souza*	73
5	Developing a More Efficient Conversation Paradigm for Learning Foreign Languages: Lessons on Asking and Answering Questions in an LSP Context *Robert A. Quinn*	87

6 Integrating Project-Based Learning into English for Specific-Purposes Classrooms: A Case Study of Engineering   101
Tatiana Nekrasova-Beker and Anthony Becker

PART II Rethinking Instructor Roles

7 The Instructor's and Learner's Roles in Learning Arabic for Specific Purposes   129
El-Hussein Aly

8 LSP Educators as Informal Career Counselors   143
Annie Abbott

PART III Exploring Workplace Realities

9 Court Interpretation of an Indigenous Language: The Experiences of an Unexpected LSP Participant   157
Mary Jill Brody

10 Señor Google and Spanish Workplace Information Practices: Information Literacy in a Multilingual World   169
Alison Hicks

Conclusion: LSP Studies and the Future of Higher Education   187
Mary K. Long

List of Contributors   191
Index   195

Figures

4.1	Q1: The Scenarios Increased My Understanding of Appropriate Behaviors in the Other Cultures	81
4.2	Q2: The Scenarios Increased My Appreciation of the Relevance of Cultural Understanding to My Career as an Officer	83
6.1	An Engineering ESP Course: Sample TLU Tasks	107
10.1	Visual Representation of the Argentine Architect's Personal Learning Environment	179
10.2	Visual Representations of Student A's Personal Learning Environment	180
10.3	Visual Representations of Student B's Personal Learning Environment	180

Tables

1.1	Which Domain Is (Would Be) Your Preferred Area of LSP Research?	19
1.2	Use of Spoken Languages among LSP Professionals in the Workplace	20
1.3	Characteristics of Authentic Written Texts in Professional Domains	20
1.4	Development of Formal Aspects of Language Use by LSP Learners	21
1.5	Use and Development of Spoken Languages by LSP Learners	21
1.6	The Characteristics of Written Texts Created by LSP Learners	22
1.7	Other Learner-Related and Pedagogical Issues	22
1.8	Programmatic Issues	23
1.9	Domain Content, History, Cultural Perspective, and Interactions with the United States	24
2.1	Activities of the Network of Business Language Educators	41
3.1	Community Placements and Internship Goals	59
3.2	Professional Activities	60
3.3	Grammar/Orthography/Vocabulary	62
3.4	Professionalism and Linguistic Growth	63
4.1	Spanish 221 Results, by Instructor	80
5.1	The Traditional Verb Chart, Present Tense	92
5.2	An Innovative Paradigm for –ar Conjugation, Present Tense	94
5.3	An Innovative Paradigm for –er Conjugation, Present Tense	94
5.4	An Innovative Paradigm for –ir Conjugation, Present Tense	95
6.1	Description of Data Collected during an NA	105
6.2	Discipline-Specific Vocabulary Identified in Corpus-Based Analyses	111
6.3	Knowledge and Abilities Targeted in Project Tasks	112
6.4	Considerations for Project Task Characteristics	115
7.1	Courses on Arabic for Specific Purposes	132
7.2	Roles of Instructors Identified through Classroom Observation	134
7.3	Roles of Learners Identified through Classroom Observation	135
10.1	Coloradan Interviewees	173
10.2	Latin American Interviewees	174

Acknowledgments

Educators and scholars in the field of languages for specific purposes form a community that is uniquely inclusive, generous, and collegial. I have benefited greatly over the years from the experience and wisdom of innumerable colleagues in the field, and many of them have provided support and encouragement for this project. In particular, I am grateful to the authors of the chapters included here for their excellent contributions and professionalism, and to the experts who provided a crucial layer of peer review for each chapter as the volume was being assembled: Helen Basturkmen, University of Auckland, New Zealand; Anne Becher, University of Colorado, Boulder; Kathleen Bollard, University of Colorado, Denver; Esther Brown, University of Colorado, Boulder; Alberto Bruzos Moro, Princeton University; Ame Cividanes, Yale University; Robert T. Conn, Wesleyan University; Carmen Vega Carney, Thunderbird School of Global Management; José M. del Pino, Dartmouth College; Michael Scott Doyle, University of North Carolina, Charlotte; Karen Easterday, University of Colorado, Boulder; Carmen Grace, University of Colorado, Boulder; Michel Gueldry, Middlebury Institute of International Studies at Monterey; Orlando Kelm, University of Texas, Austin; Mark Knowles, University of Colorado, Boulder; Manel Lacorte, University of Maryland, College Park; Roberta Z. Lavine, University of Maryland, College Park; Gillian Lord, University of Florida; Karen Malcolm, University of Colorado, Boulder; Francisco Picado, language access manager for the First Judicial District of the State of Colorado; Danielle Rocheleau Salaz, University of Colorado, Boulder; and Zane Segle, The Citadel. I am also profoundly grateful to Hope LeGro for her belief in the project and to the many professionals at Georgetown University Press for their work to bring the volume to fruition.

The project emerged from the Second International Symposium on Languages for Specific Purposes, which was held at the University of Colorado, Boulder in the spring of 2014 (http://altec.colorado.edu/lsp/). Without the help of the following individuals and groups, this event (and thus this subsequent volume) would not have been possible: the External Advisory Board, made up of Michael Scott Doyle, Barbara A. Lafford, Lourdes Sánchez-López, Sheri Spaine Long, and Mary E. Risner; the organizing committee at the University of Colorado, made up of Anne Becher, Laura Lesta-Garcia, Wladimir Márquez, Mark Knowles, Santé Jonker, and Doreen Williams; the graduate students of the Department of Spanish and Portuguese, who provided logistical support during the conference; Peter Elmore, professor and chair, and my colleagues in the Department of Spanish and Portuguese, who each provided an encouraging word along the way, and specifically to those who moderated panels and staffed the registration desk, Adriana Cabeza, Susan Hallstead, Karen Malcolm, Tania Martuscelli, Nina Molinaro, Susanna Pérez-Pàmies, and Alicia Tabler; colleagues from across campus, who also provided logistical support during the symposium; Francisco Moreno Ramírez, who traveled from Mexico to participate and provided invaluable last-minute organizational support; and Ellen Haynes and Isolde Jordan, who always listen.

This project emerges from a truly interdisciplinary institutional effort that represents the potential of languages for specific purposes to enhance global learning within higher education. Generous funding for the symposium was provided by the Department of Spanish and Portuguese, the Anderson Language and Technology Center, the Department of German and Slavic Languages and Literatures, the Program in International Affairs, Leeds Global Initiatives, the Engineering International Programs, the President's Fund for the Humanities, Pearson Publishing, and the federally funded Center for International Business Education and Research (CIBER) at the University of Colorado, Denver. I would like to offer particular thanks to the CIBER staff—Manuel Serapio, Jana Blakestad, and Melanie Ellison—for many years of crucial encouragement and support.

Finally, I am thankful, as always, for the love and support provided by my family: Rafael Moreno-Sánchez, Angela Moreno-Long, and Elaine Long.

Introduction

LSP Studies and the Creation of Translingual and Transcultural Competence

Mary K. Long

Much has been written since 2000 about the need to prepare students by enabling them to gain high-level language and cross-cultural communication proficiency that will serve them both professionally and personally in the global environment of the twenty-first century. Language and literature departments have been urged to develop multiple interdisciplinary tracks in order to prepare students across a wider array of fields.[1] Most recently, discussions about how best to stimulate students to engage in the study of languages other than English have taken on a sense of both urgency and embattlement because, from many accounts, there is a growing shortage of graduates who possess the language skills to compete globally.[2] Also, in the United States overall enrollments in higher education in languages other than English actually decreased between 2009 and 2013 by 6.7 percent (MLA 2013).[3] This situation has spurred many language and literature departments to explore ways to create new courses as well as new certificates, minors, and degree programs in hopes of attracting, retaining, and thus preparing more students.[4]

The interdisciplinary field of languages for specific purposes (LSP) studies provides many of the student-centered, multidisciplinary curricular design and research elements that have been proposed in these discussions. Moreover, LSP has a long tradition of attracting students and creating "educated speakers who have deep translingual and transcultural competence," the goal established in a 2007 report by the Modern Language Association (MLA 2007, 3).[5] The present volume responds to the growing demand for more in-depth LSP scholarship by offering ten selected, original, peer-reviewed chapters based on some of the thirty-eight presentations given at (or new topics suggested by) the Second International Symposium on Languages for Specific Purposes 2014, which was held at the University of Colorado, Boulder. This volume also builds on the work begun in *Scholarship and Teaching on Languages for Specific Purposes* (Sánchez-López, 2013), a collection of peer-reviewed scholarly articles that emerged from the First International Symposium on Languages for Specific Purposes, which met at the University of Alabama at Birmingham in April 2012.[6] Before giving an overview of the chapters in this volume, it is useful to consider LSP's history, growth, and potential.

In the United States a key LSP foundational moment came in 1946 in the area of business, when the American Institute for Foreign Trade (later known as the Thunderbird School of Global Management) became the first US institution to create an integrated curriculum in which students combined the study of languages other than English with business content and regional/cultural studies (Branan 1998). In the United Kingdom, English for Specific Purposes took hold in the 1960s and stimulated the development of materials and pedagogical approaches for a broader range of professional settings (Sánchez-López 2013, x). Since that time, global interest in the field has expanded to encompass multiple languages and professions. Results from two surveys conducted twenty-one years apart (Grosse and Voght 1990; Long and Uscinski 2012) reveal that offerings in the United States have held steady, with 58 to 62 percent of institutions reporting some level of LSP offerings, which range from one course to entire majors in a variety of languages and professions. Over the years, the sophistication and variety of courses and programs have become more deeply focused and encompass an ever-growing body of research fields (Long and Uscinski 2012; also see chapter 1 in this volume by Sánchez-López, Long, and Lafford).

LSP studies is uniquely positioned to make an impact on students' global education in a wide variety of disciplines because the field has at its center the aim of "fulfilling the communicative needs of a specific group of people within a specific professional context such as medicine, law, sciences, social work, business, translation and interpretation, etc." (Sánchez-López 2013, x). These goals lead to the development of courses and programs that focus on "the integration of language related competencies through connections to other disciplines, comparison of native and target languages and culture and communication with target culture communities" (Lafford 2012, 2). The three basic axes that define any specific purpose focus—language, culture, and the history and current state of the professional domain's content and practice—necessitate the cooperative participation of practitioners and researchers from a variety of theoretical and applied disciplinary backgrounds, including approaches falling under the umbrellas of applied and theoretical linguistics, experiential learning, literary and cultural studies, and all the professional domains.

Yet even with such dynamic elements, LSP has often been underappreciated within the larger language and literature profession in the United States, and many LSP instructors and researchers have found themselves pushed to the margins of departmental and professional communities (Long and Uscinski 2012; chapter 1 in this volume). Although this is, in part, a reflection of the hierarchies between the literature and second language acquisition programs pointed to in the MLA's 2007 report, a further explanation of this tension can be found in the fact that the field of LSP is frequently misdefined as lying exclusively on the instrumentalist rather than the constitutive side of the spectrum of language study described by the report, when in fact LSP's goals lie more in the middle of this spectrum.[7] In addition, there is often a fear that any move toward teaching students pragmatic, "useful," job-oriented skills will undermine the humanities mission to which language and literature departments are committed and also turn language departments exclusively into service departments within the power structures of higher education.

Such narrow definitions miss the full scope and potentially enriching impact of LSP courses and programs on the larger goals of a humanities-focused education, which seek to make an impact on a world where multiple cultures and discourses are being brought together at an ever-increasing rate. LSP courses and programs are far more than simple technical offerings defined by a body of specialized vocabulary; these courses and programs require students to work across disciplines and to acquire a rich depth and breadth of knowledge and skills. LSP courses and programs offer students applied knowledge and skills related to professional domains while at the same time helping them to develop the critical thinking skills and deep cultural knowledge that are at the heart of the traditional humanities education in language and literature. What has changed from the traditional approach to language and literature is not the teaching of literature, culture, critical thinking, and textual analysis, all of which should remain as key offerings within departments. The change lies in the fact that in LSP courses and programs, the categories of texts and situations being analyzed have expanded beyond literature, increasing sources of cultural information and paving the way for the critical tools of textual and discourse analysis to be applied to influential contemporary texts and discourses generated by a broad array of private, governmental, and nongovernmental institutions that seek to direct global views and practices. Thus, as students learn, for example, to discuss contracts and corporate finance, or to engage in dialogue with patients about their medical conditions, or to interpret legal discussions in a courtroom, or to carry out leadership roles in multicultural contexts at home and abroad, they are simultaneously learning to work with different and often blended cultures, assessing the needs of multiple players in order to avoid conflict and create mutually beneficial outcomes (Long 2003, 2010).

Another significant aspect of LSP courses and programs is the student-centered nature of the curricular design process. This does not so much represent a change within the language and literature disciplines. Instead, it reflects pedagogical research on the learning process, which has led to insights about the best methodologies for engaging learners.[8] As Sánchez-López (2013, x) notes,

> The specificity of LSP depends largely on the students themselves. . . . Courses are usually developed according to (1) the student level of communicative competence, (2) the urgency to use the language in a professional context, (3) the specific characteristics of such context, and (4) the design of a program that promotes the learning process. . . . For all these reasons, LSP represents the teaching of languages according to learners' characteristics, and its teaching is closely determined by these elements.

The student-centered nature of LSP creates new roles for both students and instructors. For some instructors, the idea of designing courses and programs that "[attempt] to give learners access to the language they want and need to accomplish their own academic or occupational goals" (Belcher, quoted by Sánchez-López 2013, x) may seem to promote a problematic, even dangerous, disregard for the wisdom and insights to be found in the rich and substantial body of scholarship dedicated to the literary and artistic production in languages other than English. These concerns are valid, to some degree. It is important to emphasize that LSP studies should not displace traditional literature programs but instead should be added as another curricular option that complements and extends the reach of both general language studies as well as programs focused on literature, culture, and the arts. The most successful LSP programs include courses in a variety of approaches to several disciplines and put students into contact with experts in each field while also putting them, in their LSP courses, in contact with instructors who embrace interdisciplinary openness and are able to help students connect and create bridges between multiple knowledge sources and discipline-specific methodologies (Long 2010). The student-centered approach to curricular design provides instructors with valuable opportunities as educators; and this approach also leads to deeper motivation on the part of students, which can lead to more complete knowledge retention. This greater level of motivation and engagement on the part of students allows instructors to enhance students' own understanding of what they *want* to learn in pursuit of their professional goals with the deeper contextual and content knowledge that instructors know they also *need* in order to fully understand the historical, moral, and human parameters of their professional calling. Ultimately, this can lead to a fuller integration of advanced language proficiency with both practical and critical thinking skills as well as more transcendent cultural, literary, and domain content knowledge. At the level of the individual, the practical skills enhance students' ability to get a job and compete in the global marketplace; and the critical thinking skills and cultural, literary, and domain knowledge provide them with a frame for intellectual, ethical, and emotional growth, both as individuals and world citizens as they move through the many jobs that will shape their careers. At the societal level, students will be well prepared to deal with the inherent ambiguities and complexities of the contemporary globalized world; and over their lifetime, in their careers they will in turn influence and ultimately define future policies and practices in the multiple professional fields that shape contemporary society. Thus, the field of LSP studies is one of the frontiers at which we, as instructors and scholars, have the opportunity to further society's understanding of globalization "as a process which is not just happening to us but which we can direct through analysis and critical thought" (Long 2003, 73–74).

The chapters in this book explore the many angles of LSP discussed here from new perspectives that open pathways for incorporating LSP techniques and topics into a broader spectrum of courses and programs. Chapter 1 presents the results of a nationwide survey conducted by Lourdes Sánchez-López, Barbara A. Lafford, and Mary K. Long during the spring and summer of 2014. This survey's principal objectives were to identify areas of research interest as well as research needs as defined by LSP scholars and practitioners in US higher education. Specifically, the survey identified (1) research areas in which LSP scholars and practitioners currently engage; (2) the future areas and priorities for expanding research that they identify; (3) challenges to carrying out LSP research in the United States; and (4) areas for improvement in LSP research, pedagogy, and program development.

The rest of this volume is divided into three parts. Part I comprises five chapters. In chapter 2, Mary Risner, Melissa Swarr, Cristin Bleess, and Janet Graham explain that an emphasis on language study for the professions or specific purposes at the K-12 level holds the potential to increase articulation between secondary and postsecondary institutions and to improve perceptions of foreign language learning as a valued workplace skill. The authors describe current initiatives that connect language and culture study across diverse industry contexts. Three model courses are highlighted that focus on LSP: Spanish for Leadership, Medical Spanish, and World Language and Business Leadership.

In chapter 3, Carmen King de Ramírez explores how LSP curricula that include professional community internships and service learning components can help heritage learners (HL) enrolled in language programs to meet their academic and professional goals. She provides an overview of studies that address how LSP curricula have been implemented in courses designed for HL populations, the importance of providing HLs with service learning opportunities, and new research regarding HLs who completed 135-hour professional community internships in order to obtain a minor in Spanish for the professions.

In chapter 4, LeAnn Derby, Jean LeLoup, James Rasmussen, and Ismênia Sales de Souza of the US Air Force Academy present the results of a multilevel, multilanguage project designed to integrate the concepts of intercultural competence with leadership development at the academy. The chapter reports the design and findings of the study that documented the impact of the inclusion of cultural scenarios involving an explicit leadership component in four different language courses—French, German, Portuguese, and Spanish—at beginning, intermediate, and advanced levels. Through both embedded assessments and an add-on questionnaire for participants, the data gathered support recommendations for course design modifications intended to make leadership development more visible as an integral component of foreign language learning. This project can serve as a model for other foreign language programs, both civilian and military, that seek to combine intercultural competence with leadership development. The authors provided additional materials that could not fit into the book; they are freely available on the Georgetown University Press website (press.georgetown.edu). These resources are further described in the chapter.

In chapter 5, Robert A. Quinn emphasizes the need for a more efficient approach to teaching conversation in order to strengthen the teaching of question/answer processes in career-focused, technologically delivered courses. He describes action research that led to the design of an innovative conversation paradigm, then compares and contrasts the traditional chart for teaching verb forms with a new and more effective paradigm. Because question/answer processes involve a language "universal," teachers of all languages can adapt the new paradigm, which displays, clarifies, and simplifies the give-and-take in the question/answer processes that are at the heart of communicative language teaching. Because the new paradigm combines both the input and output sides of conversation and is conceptualized as a summary rather than an instructional introduction, it reveals relationships between grammar topics that seem disparate in existing textbooks because they are categorized according to the traditional parts of speech and compartmentalized into separate chapters. The author predicts that as LSP instructors continue to improve their methodological foundation for the technological delivery of course content, the process of developing similar paradigms promises to reveal even more relationships that are not currently noticed. Discovering and analyzing these relationships may eventually help us integrate grammar topics into a more cogent, cohesive whole.

In chapter 6, which closes part I, Tatiana Nekrasova-Beker and Anthony Becker provide an example of the importance of encouraging dialogue between English for specific purposes and LSP practitioners. Their chapter presents the example of integrating project-based language learning into an engineering course for international students on which English-language and engineering content instructors collaborated. The detailed steps they provide (from needs analysis, through defining tasks and designing scaffolded activities, to the development of assessments tools) can be implemented in any course in any discipline in any language. The authors provided additional materials that could not fit into the book; they are freely available on the Georgetown University Press website. The resources are further described in the chapter.

The two chapters in part II expand on the area of the instructor's and learner's roles in unique ways. In chapter 7, El-Hussein Aly explores the roles of the instructor and the learner in courses on Arabic for specific purposes, noting that although there is a large body of literature on instructors' roles in English for specific purposes, little attention has been given to other languages used for specific purposes. Furthermore, although the role of instructor has been the focus of some studies, little attention has been paid to the contributions of learners to language learning and teaching in an LSP course. Data derived from four courses in Arabic for specific purposes through methodological triangulation indicated that the instructor plays six roles in addition to teaching; he or she (1) identifies learners' needs, (2) elicits information on learners' needs, (3) assesses learners' needs, (4) provides material that meets learners' needs, (5) evaluates the material, and (6) advises the learners. The learner performs two roles besides learning: identifying his or her needs and providing feedback. The study has clear implications for teacher training programs given that training in the various roles of instructor may contribute positively to the success of language courses for specific purposes.

In chapter 8, Annie Abbott takes a candid look at the many factors that can cause LSP faculty members to feel pulled by their university, department, and students to provide informal career services on an extracurricular basis outside the classroom and beyond the course that have heretofore been the sole domain of a campus career center. Although LSP instructors are uniquely positioned to provide career-specific linguistic and cultural insights, taking on this informal role of career counselor might mean that LSP educators carry an invisible workload, as researchers cited by Abbott have also noted. Abbott discusses how to mitigate this burden by making the invisible workload visible while also streamlining it so that as much work as possible is done only once and then reused with each cohort of students. She shows how technological platforms provide an ideal venue for high-impact informal career counseling for LSP students and provide models that can help instructors avoid the need to devote massive amounts of repetitive group or individual time to students.

Part III presents dilemmas that arise when academic training complements yet falls short of workplace needs. Both chapters in this part suggest paths to confront these circumstances. In chapter 9, Mary Jill Brody describes the experience of becoming and serving as a court interpreter in the United States for an "exotic language," Tojol-ab'al, a Maya language spoken in Chiapas State in Mexico. The chapter is organized as a discussion of a series of questions about such interpretation situations and ends with several suggestions about how this kind of work might be facilitated. Brody's background as a linguistic anthropologist informs her work as an interpreter, and the differing goals and perspectives of these two approaches inform her analysis. The language of the law is an LSP par excellence, and interpretation is hampered by many factors. She identifies cultural barriers, ethnolinguistic barriers, and translation barriers to carrying out the work of court interpretation. And her suggestions for facilitating court interpretation include building in extra time for the interpreter and being open to cultural differences.

In chapter 10, Alison Hicks asks the question "What does the term 'information literacy' mean?" in order to open a deeper discussion about the nature of workplace information literacy, positioning it as a skill that is both essential for the workplace yet underdeveloped within higher education. She explores what information literacy looks like within the globalized, multilingual environments that language learners enter upon graduation and how these realities can be scaffolded in the classroom. After positioning her discussion within the most current research and thinking on the topic, she explores results from twelve semistructured interviews that she carried out with Spanish-speaking working professionals in Argentina, Chile, and the United States. Encompassing a variety of professions, these interviews were designed to provide a snapshot of both bilingual and Spanish-language information practice in the workplace as well as to serve as teaching and learning resources for the classroom. Hicks concludes by describing how workplace information is starting to be introduced in the classroom at the University of Colorado, Boulder. Throughout the chapter, she situates the concept of workplace information literacy within the goals of world language learning in order to start a much broader conversation about the possibilities and the potential of workplace information literacy within the classroom.

Notes

1. Two MLA studies (2007, 2009) thoroughly explore the multiple angles of these concerns.
2. E.g., as Risner and colleagues note in chapter 2 of this volume, "The United Kingdom's *Languages: The State of the Nation* ... claim[s] that there is 'strong evidence of a growing deficit in foreign language skills at a time when globally the demand for languages is expanding.'"
3. This decrease has not completely erased gains made in the past decade, and it is important to note that overall enrollments in languages other than English are still higher now than they were in the first decade of the twenty-first century (though still lower than the peak enrollments of the mid-1960s). Nevertheless, the goal is to increase enrollments (for all the reasons listed above), and furthermore, in the current budgetary climate of higher education, any drop in enrollments can threaten administrative support of programs.
4. The thorough and thoughtful articles in volume 23, number 2, of the *ADFL Bulletin* (ADFL 2015) provide a useful overview of current concerns around these issues.
5. Historically, the nomenclature for the field has followed a pattern of linking the language and the professional focus or specific purpose together; e.g., French for business and medical Spanish. Mike Doyle reflects on the importance of a nomenclature change for the full indication of all that is included in business language studies: "Although it has existed for many decades in the national curriculum of US higher education, the study of languages for business purposes has lacked a more serviceable and academically communal name—a more rigorous toponymic identity—by which to identify itself as a theory-based field of scholarship. The intention here is to propose for consideration a name modification for an existing field and provide some reflections regarding its evolution, theory, and method. In keeping with the rise of interdisciplines in other 'studies' programs, business language's empirically definable domain of inquiry, pedagogy, and curriculum development should more appropriately be known as Business Language Studies" (Doyle 2012, 105). These observations are pertinent for the entire field of LSP studies, and the nomenclature LSP studies is used in this introduction in order to reflect its nature as a theory-based field of scholarship.
6. The joint Third International Symposium on Languages for Specific Purposes / CIBER Business Language Conference took place at the downtown Phoenix campus of Arizona State University in March 2016.
7. "At one end, language is considered to be principally instrumental, a skill to use for communicating thought and information. At the opposite end, language is understood as an essential element of a human being's thought processes, perceptions, and self-expression; and as such it is considered to be at the core of translingual and transcultural competence. While we use language to communicate our needs to others, language simultaneously reveals us to others and to ourselves. Language is a complex multifunctional phenomenon that links an individual to other individuals, to communities, and to national cultures" (MLA 2007, 3).

8. Though "most researchers agree that LSP pedagogy has been consistently learner-centered, long before the term became main-streamed in pedagogy" (Sánchez-López 2013, x).

References

ADFL (Association of Departments of Foreign Languages). 2015. *ADFL Bulletin* 43, no. 2. https://adfl.mla.org/bulletin/issue/adfl.43.2.

Branan, Alvord G. 1998. "Preface." In *Spanish and Portuguese for Business and the Professions*, edited by T. Bruce Fryer and C. Gail Guntermann. Lincolnwood, IL: AATSP / National Text Book Company.

Doyle, Michael Scott. 2012. "Business Language Studies in the United States: On Nomenclature, Context, Theory, and Method." *Modern Language Journal* 96, no. s1: 105–21. doi: 10.1111/j.1540-4781.2012.01276.x0026-7902/11/105-121.

Grosse, Christine Uber, and Geoffrey M. Voght. 1990. "Foreign Language for Business and the Professions at US Colleges and Universities." *Modern Language Journal* 74, no. 1: 36–47.

Lafford, Barbara A. 2012. "Languages for Specific Purposes in the United States in a Global Context: Commentary on Grosse and Voght (1991) Revisited." *Modern Language Journal* 96, no. s1: 1–27. doi: 10.1111/j.1540-4781.2012.01294.x 0026-7902/11/1-27.

Long, Mary K. 2003. "Globalization or Colonization? Teaching Culture for Business while Promoting Social Equity: A Comparative Study of the Use of a Canonical Definition of Latin American Identity in Latin American Literature and Philosophy with the Use of This Same Definition of Identity in the Marketing of Latin America and Latin American Products." *JOLIB: Journal of Language for International Business* 14, no. 1: 71–85.

———. 2010. "Spanish for the Professions Degree Programs in the United States: History and Current Practice." In *How Globalizing Professions Deal with National Languages: Studies in Cultural Studies and Cooperation*, edited by Michel Gueldry. Lewiston, ME: Edwin Mellen Press.

Long, Mary K., and Isabella Uscinski. 2012. "Evolution of Languages for Specific Purposes Programs in the US: 1990–2011." *Modern Language Journal* 96, no. s1: 173–89. doi: 10.1111/j.1540-4781.2012.01303.x0026-7902/11/173-189.

MLA (Modern Language Association). 2007. *Foreign Languages and Higher Education: New Structures for a Changed World*. New York: MLA. www.mla.org/pdf/forlang_news_pdf .pdf.

———. 2009. *Report to the Teagle Foundation on the Undergraduate Major in Language and Literature*. New York: MLA. www.mla.org/pdf/2008_mla_whitepaper.pdf.

———. 2013. *Enrollments in Languages Other Than English in United States Institutions of Higher Education*. New York: MLA. www.mla.org/pdf/2013_enrollment_survey.pdf.

Sánchez-López, Lourdes, ed. 2013. *Scholarship and Teaching on Languages for Specific Pur-*

poses. Birmingham: University of Alabama, UAB Digital Collections. http://contentdm.mhsl.uab.edu/cdm/compoundobject/collection/faculty/id/161/rec/19.

Sánchez-López, Lourdes, Mary K. Long, and Barbara A. Lafford. 2017. "New Directions in LSP Research in US Higher Education." In *Language for Specific Purposes: Trends in Curriculum Development*, edited by Mary K. Long. Washington, DC: Georgetown University Press.

1 | New Directions in LSP Research in US Higher Education

Lourdes Sánchez-López, Mary K. Long, and Barbara A. Lafford

In contrast to other parts of the world, where the field of (non-English) languages for specific purposes (LSP) has a well-established research tradition, in the United States, LSP has historically been an applied field with little funding, support, or recognition for in-depth research.[1] However, this is changing, as interest in LSP research and in the development of LSP course and program offerings continues to expand in higher education in the United States (Doyle 2012, 2013; Doyle and Gala 2014; Lafford 2012a, 2012b; Spaine Long 2010, 2013). For instance, course and program offerings in LSP (business, the health care professions, translation and interpretation, law enforcement, etc.) have increased throughout the country over the last twenty years (Long 2013; Long and Uscinski 2012; Sánchez-López 2010, 2012). Similarly, the number and variety of scholarly publications, conferences, symposia, and pedagogical materials in LSP have also multiplied in recent years (Lafford 2012a, 2012b; Spaine Long 2010; Sánchez-López 2013). The authors (who have been key participants in the LSP national dialogue for over a decade) were motivated by the enthusiastic discussion that evolved during the First International Symposium on Languages for Specific Purposes (2012) and the subsequent scholarly volume *Scholarship and Teaching on Languages for Specific Purposes* (Sánchez-López 2013). These discussions highlighted the urgent need for a stronger research agenda and the joining of forces to investigate the overall current state of LSP research in higher education in the United States. This chapter presents the results of a nationwide survey conducted during the spring and summer of 2014. The principal objectives of the study were to identify areas of research interest as well as research needs as defined by LSP scholars and practitioners in US higher education.

The need for a stronger LSP research agenda in the United States to strengthen the non-English LSP field has been a focal point of discussion in recent years.

In addition to the importance of research to a deeper understanding of human interaction within the global setting and to the development of solid, comprehensive curriculum and course materials, a stronger LSP research agenda will play a key role in solidifying the status of non-English LSP within academia. Lafford (2012b) suggested that non-English LSP in higher education in the United States must follow the lead of the fields such as CALL (computer-assisted language learning), translation studies, and ESP/EAP (English for specific purposes / English for academic purposes) internationally so that it grows into a recognized and valued subfield of applied linguistics. It will be only then, she maintains, that non-English LSP will obtain the place it deserves in the academy. Doyle, in his keynote address at the First International Symposium on Languages for Specific Purposes (2012) and in his subsequent essay in *Scholarship and Teaching on Languages for Specific Purposes* (2013), also addressed the need for a stronger research agenda in LSP studies (particularly in non-English LSP) while strengthening pedagogies and resources. In his essay, he called for the development of "non-English LSP theory development working groups to further develop theoretical cartographies and narratives" (2) and urged non-English LSP scholars and educators to expand on their work in theory and methodology to develop a general theoretical model, "essential to the maturation of the field" (First International Symposium on Languages for Specific Purposes 2012, 11). Both his keynote address and essay generated a rich and ongoing discussion among participants about the immediate need to strengthen the LSP agenda.

In search of clarity and understanding of the national LSP arena status, Long (2013) conducted a study of the LSP job announcements posted on the Modern Language Association (MLA) Foreign Language Job Information List. Her study intended to find answers to the new state of the foreign language profession in light of the 2007 MLA report "Foreign Languages and Higher Education: New Structures for a Changed World," which recommended that the language disciplines decenter away from literature and design programs that are more directly related to everyday life and applied contexts (MLA 2007). Long's article shed new light on foreign language professions by presenting a multiyear analysis of LSP MLA job announcements. Her results concluded that there does not seem to have been a dramatic increase in the quantity of LSP positions but rather a steady demand at a level that is similar to other less common research fields. However, there are indications that the LSP positions are becoming better defined as announcements move away from the "laundry list" format to specific visions for new programs. Also, Long noted that there is a slight increase in tenured and tenure track primary LSP positions and that these positions are also slowly becoming more focused on specific regional and-or discipline needs. Nevertheless, these announcements do not present a unified vision of LSP research fields. In the job descriptions analyzed by Long, LSP positions are coupled with requirements for a variety of advanced degrees—including literature and cultural studies, applied linguistics, second language (L2) acquisition, and occasionally simply a specialization in a specific LSP area (i.e., Spanish for business) with no degree requirement listed at all. The complex, multidisciplinary nature of LSP job descriptions is emblematic of the central tensions and dilemmas for LSP research in the United States and has led scholars from both literary/cultural studies and from applied linguistics to similar conclusion in relation to preparing future professors for the field. In her study, Long concluded that rather than decentering completely off of literature, that the most feasible approach to providing PhD candidates with well-rounded preparation for the demands of the job market would be for doctoral programs with a strong literature tradition to gradually expand into complementary LSP areas. Similarly, as part of the solution to the overall lack of adequate academic training for LSP instructors, Lafford (2012b, 16) proposed the development of LSP tracks within established applied linguistics graduate programs "in order to produce applied linguists with a solid LSP academic foundation."

The main objectives of the First International Symposium on Languages for Specific Purposes (2012) were to bring together both English and non-English LSP scholars and practitioners to create a much-needed national infrastructure; to serve as a venue to share and generate debate, thoughts, and new ideas; and to serve as a springboard for the development of a larger platform that could strengthen the non-English LSP field because "collaboration, integration and unity are key elements for the success of our growing field" (Sánchez-López 2013, vii). With the overwhelming success of the Second International Symposium on Languages for Specific Purposes (2014) and the Third International Symposium on Languages for Specific Purposes / CIBER Business Language Conference (2016), the infrastructure has been solidified, the network has been amplified, and the pathway to a stronger discipline has clearly been established. Most important, the assertion made by Doyle and others that the non-English LSP discipline must strengthen its research agenda to achieve meritorious recognition is now more prominent than ever. Furthermore, the importance of a solid research agenda goes far beyond simply solidifying the status of the LSP discipline and points to the central role of universities in creating and transmitting knowledge. For example, as Lafford (2013) has noted, studies of acquisition of L2s in LSP and workplace settings can shed light on the effect of context on L2 acquisition in general. Research can also shape the ethical direction of the field. For example, from the perspective of cultural interaction, a deeper understanding of historical and cultural contexts of domains such as business, medicine, and law can help to ensure equitable interactions in the global setting (Long 2003). As interest in the LSP discipline grows nationwide, it is essential that processes of creating new undergraduate and graduate programs be informed by ongoing research that will continue to enrich and inform the field. The main objective of our study is to help give the above-mentioned research agenda a better-defined direction with a more meaningful and common purpose.

Research Questions

Through this survey, we sought to answer four specific research questions: (1) What are the research areas in which LSP scholars and practitioners currently engage? (2) What future areas and priorities for expanding research do they identify? (3) What are the challenges for carrying out LSP research in the United States? and (4) What are areas for improvement in LSP research, pedagogy, and program development?

Methodology

The field of LSP incorporates a variety of academic disciplines and content domains. We strove to reflect the richness of the field in both the design of the survey instrument and the selection of participants.

Survey Instrument

The survey was developed during the fall of 2013 and distributed via Survey Monkey in two rounds during the spring and summer of 2014.[2] The survey consisted of a maximum of fifty-three questions. For respondents who stated that they are not engaged or interested in LSP research, the survey automatically skipped a large number of the questions. Questions 1 through 11 asked about respondents' demographic information, such as gender, title, qualifications, type of institution, state, position, and degree. Questions 12 through 21 asked about respondents' language program characteristics, such as languages offered, LSP offerings, and LSP faculty. Questions 22 through 53 concentrated on LSP research. In particular, questions 23 and 24 asked about whether or not the respondent was engaged in LSP research or would like to be engaged in it. If the answer to these two questions was no, then the survey finished. If the answer was yes, then the survey continued until the end. Questions 26 through 33 asked about the topics that constitute the focus of the respondent's LSP research. Questions 34 through 37 asked about the respondent's preparedness and training to conduct LSP research. Questions 38 through 51 focused on LSP research interests, including topics, domains, instruments, types of analysis used, and LSP research area priorities. Finally, questions 52 through 53 asked respondents for their opinions about LSP needs for improvement in general and challenges to LSP research. A summary and an analysis of the data are presented and discussed below. Although the data sample is not large, it provides the authors with a clearer understanding of the current state of LSP research in American higher education, with more informed data about its perceived challenges and priorities and about who LSP researchers currently are or potentially will be in the near future.

Domain areas in the survey reflect the offerings nationwide based on previous surveys, program reviews, and trends at national conferences. Research fields have been defined by (1) existing research and (2) the authors' knowledge of the field from the perspectives of L2 acquisition and applied linguistics as well as literary and cultural studies. It is important to note that the authors recognize that some domain/research areas—for example, translation and interpretation, exist independently from the field of LSP—but they also represent a specific LSP domain and research area with unique LSP characteristics and therefore were included in the survey.

Participants

The survey was sent to previously identified LSP scholars and practitioners in higher education in the United States as well as a random sample of department chairs and directors listed by the Association of Departments of Foreign Languages and the MLA. The survey was sent to a total of 528 individuals, via e-mail messages. Fourteen messages came back as undeliverable, and 18 came back with "out-of-office" notices. Of the 426 e-mails that went through, 150 people (35 percent) answered at least part of the survey. The data show that there was a broad range of languages, types of departments, and LSP programs represented in this survey. There were twice as many female respondents (69 percent) as males (31 percent). Eighty percent of participants have a PhD, and 78 percent are tenured or tenure track faculty. Sixty percent teach at a research institution, while 21 percent work at liberal arts institutions and 9 percent teach at community colleges. More than half the participants (58 percent) have taught LSP.

Forty-four of 114 respondents (39 percent) replied yes to the question "Are you currently engaged in LSP research?" Of the 70 individuals who indicated that they are not currently engaged in LSP research, another 28 (40 percent) stated that they would be interested in conducting research in the future. It is these 72 respondents (44 of whom are already engaged in research and 28 of whom are interested in conducting research) who provide the most pertinent insights in response to the questions about current and future research fields.

Presentation of percentages in the analysis of data are meant to aid in quantifying results. No statistical analysis has been performed, because the point of the survey was not to determine statistically significant cause-and-effect relationships but rather to get a snapshot of current issues related to LSP research.

Survey Results

The results of the survey, which are presented in this section, address these topics: preferred research domain areas, topics that do (or would) constitute the focus of LSP research, research areas that will most benefit students, areas that affect LSP research production, research preparedness and interest in research training, the need for improvement in LSP areas, and the greatest obstacles to conducting LSP research. This results section is followed by a discussion of the results, recommendations for future LSP research, and suggestions for removing the obstacles that currently hinder the production of LSP research.

Preferred Research Domain Areas

Both those engaged in research and those who would like to carry out research in the future were asked to rank thirteen domain areas in response to the question "Which domain is (or would be) your preferred area of LSP research? (Mark all that apply)." Table 1.1 shows these domain areas in order of preference for current research in the left-hand column and provides data on future interest areas in the right-hand column.

The top six preferred domain areas for those currently engaged in research were as follows: business (46 percent), culture (46 percent), translation (36 percent), academic purposes (33 percent), service learning / community engagement (31 percent), and health care (28 percent). Among those who would be interested in conducting research in the future, there was a marked increase in interest in the areas of business and academic purposes among the top six current research domain areas. However, overall, the largest differences in interest, between current and future domain areas (respectively) for research interests are seen in diplomacy (5 vs. 30 percent), international development (7 vs. 27 percent), academic purposes (33 vs. 43 percent), and interpretation (10 vs. 20 percent). Throughout the study, only differences of 10 percent or more are considered to be notable changes.

Topics That Do (or Would) Constitute the Focus of LSP Research

The section of the survey on topics that do (or would) constitute the focus of LSP research delved deeply into the details of the varied focuses of LSP research,

Table 1.1 Which Domain Is (Would Be) Your Preferred Area of LSP Research? (Check all that apply)

Domain	Engaged in Research (number of responses; 39 total responses)	Interested in Engaging in Research (number of responses; 30 total responses)
Business	18 (46%)	10 (33%)
Culture	18 (46%)	13 (43%)
Translation	14 (36%)	9 (30%)
Academic purposes	13 (33%)	13 (43%)
Service learning / community engagement	12 (31%)	12 (40%)
Health care	11 (28%)	8 (27%)
Law	5 (13%)	5 (17%)
Social work	4 (10%)	5 (17%)
Interpretation	4 (10%)	6 (20%)
Media / journalism	3 (8%)	4 (13%)
International development	3 (8%)	8 (27%)
Diplomacy	2 (5%)	9 (30%)
Tourism	1 (3%)	2 (7%)
Other	9 (23%)	3 (10%)

which span areas traditionally defined by applied linguistics / L2 acquisition and others that fall more within the realms of communication, history, and cultural studies. The authors combined their years of experience in the field of LSP along with their different backgrounds in linguistics, L2 acquisition, and literary and cultural studies to create this list, which includes both established research areas and areas that we consider have potential for growth. These questions addressed a total of eight overarching categories, with a number of subcategories within each. Tables 1.2 through 1.9 provide the complete list of options. In our discussion, we limit ourselves to a consideration of the dominant trends.

Table 1.2 shows the results for the category *use of spoken languages among LSP professionals in the workplace*. Those who are currently engaged in research focus most on registers (73 percent), followed by pragmatics (69 percent), conversational structures (65 percent), selection of language (50 percent), and structure of professional presentations (46 percent) in workplace settings. New research interests show an increase in research interests related to conversational structures (65 vs. 82 percent) and the structure of professional presentations (46 vs. 64 percent).

Table 1.3 shows the results for the research area *characteristics of authentic*

Table 1.2 Use of Spoken Languages among LSP Professionals in the Workplace (Check all that apply)

Topic Subcategory	Engaged in Research (number of responses; 26 total responses)	Interested in Engaging in Research (number of responses; 22 total responses)
Formal vs. informal registers	19 (73%)	15 (68%)
Pragmatics	18 (69%)	15 (68%)
Conversational structures	17 (65%)	18 (82%)
Selection of language	13 (50%)	10 (46%)
Structure of professional presentations	12 (46%)	14 (64%)

Table 1.3 Characteristics of Authentic Written Texts in Professional Domains (Check all that apply)

Topic Subcategory	Engaged in Research (number of responses; 27 total responses)	Interested in Engaging in Research (number of responses; 22 total responses)
Reflection of cultural perspectives	24 (88%)	18 (82%)
Genre-specific features	16 (59%)	15 (68%)
Other	8 (30%)	2 (9%)

written texts in professional domains. Interestingly, current researchers focus more on cultural perspectives (88 percent of current researchers vs. 82 percent of future researchers), while future researchers are more interested in genre-specific features (59 percent of current researchers vs. 68 percent of future researchers).

In relation to the *development of formal aspects of language use by LSP learners in workplace environments and LSP classrooms* (table 1.4), there is high and steady interest in semantics (vocabulary) (96 vs. 96 percent) and syntax (91 vs. 100 percent), both currently and for the future, and a marked increase, above 10 percent, in interest in the areas of morphology (70 vs. 86 percent) and phonetics/phonology (52 vs. 73 percent).

The next two questions pertain to *oral and written language production by LSP learners in the workplace and within LSP classrooms.* Table 1.5 shows that with regard to spoken language, all four options (pragmatics, conversational structures, language selection, and professional presentation) are considered highly interesting by both current and future researchers. The largest difference can be seen in

Table 1.4 Development of Formal Aspects of Language Use by LSP Learners in Workplace Environments and LSP Classrooms (Check all that apply)

Topic Subcategory	Engaged in Research (number of responses; 23 total responses)	Interested in Engaging in Research (number of responses; 22 total responses)
Semantics	22 (96%)	21 (96%)
Syntax	21 (91%)	22 (100%)
Morphology	16 (70%)	19 (86%)
Phonetics/phonology	12 (52%)	16 (73%)

Table 1.5 Use and Development of Spoken Languages by LSP Learners in the Workplace and LSP Classrooms

Topic Subcategory	Engaged in Research (number of responses; 23 total responses)	Interested in Engaging in Research (number of responses; 23 total responses)
Pragmatics	21 (91%)	20 (87%)
Conversational structures	19 (83%)	21 (91%)
Language selection	17 (74%)	20 (87%)
Professional presentations	17 (74%)	20 (87%)

the categories of language selection and professional presentations, which both increased from 74 to 87 percent.

With regard to LSP learner written language, table 1.6 shows that cultural perspectives are equally important to both current and future researchers (92 and 91 percent), while the category of genre-specific features of nonnative speakers' LSP texts shows an increase in interest, from 72 percent of current researchers to 91 percent of future researchers, which brings it on par with cultural perspectives.

In the area of *other learner-related/pedagogical issues* (table 1.7), the top five issues are the development and assessment of intercultural competence, heritage learner development in internships and in the classroom, LSP learner motivations, language learning strategies, and communication strategies. Future researchers are less interested in the areas of language learning strategies (57 vs. 41 percent) and heritage learner language development (70 vs. 32 percent). Instead, this group shows an increased interest in communication strategies (53 vs. 73 percent), assessment of language skills (47 vs. 73 percent), identity formation (33 vs. 46 percent), and social networks (23 vs. 68 percent).

Table 1.6 The Characteristics of Written Texts Created by LSP Learners in Workplace Settings and LSP Classrooms

Topic Subcategory	Engaged in Research (number of responses; 25 total responses)	Interested in Engaging in Research (number of responses; 22 total responses)
Cultural perspectives	23 (92%)	20 (91%)
Genre-specific features	18 (72%)	20 (91%)

Table 1.7 Other Learner-Related and Pedagogical Issues

Topic Subcategory	Engaged in Research (number of responses; 30 total responses)	Interested in Engaging in Research (number of responses; 22 total responses)
Development and assessment of intercultural competence	21 (70%)	17 (77%)
Heritage learners language development in CSL/internship and LSP classrooms	21 (70%)	7 (32%)
LSP learner motivations	18 (60%)	13 (59%)
Language learning strategies	17 (57%)	9 (41%)
Communication strategies	16 (53%)	16 (73%)
LSP learner attitudes	15 (50%)	10 (46%)
Assessment of language skills of LSP learners in CSL internships and LSP classrooms	14 (47%)	16 (73%)
Identity formation in LSP interns in CSL/internships and LSP classrooms	10 (33%)	10 (46%)
Development of social networks in LSP interns in CSL/internships and LSP classrooms	7 (23%)	15 (68%)
Other	5 (17%)	1 (5%)

Table 1.8 addresses research in relation to *programmatic issues*. Top current programmatic issues are LSP materials development and LSP course development, followed by LSP service learning, LSP course assessment, and LSP program assessment. The biggest increases in interest between current and future research are in the areas of differences and similarities between LSP and language for general purposes (32 vs. 62 percent), the effectiveness of methodology/pedagogical

Table 1.8 Programmatic Issues (Check all that apply)

Topic Subcategory	Engaged in Research (number of responses; 34 total responses)	Interested in Engaging in Research (number of responses; 21 total responses)
LSP materials development	24 (71%)	14 (67%)
LSP course development	21 (62%)	15 (71%)
LSP service-learning/community engagement at home and abroad	15 (44%)	9 (43%)
LSP course assessment	14 (41%)	10 (48%)
LSP program assessment	14 (41%)	8 (38%)
Application of technology to teaching of LSP	13 (38%)	10 (48%)
Effectiveness of methodology/pedagogical interventions in the LSP classroom	13 (38%)	14 (67%)
Differences and similarities between LSP and languages for general purposes	11 (32%)	13 (62%)
LSP instructor training	11 (32%)	13 (62%)
Current state of LSP	11 (32%)	12 (57%)
LSP instructor assessment	11 (32%)	6 (29%)
History of LSP	4 (12%)	5 (24%)

interventions (38 vs. 67 percent), the current state of LSP (32 vs. 57 percent), the history of LSP (12 vs. 24 percent), and application of technology to the teaching of LSP (38 vs. 48 percent).

Table 1.9 covers a variety of topics related to domain content, history, cultural perspectives, and interactions with the United States. The greatest amount of current research is being carried out in the areas of cultural perspectives (of any variety) (61 percent), and this topic remains stable in relation to future research interests (62 percent). The areas that show the greatest trends of increased interest between current and future perspectives are as follows (ordered from greater to lesser differences):

- Perceptions of US involvement/impact in the affairs of the target language culture abroad from the perspective of that culture (14 vs. 48 percent).
- History of the US involvement/impact in the domain in the target language culture abroad (11 vs. 38 percent).
- History of domain content (4 vs. 29 percent).

Table 1.9 Domain Content, History, Cultural Perspective, and Interactions with the United States

Topic Subcategory	Engaged in Research (number of responses; 28 total responses)	Interested in Engaging in Research (number of responses; 21 total responses)
Cultural perspective (of any variety)	17 (61%)	13 (62%)
Contemporary view of domain content and practice in general target language culture	8 (29%)	12 (57%)
Comparative study of domain content and practices between target and native culture workplace setting	7 (25%)	12 (57%)
Perception of the English dominant culture in the United States from the perspective of target language culture in the United States	7 (25%)	9 (43%)
Perceptions of US involvement/impact in the affairs of the target language culture abroad from the perspective of that culture	4 (14%)	10 (48%)
History of the US involvement/impact in the domain in the target language culture abroad	3 (11%)	8 (38%)
History of domain content	1 (4%)	6 (29%)
Other	3 (11%)	2 (10%)

- Comparative study of domain content and practices between the target and native culture workplace setting (25 vs. 57 percent).
- Contemporary views of domain content and practice in the general target language culture (29 vs. 57 percent).
- Perception of English as the dominant culture in the United States from the target culture perspective (25 vs. 43 percent).

Finally, the last question in the area of research topics reveals that 94 percent of respondents believe that LSP / community service learning (CSL) / internship research should be carried out in both foreign (abroad) and domestic environments.

Research Areas That Will Most Benefit Students

In addition to the questions about current and future research areas and potential interest on the part of researchers, another perspective that we took to establish research priorities was to ask participants to rate, in order of importance, five of twenty-six research areas from which participants believe their *students* would benefit the most. The area names are the same used for the overarching categories from the current and future research questions. Appendix 1A shows the survey question with all twenty-six research areas. In the discussion here, we consider the top eleven research priorities in descending order of importance. Respondents were asked to list the top five priorities in order from one to five, with one being the most important and five being the least important.

The results show that respondents consider the most important priorities to be related to understanding native speaker oral and written modes in professional contexts, with professional oral language use by native speakers in the workplace (2.35; response count, or RC: 52/60) and the characteristics of written professional documents (2.54; RC: 37/60). The next three areas are related to the meta-themes of LSP teaching methodology (2.64; RC: 28/60), program development (2.72; RC: 18/60), and development and assessment of intercultural communicative competence in the LSP classroom (2.72; RC: 29/60). Cultural perspectives and contemporary views are next, with a score of 2.84 for each (RC: 37 and 32/60, respectively) followed by development and assessment of nonnative speaker oral and written LSP usage in the classroom (2.86; RC: 28/60) and community engagement at home and abroad (2.87; RC: 23/60). The last two of the top eleven are LSP instructor training (2.94; RC: 34/60) and LSP learner communication strategies (2.95; RC: 37).

Areas That Affect LSP Research Production

The survey includes questions about several factors that can affect the production of LSP research: research preparedness and interest in research training; areas in greatest need of improvement in the field of LSP overall; and, finally, the greatest obstacles to conducting LSP research.

Research Preparedness and Interest in Research Training

Only 26 percent of respondents self-identify as being well or extremely well prepared to carry out LSP research. The most attractive forms of research training would be face-to-face short workshops (82 percent), webinars (82 percent), and online short courses (77 percent). Eighty-eight percent of respondents would take advantage of such training, but only one-third (33 percent) want continuing education credits for that training.

Need for Improvement in LSP Areas

Appendix 1B shows all sixteen areas included in the question about which LSP areas most need improvement. Here we present the results for the top eight. The number one area in need of improvement is quality of LSP materials (1.79; RC: 86/88). This corresponds to the research priorities shown above, which are related to native speakers in the workplace, because increased results in these areas of research would make it possible to create more authentic materials. The remaining areas in need of improvement relate mostly to the ongoing need for formalized institutional recognition of all issues related to LSP as a field. The priorities in this area would be to first improve faculty support and overall recognition of LSP as a field (1.86; RC: 85/88) and then to increase LSP instructor training (1.98; RC: 82/88). Strengthening the field would also involve supporting more successful implementation of internships (1.98; RC: 80/88) as well as implementation of community and community service learning partnerships (2.01; RC: 79/88). Opportunities for LSP professional development (2.02; RC: 81/88), expansion of LSP course offerings (2.10; RC: 81/88), and more LSP conferences (2.13; RC: 82/88) were also among the areas in need of improvement.

The Greatest Obstacles to Conducting LSP Research

Not surprisingly, many of the points made in the previous two categories are echoed in the questions related to obstacles to conducting LSP research. The responses show that the primary obstacles to LSP research are a lack of institutional rewards (2.10; RC: 60/60), a lack of recognition of LSP as a field (2.13; RC 54/60), and a lack of research training (2.24; RC: 56/60), followed by a lack of LSP infrastructure (organizations, 2.41, RC: 56/60; conferences, 2.43, RC: 56/60; publication venues, 2.46, RC: 56/60), a lack of appropriate LSP assessments (2.49; RC: 53/60), and a lack of interest by LSP practitioners in carrying out LSP research (2.71; RC: 54/60).

The following summary provides a different view of these challenges to LSP research grouped into institutional and disciplinary challenges, beginning with the factor that the results indicated as the most important.

A. Institutional
1. Lack of institutional rewards.
2. Lack of departmental and institutional recognition.
3. Resistance to change.
4. Lack of interest in LSP.

B. Disciplinary
      1. Lack of recognition of LSP as a field.
      2. Lack of graduate programs in LSP.
      3. Lack of faculty research training in LSP.
      4. Lack of LSP pedagogical training for faculty.
      5. Few LSP professional organizations, conferences, and publication venues.
      6. Lack of appropriate LSP assessment.
      7. Lack of interest in LSP by practitioners.

Interestingly, respondents believe that there exists a somewhat balanced combination of research challenges, which stem from institutional historical traditions in American higher education and challenges that derive from the LSP discipline itself. This summary of challenges to LSP research illustrates how a vicious cycle emanates from the institutional side, moves to the discipline-specific side, then bounces back to the institutional side again, and so forth. Each set of challenges has an impact on and is affected by the other, creating a flowing cycle with a boomerang effect. For example, if institutions maintain a historically hierarchical system with traditional disciplines on top, and then newer, applied disciplines are placed at a secondary level, it is difficult for these new disciplines—without the appropriate support—to develop the kind of graduate and teacher training programs and level of scholarship necessary to advance to the top of the institutional strata.

Discussion and Recommendations

As noted in the introduction, the need for a stronger LSP research agenda in the United States as a prerequisite for reinforcing the non-English LSP field and elevating its status in academe has been a focal point of discussion in recent years. This chapter has presented the results of a nationwide survey conducted to identify areas of research interest, as well as research needs, as recognized by LSP scholars and practitioners in US higher education. The survey results have revealed a rich diversity of interests, topics, and potential disciplinary approaches that reflect the complexities of the contemporary global context, which seems to simultaneously demand research that furthers theoretical knowledge while also mapping out best practices for applying this knowledge to human interactions. The survey results have helped the authors identify research areas where LSP scholars and practitioners are currently engaged as well as the main future areas and priorities for expanding research. The results have also shed important light on the main challenges and obstacles to carrying out LSP research in the United States, as well as the principal areas for improvement in LSP research, pedagogy, and program development. These results are useful to help give the LSP research agenda a better-defined direction with a more meaningful and common purpose.

Of particular importance, the study results have identified that the top six current research domain areas coincide with the future top research interests: business, culture, translation, academic purposes, service learning / community engagement, and health. Furthermore, the top four domains with the highest increase between current and future research areas are diplomacy, international development, business, culture, and interpretation. These results not only reflect stability in the field but also a future potential shift that suggests changes in the world related to globalization. To this end, some implications may be the ample possibilities of collaborations among English and non-English LSP scholars around the world to build an international network of scholars and practitioners with common goals. Another direct implication is the necessity to establish more and stronger partnerships with international companies and organizations for formalized LSP service learning and internships. In a similar way, an increased interest in diplomacy, international development, business, culture, and interpretation indicates an awareness of the economic and social effects of globalization and the need to communicate with newer societies for professional purposes. These results may also indicate a future need to develop and offer new LSP courses and programs based on these increasing interests. This information is useful now for current administrators and program directors as they develop and revise existing strategic plans, conduct program assessments, and look into expanding collaborative and interdisciplinary efforts through external grants and institutional seed funds. Finally, these results can be also useful to publishers, editors, and conference organizers as they prepare volume and conference themes.

Another important conclusion gleaned from the results is the fact that the top two research areas believed to be most directly beneficial to students—*understanding native speakers' oral and written modes in professional contexts with professional oral language use by native speakers in the workplace* and the *characteristics of written professional documents*—do not coincide directly with current or future research. This indicates that there are specific new avenues to explore, where LSP scholars can engage in more formal and traditional types of theoretical linguistics research (e.g., conversation and discourse analysis). Other more applied research areas also listed as being beneficial to students (*LSP teaching methodology, program development, instructor training,* and *development and assessment of intercultural communicative competence in the LSP classroom*) fall within current research areas. This indicates that the research that is currently being conducted potentially has an immediate pedagogical application, necessary for the establishment, sustainability, and growth of the field. Finally, other areas of research regarded as beneficial to students are *cultural perspectives, contemporary views, the development and assessment of nonnative speaker oral and written LSP usage in the classroom,* and *community engagement at home and abroad.* This variety of perceived beneficial areas indicates that there are ample opportunities and possibilities for an array of research areas, from theoretical linguistics to pedagogy to applied linguistics to cultural studies, which can lead to more and more fruitful interdisciplinary, interdepartmental, and external (with companies, health care entities, agencies, etc.) collaborations and partnerships.

A third important conclusion is that the survey results have identified several factors that can challenge the production of LSP research. For example, only one-fourth of respondents feel adequately prepared to carry out LSP research. This is related to the fact that most current LSP scholars in the United States do not have a formal background in LSP, falling into a large category of LSP self-trained linguists, applied linguists, and cultural studies experts. Results suggest that LSP training workshops, webinars, and online short courses would be beneficial and welcomed by current researchers and practitioners and also indicate the need to develop graduate courses in order to prepare future LSP scholars, both from the perspective of applied and theoretical linguistics and from that of literary and cultural studies.[3] Other primary obstacles to LSP research that were identified are a lack of institutional rewards, a lack of recognition of LSP as a field, a lack of LSP infrastructure (organizations, conferences, and publication venues), a lack of appropriate LSP assessments, and a lack of interest by LSP practitioners in carrying out LSP research. This last point may be a direct consequence of the previous challenges identified, all of which form a vicious cycle difficult to overcome unless specific measures are addressed. Unfortunately, unless the non-English LSP research agenda in the United States grows, strengthens, and solidifies, most of the challenges identified will not improve. Furthermore, unless some of these challenges (institutional rewards and adequate recognition of LSP discipline) improve, the non-English LSP research agenda will not be strengthened in a meaningful and visible way.[4]

Nevertheless, concrete steps can be taken to eliminate some of the obstacles faced by LSP researchers. First, university and department administrators and researchers themselves must take an honest look at hierarchies of research values in relation to current pressures, both to increase enrollments and to prepare US students for careers without losing sight of the primary role of universities and the scholars they employ in the creation of knowledge. Both theoretical and applied research are vital to achieving all these goals, yet within the rewards structures of higher education, theoretical research is often privileged over applied. Concomitantly, in fields focused on providing students with the knowledge and skills to secure specific employment, research that is aimed at producing historical, theoretical, and critical insights is often scorned as impractical and even superfluous. Yet increased economic, political, and environmental pressures on the global population will create an ever-more-urgent need for multilingual world citizens who possess both applied skills and historical and theoretical knowledge as well as critical analysis abilities that will enhance cross-cultural communication and cooperation in a variety of professional settings. It is clear from this survey that LSP studies is a field uniquely positioned to provide the research necessary to meet these global needs. To this end, universities and their academic departments must be open to the multidisciplinary nature of LSP studies. LSP scholars, for their part, must continue to pursue research and to serve as peer reviewers for the work of their colleagues, with confidence that increased research production will continue to solidify and formalize the field. The results of this survey point to a vibrant and engaged community of such researchers.

Appendix 1A

Question 50. From which LSP research areas do you think that your LSP students would benefit the most? Indicate only your top five selections, with number one being the highest priority. 1 2 3 4 5

- Professional language use by NSs [nonnative speakers] in workplace
- Characteristics of written professional documents
- Development/assessment of LSP oral and written learner language in LSP classrooms
- Development/assessment of LSP oral and written learner language in CSL/internships
- Development/assessment of intercultural competence in LSP classrooms
- Development/assessment of LSP intercultural competence in CSL/internships
- LSP learner attitudes/motivation
- Development of social networks
- LSP learner/communication strategies
- Identity formation in LSP interns in the workplace
- LSP teaching methodology
- LSP instructor training
- LSP instructor assessment

- Application of technology in LSP courses/internships
- LSP course development
- LSP course assessment
- LSP program development
- LSP program assessment
- LSP materials development
- CSL/community engagement at home and abroad
- Comparative study of domain content and practices between target and native culture workplace settings
- Contemporary societal, political, economic views of domain content and practice in the general target language cultures (whether abroad or in the United States)
- History of domain content and practices in the target language culture (whether abroad or in the United States), e.g., history of corporate development in Argentina, or history of small Hispanic-owned businesses in Denver, or history of Korean concepts of IV delivery of vitamin solutions as vital health service
- History of US involvement/impact in the domain in the target language cultures abroad (e.g., the history of the United Fruit company in Central America; military intervention to protect US investments; or, on the "positive" side, US postwar aid and medical/nutritional training programs)
- Perceptions of US involvement in the affairs of the target language culture abroad from the perspective of that culture, i.e., How are the "good works" or donation of goods and services in a voluntourism or missionary trip received/perceived by the host culture; how does US military/political intervention in the past still shape contemporary interpretations of US nationals operating in the host setting?
- Perceptions of English dominant culture in the United States from the perspective of target language cultures in the United States

Appendix 1B

Question 52. In your view, please indicate the overall need for improvement in the following LSP areas by using the following ratings: 1, extremely needed; 2, very needed; 3, somewhat needed; 4, not very needed; 5, not needed; or 6, not at all needed:

- Community partnerships for CSL/internships
- Expansion of LSP course offerings

- Expansion of LSP program offerings
- Faculty support and recognition for LSP as a field
- LSP conferences, symposia, and workshops
- LSP instructor assessment
- LSP instructor training/preparation
- LSP learner outcomes assessment
- LSP program assessment
- LSP program development preparation
- Professional development of LSP instructors in the field
- Quality of LSP materials (textbooks, websites, etc.)
- Quality of LSP scholarly publications
- Quantity of LSP scholarly publications
- Successful implementation of SL/internships
- Use of technology in LSP instruction

Notes

1. The field of English for specific purposes (ESP) has an established research tradition both within the United States and abroad. However, within US institutions of higher learning, ESP is taught within ESL/TESL programs, which are traditionally not housed in the non-English language departments. The emphasis in this survey on issues of research in LSP field is not meant to imply that LSP research should develop entirely independently of ESP, for there are many shared issues. Nevertheless, there are also realities specific to research and teaching in the area of LSP, and the focus of this article is primarily on those realities. Possible links between LSP and ESP theory, pedagogy, and practice will be discussed in the conclusions.
2. The authors are grateful to Izabela Uscinski for her invaluable work with Survey Monkey throughout the length of the project.
3. There are already some early models for such graduate courses. For example, Ruggiero (2014) has published about the creation of graduate courses for languages for specific purposes that include elements of cultural studies and social engagement.
4. On the bright side, since our survey was distributed in 2013, significant steps to improve and solidify the LSP infrastructure have been taken in the areas of LSP conferences and publication venues. The International Symposium on Languages for Specific Purposes (ISLSP) has become an established biannual academic gathering with a critical partnership with CIBER, starting from the Third ISLSP, which met at Arizona State University–Phoenix in 2016. Future joint ISLSP/CIBER Business Language Conferences are already scheduled for 2018 and 2020, and venues have been discussed for 2022. In parallel and as a direct consequence of the ISLSPs, LSP publication venues are also increasing, with the publication of this volume and a later volume, *Language for Specific Purposes: Developing Skills to Serve Domestic and International Communities*

(working title), edited by Barbara A. Lafford and Carmen King de Ramírez. Finally, a last important step to solidify the LSP infrastructure is the current progress that is being made toward the establishment of an LSP professional association in the United States.

References

Doyle, Michael S. 2012. "Business Language Studies in the United States: On Nomenclature, Context, Theory and Method." *Modern Language Journal* 96, no. s1: 105–21. doi: 10.1111/j.1540-4781.2012.01276.x 0026-7902/11/105–121.

———. 2013. "Continuing Theoretical Cartography in the Languages for Specific Purposes Era." In *Scholarship and Teaching on Languages for Specific Purposes*, edited by Lourdes Sánchez-López. Birmingham: University of Alabama, UAB Digital Collections. http://contentdm.mhsl.uab.edu/cdm/singleitem/collection/faculty/id/163/rec/2.

Doyle, Michael S., and Candelas Gala, eds. 2014. "Spanish for the Professions and Other Purposes." Special Issue of *Cuadernos de ALDEEU* (Asociacion de Licenciados y Doctores Espanoles en Estados Unidos) 28 (Autumn). https://clas-pages.uncc.edu/michael-scott-doyle/wp-content/uploads/sites/264/2012/12/Doyle-editing-co-author-Spanish-at-the-United-States-Air-Force-Academy-Developing-Leaders-of-Character-as-an-LSP-Curricular-Model.pdf.

First International Symposium on Languages for Specific Purposes. 2012. University of Alabama at Birmingham, April 12–13.

Lafford, Barbara. 2012a. "The Evolution of Languages for Specific Purposes: Update on Grosse and Voght (1991) in a Global Context." *Modern Language Journal* 96, no. s1. doi: 10.1111/j.1540-4781.2012.01294.x 0026-7902/11/1–27.

———. 2012b. "Languages for Specific Purposes in the United States in a Global Context: Commentary on Grosse and Voght (1991) Revisited." *Modern Language Journal* 96, no. s1: 1–27. doi: 10.1111/j.1540-4781.2012.01294.x0026-7902/11/1–27.

———. 2013. "The Next Frontier: A Research Agenda for Exploring Experiential Language Learning in International and Domestic Contexts." In *Selected Proceedings of the 16th Hispanic Linguistics Symposium*, edited by Jennifer Cabrelli Amaro, Gillian Lord, Ana de Prada Pérez, and Jessi Elana Aaron. Somerville, MA: Cascadilla Proceedings Project.

Long, Mary K. 2003. "Globalization or Colonization? Teaching Culture for Business while Promoting Social Equity: A Comparative Study of the Use of a Canonical Definition of Latin American Identity in Latin American Literature and Philosophy with the Use of This Same Definition of Identity in the Marketing of Latin America and Latin American Products." *JOLIB: Journal of Language for International Business* 14, no. 1: 71–85.

———. 2013. "Language for Specific Purposes Job Announcements from the Modern Language Association Job Lists: A Multiyear Analysis." In *Scholarship and Teaching on Languages for Specific Purposes*, edited by Lourdes Sánchez-López. Birmingham: University of Alabama, UAB Digital Collections. http://contentdm.mhsl.uab.edu/cdm/singleitem/collection/faculty/id/165/rec/7.

Long, Mary K., and Izabela Uscinski. 2012. "Evolution of Languages for Specific Purposes Programs in the United States: 1990–2011." *Modern Language Journal* 96, no. s1: 173–89. doi: 10.1111/j.1540-4781.2012.01303.x 0026-7902/11/173–189.

MLA (Modern Language Association). 2007. *Foreign Languages and Higher Education: New Structures for a Changed World*. New York: MLA. www.mla.org/pdf/forlang_news_pdf.pdf.

Ruggiero, Diana. 2014. "Graduate Courses in Languages for Specific Purposes: Needs, Challenges, and Models." *Global Business Languages* 19, no. 5: 55–69. http://docs.lib.purdue.edu/gbl/vol19/iss1/5/.

Sánchez-López, Lourdes. 2010. "El español para fines específicos: La proliferación de programas creados para satisfacer las necesidades del siglo XXI." *Hispania* 93, no. 1: 85–89. doi:129.219.247.33.

———. 2012. "Spanish for Specific Purposes." In *Encyclopedia of Applied Linguistics*, edited by Carol Chapelle. Oxford: Wiley Blackwell.

———. 2013. "Introduction." In *Scholarship and Teaching on Languages for Specific Purposes*, edited by Lourdes Sánchez-López. Birmingham: University of Alabama, UAB Digital Collections. http://contentdm.mhsl.uab.edu/cdm/compoundobject/collection/faculty/id/161/rec/19.

Spaine Long, Sheri, ed. 2010. "Special Section: Curricular Changes for Spanish and Portuguese in a New Era." *Hispania* 93, no. 1.

Second International Symposium on Languages for Specific Purposes. 2014. University of Colorado, Boulder, April 17–19. http://altec.colorado.edu/lsp/index2014.shtml.utf8.

Third International Symposium on Languages for Specific Purposes / CIBER Business Language Conference. 2016. Arizona State University, March 17–19. https://cls.asu.edu/lsp2016.

PART I
New Directions in LSP Curriculum Development

2 | Developing and Implementing LSP Curricula at the K-12 Level

Mary Risner, Melissa Swarr, Cristin Bleess, and Janet Graham

Multiple reports on desirable job skills for the future assert the need for global communication and intercultural skills to succeed in today's increasingly interconnected economies (Economist Intelligence Unit 2012; Language Flagship 2009; Workforce 20/20 2011–13; Fenstermacher 2013). In spite of these reports, others, such as the United Kingdom's *Languages: The State of the Nation* (Tinsely 2013), claim that there is "strong evidence of a growing deficit in foreign language skills at a time when globally the demand for languages is expanding." A 2014 US report, *Language Enterprise, Languages for All?* (Abbott et al. 2014), also cites an increased demand for language skills but points to a lack of preparedness in education to give students this training. So what curriculum changes can be made to meet this demand to adequately prepare students with the language and culture skills they need for the twenty-first-century workplace?

Fryer (1986) pointed out four reasons for integrating business terminology into language curricula: (1) the need to function in an international business environment, (2) the need to communicate in an increasingly linguistically diverse society, (3) the need for real-world communication skills, and (4) the fact that general *business* skills are a part of everyday life. His arguments are even more relevant today and apply across disciplines such as health care; law; education; and science, technology, engineering, and mathematics. Applying strategies for languages for specific purposes (LSP) in language course design is one way to prepare students with advanced communication and cross-cultural skills while helping them see how they can apply these skills in their personal and professional lives.

The purpose of this chapter is to emphasize the importance of connecting foreign language and culture study to professional contexts and real-world applications, starting at the secondary level. In this chapter we first provide an overview of LSP at the secondary level and highlight K-12 initiatives to date. We then describe three models currently being offered in the areas of leadership, health care, and global business. The chapter concludes with recommendations for how to continue to develop K-12 LSP models.

The Current State of LSP Curricula in Secondary Education

Crouse (2013) describes LSP as a focus on helping students discover and practice the types of language they need to meet their specific professional goals. Long (2010, 37) provides a more extensive definition of LSP, highlighting the shift in text content and real-world content in the curricula: "Spanish [or any other language] for any 'professional use' is much more than a technical course and in fact requires both the critical thinking skills and cultural knowledge that are at the heart of traditional humanities education in language and literature. What has changed from the traditional approach to language and literature is not the teaching of literature, culture, critical thinking and textual analysis, but rather the sorts of texts and situations being analyzed."

Doyle (2013, 3) states that Spanish for business at the postsecondary level has "evolved from curricular margin to mainstay," and recent findings by Long and Uscinski (2012) show that LSP courses are now solid curricular options and are increasing in variety across languages and professions. LSP courses and publications are still sparse at the secondary level but are growing gradually through a variety of initiatives, many supported by the US Department of Education (DOE) funding through the Centers for International Business Education and Research (CIBERs).

The K-12 literature that is available emphasizes business language specifically, with less reference to other professional fields such as health care, law, or translation. Grosse's (1988) study aimed to determine to what extent business language had been integrated into the secondary curriculum. She gathered data by surveying the state foreign language supervisors of the twenty most populous states and consulted district foreign language supervisors to get more detailed responses where necessary. Findings were that very few states offered business language courses or included them in state course listings. Massachusetts, Tennessee, Virginia, and Louisiana reported having some form of business language course offering, but only Florida and Wisconsin had "Spanish for business" in their state course directories. In response to a question regarding the future implementation of business language courses, supervisors did not foresee such offerings, because they felt that other state mandates took priority in the curriculum and that students barely had time to master basic Spanish without adding on specialized language. In light of the findings in the secondary environment of the time, Grosse's recommendation was for teachers, where possible, to integrate supplementary units into their already-existing courses.

As a follow-up to Grosse's study at the secondary level twenty years later, Risner (2006) presented a paper on the state of business language in secondary schools at the 2006 Annual CIBER Business Language Conference. She contacted each state supervisor with programs listed in Grosse's 1988 results. None reported any business language or LSP activity. However, courses may have been available that were not known by each state. Through other sources, it was found that Florida did have high school Spanish for business and for health care courses (Port Charlotte) and that California offered business Spanish (San Diego) at the time. The Purdue CIBER International Business Education Outreach Initiatives for the K-12 Level (CIBER 2008) served as a supplemental source for identifying K-12 CIBER-funded activities, including curriculum development, international fairs, workshops, and meetings on how to promote business language at the K-12 level; but there were no official course offerings.

Two other sources addressing secondary business language by Fryer (1986) and Takami (2010) focus more on suggestions for K-12 curriculum design rather than assessing the business language presence at the K-12 level. Fryer (1986) suggested integrating business language content at the secondary level by developing proficiency-based units pegged to the standards of the American Council on the Teaching of Foreign Languages (ACTFL) rather than specialized courses. He also proposed using case studies in the classroom and making interdisciplinary connections with economics. Takami (2010) uses examples of high school business Japanese units to illustrate how national foreign language standards can be aligned with the business language curriculum.

A key contribution to the promotion of LSP in K-12 is the fact that ACTFL, with more than 11,000 members (many teaching at the K-12 level), is now taking more decisive action to promote the importance of language and career connections across the disciplines. The 2013 issue of *The Language Educator* was a prime example—it included the article "Languages for Specific Purposes in the 21st Century," by Crouse (2013), which highlighted current LSP initiatives in K-12 and across a variety of disciplines.

Another K-12 article proposes secondary LSP training through annual state foreign language conferences (Risner and Markley 2013). The authors present a model for an LSP-themed state conference to raise awareness of the professional applications of language to student careers, promote connections with state and local industry professionals, and help teachers design and implement future LSP course offerings.

K-12 Initiatives

Encouraging K-12 activities by including them as a competitive priority in DOE grant proposals for CIBERs has helped promote K-12 projects during the last fifteen years. For instance, the Purdue CIBER published a manual of CIBER-funded K-12 outreach activities that promoted the area of business language in 2003, 2005, and 2008. The K-12 Business Language Conference sponsored by the Florida International University CIBER is in its seventh year. The University of Pennsylvania CIBER business language summer institute has been offered since 2002. In 2011 LSP began to be included as a track at the Florida Foreign Language Association, and continues to be offered.

With the goal of addressing the challenges mentioned above of integrating LSP into secondary schools' programs, the Network of Business Language Educators (NOBLE) was established with support from two DOE Title VI centers at the University of Florida, the Center for Latin American Studies, and the CIBER (Risner 2009a, 2009b, 2011). The NOBLE project began in 2009 as a community of practice to bring together educators interested in curriculum development and program building that seeks to integrate the study of foreign languages and cultures across disciplines. Some NOBLE activities to date that meet the needs of furthering LSP integration in K-12 are listed in table 2.1.

Three Models

A compelling case has been made for the benefits for students, language programs, and society at large of connecting language learning to other aspects of students' lives, including their future professions (Chen 2014; Fryer 1986; Klein 1988; Morrison 2014). This section of this chapter uses Long's (2010) definition of LSP to inform three innovative course models developed and delivered by high school teachers in Colorado, Kansas, and Pennsylvania. The courses cover three diverse professional areas: Spanish for leadership, medical Spanish, and world language and business leadership. In addition to the five Cs of language education—communication, cultures, connections, comparisons, and communities—these courses address the ACTFL *21st-Century Skills Roadmap*'s interdisciplinary themes of entrepreneurial, health, and financial literacy, respectively (ACTFL 2011).

All three courses are unique at the K-12 level, where the shift from traditional language and literature courses to LSP-based content is less common and even more difficult to implement than at the postsecondary level. Each has been developed to entail minimal costs, thanks to the vision, time, and dedication of the

Table 2.1 Activities of the Network of Business Language Educators

Activity	Need Filled
Workshops	Provide training and resources for teachers
Advocacy videos	Provide materials to convince administrators of value of language/culture
Exhibit booths at conferences	Raise national awareness of LSP across languages (ACTFL, SCOLT, AATSP, etc.)
Organize and copresent with K-12 teachers	Empower K-12 teachers with voice to showcase their work
Sponsor teacher attendance at LSP conferences	Provide free professional development for teachers
State conference theme/strand	Raise awareness of LSP for teachers who can attend only local conferences
Compile/develop/contribute curriculum materials	Increase availability of materials for other K-12 teachers
Webinar series	Provide affordable and easily accessible training
Social media / monthly LSP newsletter	Raise awareness of LSP news, resources, and events

teacher creating the course. Each model describes the motivation for developing the courses, key components of coursework, and outcomes.

Spanish for Leadership

There were at least two reasons for proposing to teach the "Spanish for leadership" course at a high school in Colorado. First, students needed additional Spanish offerings (besides advanced placement Spanish and advanced conversation) because the enrollment of sophomores in Spanish 4 classes had increased. Second, there was a demand for a course that would give students a further advantage in their future career options.

Course Structure
The course was structured as a one-credit offering in a public high school. The course is on the accelerated block schedule, which means the class meets every day for 85 minutes for one semester. If the course were offered in a traditional

school schedule, the class would meet every day for 50 minutes all year long. The prerequisite for this course was being able to communicate at an intermediate-mid level, according to the ACTFL Proficiency Scale, which meant completion of a level IV course or outside experience (ACTFL 2012). The course was divided into four major units: business skills, career interest projects, qualities and characteristics of good leaders, and business and cultural etiquette.

Course Activities

A fundamental goal of this course was that students would acquire real-life skills in Spanish that they would be able to transfer to any future job. The course was called "Spanish for Leadership" to attract students who were interested in all different types of careers. Offering the course with a more specific focus could have deterred students from enrolling and could also have limited the type of content included. In alignment with ACTFL benchmarks, the purpose of this course was to have the students gain confidence in their ability to use Spanish in all three modes of communication—interpersonal, presentational, and interpretive; to develop cultural competence; and to acquire skills applicable to their future careers. The basic business skills taught in this course included topics such as creating a résumé and cover letter, business cards, business letters and e-mails, training manuals for jobs students currently have, and professional communication skills for the telephone and other media. An emphasis was also placed on looking at the differences between samples from the United States and Spanish-speaking countries in order to start to increase their cultural competency.

Students did individualized projects based on their career interest. In these projects, they researched specialized vocabulary and investigated potential universities and programs for study abroad where they could further their studies. Students also looked at what a professional in a particular field does on a typical day and the salary they could expect to earn.

The largest unit of the course was about the qualities and characteristics of good leaders. According to Spaine Long and colleagues (2014, 14), "Careful selection of materials, examples and face-to-face encounters will help guide learners toward observing cultural-specific interactions that highlight leaders, followers, and positive/negative global citizens. In addition, it is precisely this variation and differentiation in the meld of culture and leadership that necessitate critical thinking on the part of learners grappling with the challenge of finding the best ways to effect appropriate intercultural interactions." Students looked at past and present world leaders, as well as at leaders in their own community, and reported on why they thought they were good leaders.

The Spanish version of John C. Maxwell's (1999) *21 Indispensable Qualities in a Leader* was then used to thoroughly examine the characteristics of a good leader, and students did a more in-depth analysis of the leaders researched in their previous reports. Students also did a self-inventory of their leadership skills and identified the areas of leadership where they were strong and weak. They looked at how their strengths could be used and how their weaknesses could be overcome. Based on the work of James March of the Stanford Graduate School of Business, students analyzed the leadership qualities of the literary character Don Quixote (Zich 2003). We concluded the leadership unit by playing our version of the television show *The Apprentice*, with two teams competing weekly in different challenges. Each week a different student was the project leader and the rest of the members were his or her team. This activity allowed students to use the leadership skills discussed in this unit. It also gave students the opportunity to practice teamwork in the target language. This is an example of another ACTFL benchmark showing how students can "make presentations in a generally organized way on school, work, and community topics, and on topics [they] have researched [and] can make presentations on some events and experiences in various time frames," which is compliant with intermediate high presentational speaking (ACTFL n.d.).

The last major unit was on cultural and business etiquette, focusing on the differences and similarities among Spanish-speaking countries. Due to changing demographics, the future workforce will need the ability to work with people of different cultures whether they are in the United States or abroad (Singmaster 2013). To prepare for this future, students studied how to behave when meeting and greeting someone, in business meetings, at business luncheons or dinners, at social gatherings, and when gift giving. Skype was used, and live guest speakers from various countries were brought in so that the students could interview them and verify, clarify, and extend what they had learned in class about the different cultural expectations. An optional capstone component of the course was a summer study abroad opportunity in Costa Rica, of which 50 percent of the students took advantage.

Course Development

In order to offer this course, approval from the principal was needed. Once approval was granted, research was done to create a curriculum—for example, by attending conferences, such as the K-12 Language for Business Conference at Florida International University in January each year and the annual CIBER conference held at a different university campus each year. Once all the needed information was gathered, the course had to be approved by the school board and the superintendent, who in turn required the support of the teachers in the district as well as of community members, such as parents and students. A survey was sent out to students and parents, and a meeting was held for the other language teachers in the district.

Once the course was approved, the challenge was getting enough students to enroll to make it a viable option. The course was well advertised during the enrollment period. Infographics, such as the one created by Best Colleges Online titled "Bilingualism across the US" (ACTFL n.d.) are an easy way to share this information with all stakeholders (Mortiz-Saladino 2015). Through Google searches using keywords from the curricular units, articles, videos, and charts were found to be used as additional material to promote the value of the course.

Outcomes

Students who took this course were very excited to be able to actually use all the Spanish they had learned in real-life situations. They saw added value to their own lives in this course and enjoyed being able to look ahead to a bilingual future. After taking this course, every single student said he or she planned to continue to study Spanish at the university level and hoped to study abroad. Some of the comments in a postcourse survey included: "It [the course] showed us how the real world works in a way and gave us skills that would benefit us in the competition for future jobs." "It covered a lot of different topics in a globalized world." "I learned phrases that made my Spanish sound less basic and how to present myself in a more professional manner."

Spanish for Health Care

The "Spanish for Health Care" course in Pennsylvania was created to provide a course that would be valuable for secondary students wishing to study a profession in health, or those entering the workforce in a health-related field. The goal was to provide a proficiency level that would allow for meaningful patient communication beyond basic skills. In this level V high school course, students can utilize language skills in connection with health themes, increase proficiency, and add real-world applications for a specific purpose that fulfill needs in the local community. By combining academic efforts with students' long-term goals, students may also become more motivated to learn (Chen 2014). In the first cohort of Spanish for Health Care, having a sense of purpose seemed to provide intrinsic motivation for success. College- and vocation-bound students were eager registrants for volunteer positions in the local community, including those of emergency medical technicians and firemen.

Course Structure

The course was designed for delivery in a public school district and is a standard high school course worth one credit. Given that the course was originally designed on a block schedule format, its class sessions meet daily for approximately 90 minutes for one semester but may easily be adjusted to a traditional schedule that meets daily for the academic year. The prerequisite is the successful completion of Spanish I through IV with an average of "C" or better to ensure that students are capable of meeting the expectations of the course. The course had a broad scope that exposed students to several areas in health care but that also emphasized communication over grammar and writing. There was consistent informal feedback from local nursing students that their communication in the workplace revolved around patient demographics, main health concerns, patient instructions, ethics involved in interpretation, and dealing with making or changing appointments. Focusing on these types of activities in the course helps students "communicate on very familiar topics using a variety of words and phrases that they have practiced and memorized" (ACTFL n.d.). Beyond these communicative tasks and related vocabulary, the remainder of the course was developed to touch on very basic areas related to health, such as the patient and general health, car accidents and first responders, prescriptions and instructions, depression and suicide, childhood illnesses and well visits, sports injuries and therapies, interpretation, doctor–patient relationships, home remedies, and patient discharge and home care instructions.

Course Activities

To reinforce the course's goals of increased proficiency and confidence in verbal communication, course activities encouraged impromptu and uninhibited speech and downplayed an emphasis on perfecting grammatical structures. To accomplish these goals, rote skills and traditional grammar assessments were minimized and production tasks were maximized. Students were encouraged to acquire proficiency both through Spanish–English translation of terms and also through circumlocution in Spanish, thus moving their interpersonal communication skills out of the novice and into the intermediate range. This allowed learners to become more self-directed and helped them not only gain communicative competence but also reach the next level of competence because they were using their language skills to "participate in conversations on a number of familiar topics using simple sentences." Some students were able to reach intermediate-mid level by "participating in conversations on familiar topics using sentences and series of sentences" (ACTFL n.d.). This was demonstrated during the progression of the course as students gained confidence and began speaking more voluntarily and using sentences and paragraphs. Encouraging students to fully utilize language skills and think in the target language, rather than rely on English translations, helped to increase their proficiency and motivation. (This was demonstrated during one component of the final examination, whereby each student interviewed the teacher and took a complete health history.) Informal proficiency gains were realized, and it became evident that teachers do facilitate the learning process, but they also need to recognize that the students must be responsible and active learners in the language acquisition process (Lessard-Clouston 1997). This increase in confidence and speaking ability could also be attributed to an emphasis on course activities that promoted production only in the target language, such as describing common items, describing scenes, and creating stories from images, role-playing, a grab-bag of patient complaints, Password, and so on. Students were engaged in communication-based and student-centered activities to promote language production during the majority of the classroom time. Students practiced interpretation among patient, doctor, and health care workers in various role-play situations. Students worked diligently to utilize synonyms, antonyms, and other language skills to communicate with the "patient." Students used authentic videos and texts to learn about topics and themes related to health and were required to demonstrate growth in the topics and themes in addition to demonstrating language skills. This growth was measured using traditional formative and summative assessments as well as consistent practice of interpreting native speaker videos and audio files conforming with the benchmark on how students "can understand the main idea in short, simple messages and presentations on familiar topics and can understand the main idea of simple conversations that [they] overhear" (ACTFL n.d.).

Course Development

Because of the specialized content, teachers may have more flexibility regarding curricula and may be able to adjust course design, but one of the greatest challenges for course development was the lack of available resources. The school district may not be in a financial position to supply paid time for curriculum development or to purchase textbooks. Additionally, locating appropriate curricular materials for specialized language training and appropriate for the language level posed a challenge. Armed with informal feedback, course units were developed by beginning with a topic and goal for each unit, developing pertinent vocabulary and accompanying grammatical structures, and then finally creating activities and assessments.

Outcomes

Student and family responses to the Spanish for Health Care course were positive. Because it offered a divergence from traditional skill-and-drill or grammar-heavy course content, students found it appealing. Additionally, many wished to have the course on their high school transcript as they moved toward careers in a field of health care or on to college. Students' early production in Spanish—stunted by a dependence on English–Spanish translation—gave way to increased proficiency as students embraced strategies that depended on using the target language they had mastered to communicate more fluently, such as circumlocution, gestures, and pointing to indicate physical objects and items. Both parental and student feedback were positive. Families appreciated the bridge that the course created between education and vocation; students appreciated the increase in proficiency levels as they were able to participate in conversations on familiar topics, speak in sentences, and exchange information about familiar topics using phrases and simple sentences (ACTFL n.d.).

World Language and Business Leadership

The Center for Advanced Professional Studies (CAPS) is an innovative high school established in 2009 in the Blue Valley School District, in the Kansas City metropolitan area, that focuses on profession-based learning, where students are paired with local businesses and professionals to work on real-world client projects in a just-in-time learning environment. The global business course was recently expanded to include advanced-level world language students to provide an opportunity to increase language proficiency in an authentic work environment. Enrollment in CAPS requires three class periods per day and is open to students who attend any of the nearby partner high schools for the remainder of their school day.

In the spring of 2014, the pilot course integrating the language component for students at the intermediate-mid benchmark level was initiated. The students were able to participate in conversations on familiar topics using sentences and series of sentences. They could handle short social interactions in everyday situations by asking and answering a variety of questions while they interacted with corporate business partners, displaying their interpersonal communication skills. The course was named "World Language and Business Leadership," and it was officially launched in the fall of 2014. The program format involves high school students working directly with external clients on real-world projects while utilizing their Spanish interpersonal, presentational, and interpretive skills.

Course Structure

The World Language and Business Leadership course is offered two periods per day for one semester, and students may enroll in the course for a second semester. While all instruction is in English, the prerequisites for enrolling in this two-period class are concurrent enrollment at their respective traditional high school in advanced placement Spanish 5 or advanced placement French 5; Honors or Spanish 4, French 4, or German 4; and the proficiency to use their target language at a company project.

Students receive one high school credit per semester as a business elective course. The students are concurrently part of the "Global Business" course, which emphasizes marketing, introduction to business, and entrepreneurship. They also have the option of enrolling in a concurrent university credit in marketing for the first semester and in Introduction to Business and Introduction to Global Business for the second semester. In addition, "World Language and Business Leadership" students engage in external client projects focused on utilizing their target language of study in real-world workplace settings.

Course Activities

The course begins with classic Harvard Business School case studies on the principles of marketing and the five forces of business. After the case studies are reviewed in English by the entire class, the world language students review them in Spanish. Through this activity, they demonstrate intermediate-mid to intermediate-high level as they can easily understand the main idea of texts related to studies, and can sometimes follow stories and descriptions about events in various time frames in Spanish (ACTFL n.d.).

The remaining part of the curriculum is made up of contemporary articles on globalization and cross-cultural skills, and the course relies on guest speakers and field trips to instruct students firsthand about international business practices. Guest speakers visit the class weekly, and many have extensive international experience, giving students the opportunity to hear about various careers in global business. Examples of speakers include a bank's foreign exchange trader, a buyer for a holiday ornament supply company who regularly travels to China to design and purchase goods, a consultant who manages a global process outsourcing group, a salesperson who works for a high-technology communications firm, and a university student who shares information about his Arabic studies while studying abroad. Field trips are another key component of the program, and students have the opportunity to visit numerous multinational companies with large manufacturing, distribution, and retail centers in the area. A special emphasis is placed on locating companies that utilize target languages such as Spanish, French, and German in the workplace.

General cross-cultural competencies are introduced, and students are exposed to cultural differences in business, such as hand-shaking, greetings, the use of chopsticks, and other types of protocol. Business strategies are explained, and students learn how large corporations change and adapt many components when they expand globally, such as tailoring their advertising, training procedures, and business structures to local cultures.

Profession-based learning is the key component of the CAPS educational model, and students are assigned to work with external client partners on specific business projects that are organized by the instructors. These vary based on the clients' needs. Some examples of client projects for the course include researching and writing a Latino marketing strategy for H&R Block, translating key website terms for Garmin, interacting with Garmin's bilingual call center, and translating cultural and press release documents for the Mexican Consulate. The instructors have initially organized partnerships with global corporations that are headquartered in the city; but as the course expands, they will work with local small businesses that employ immigrant workers (e.g., landscape and construction firms) that require student work in target languages.

Course Development

Once the school district determined the need for the World Language and Business Leadership course in the fall of 2013, the lead instructor immediately began forming a committee to help develop the curriculum. The CAPS program director created the trademarked rapid curriculum prototyping process, which allows the school to identify industry needs and to work backward to design courses that teach those skills at the high school level in alignment with skills that industry is looking for in university graduates.

The first phase—recruiting the committee—took about one month. The key to the program's success is to invite key industry leaders and external business partners to become a part of the process to determine industry needs for cross-cultural competencies and world language skills. Two professors from different universities were invited to join the committee in addition to key district partners—such as department heads and lead teachers. The second six-week phase was to write the curriculum document, with edits and approvals by all the key players on the committee. The next step was to try out the plan with a pilot student. The Latino marketing director of H&R Block and the global website manager of Garmin (both of whom were members of the curriculum design committee) immediately offered to provide work experiences for a single pilot student in the upcoming spring 2014 semester.

Outcomes

The initial pilot student completed her semester of profession-based learning and graduated from high school. The experience of utilizing her Spanish-language skills by working within two major global corporations increased her confidence. In addition, her language proficiency and cultural competency improved, as she was able to interact and speak Spanish with native speakers from several different countries. She was able to understand the main idea in conversations that she overheard through interpretive listening at the intermediate-mid level (ACTFL n.d.). Based on her high school experiences in this course, she has decided to major in international business at the university level and to obtain a minor in Spanish.

In the fall of 2014—the inaugural semester for the World Language and Business Leadership course—students were invited to attend a Latin American sales meeting and sit in on a discussion between the Brazilian and Mexican sales managers, which was conducted in Spanish. The students were fascinated to see how the conversation switched interchangeably between Spanish and English, and the corporate partners made the students feel so welcome that they posed a few questions in Spanish to the sales managers. Because the CAPS focus is profession-based learning, the instructors can rapidly adapt and modify the curriculum in a real-time environment, which is an advantage because students in numerous disciplines—such as engineering, medicine, education, law, and bioscience—have also expressed an interest in utilizing their cultural and language skills in a workplace environment.

Recommendations and Conclusion

With planning and preparation, anyone can adopt these innovations, either by incorporating activities or mini-units into existing courses or by designing entire courses like those described here. A first volume of sample K-12 LSP lesson plans is now available for free downloading at the NOBLE website (www.nble.org). The following are a few key considerations to infuse LSP into your curriculum:

- Consider teaming with another teacher to share the workload.
- Utilize the help of a mapping system to look at your scholastic calendar and determine basic units of study; from there, map goals, teaching objectives, and final activities and assessments required to meet the goals within the allotted time frame.
- Consider utilizing student portfolios and-or pre/post-assessment results to support course objectives and drive instruction.
- Utilize survey results from the target student audience and consider responses when creating course content and objectives.

- The key to any program's success is buy-in from all key stakeholders, including industry partners, education colleagues, parents, and community members.

Profession-based learning requires that instructors spend a considerable amount of time outside the classroom developing relationships with industries in their community in order to place high school students in real-world projects. This is a critical success factor for an innovative educational model to succeed.

Many large global corporations are expanding their market segments in the United States, and it has been forecasted that there will be a shortage of bilingual professionals graduating from universities in the next ten to twenty years to fulfill this growing marketplace demand for a culturally competent workforce. World language students who have early exposure to practical and industry applications in a real-world context may be more likely to continue their studies at the university level and pursue careers that utilize both language proficiency and other professional skills. Thanks to the efforts of many NOBLE collaborators, including the three teacher/authors featured here, progress has been made; more K-12 resources are available, there is a growing network of K-12 teachers developing courses and materials, and positive outcomes have been documented and reported in the literature. The need for advocacy to decision makers at the local, state, and national levels persists; without this, the necessary funding and support to provide more training for teachers interested in LSP course development will not be forthcoming. Similarly, an organized movement connecting teachers and schools to industry professionals and workplace contexts would give momentum for the types of programs that provide today's high school students with the skills they will need in the global workplace of their future.

References

Abbott, Marty, Richard D. Brecht, Dan E. Davidson, Hans Fenstermacher, Donald Fischer, William P. Rivers, Robert Slater, Amy Weinberg, and Terrence Wiley. 2014. *Language Enterprise, Languages for All? Final Report: Can All US Residents Have the Opportunity to Learn A Second Language?* http://www.languagepolicy.org/wp-content/uploads/2014/04/Languages-for-All-Final-Report.pdf.

ACTFL (American Council on the Teaching of Foreign Languages). No date. "NCSSFL-ACTFL Global Can-Do Benchmarks." www.actfl.org/global_statements.

———. 2011. *21st-Century Skills Roadmap.* www.actfl.org/sites/default/files/pdfs/21stCenturySkillsMap/p21_worldlanguagesmap.pdf.

———. 2012. *Proficiency Guidelines 2012.* www.actfl.org/publications/guidelines-and-manuals/actfl-proficiency-guidelines-2012.

Chen, Ingfei. 2014. "How a Bigger Purpose Can Motivate Students to Learn." KQED News, August 18. ww2.kqed.org/mindshift/2014/08/18/how-a-bigger-purpose-can-motivate-students-to-learn/.

CIBER (Centers for International Business Education). 2008. *International Business Education: Outreach Initiatives for Grades K–12*. http://ciberweb.msu.edu/NationalImpact/K-12-2008.pdf.

Crouse, Douglass. 2013. "Language for Specific Purposes in the 21st Century." *Language Educator* 8, no. 3: 32–38. www.actfl.org/sites/default/files/pdfs/TLE_pdf/TLE_Apr13_Article.pdf.

Doyle, Michael Scott. 2013. "Continuing Theoretical Cartography in the LSP Era." In *Scholarship and Teaching on Languages for Specific Purposes*, edited by Lourdes Sánchez-López. Birmingham: University of Alabama, UAB Digital Collections. http://contentdm.mhsl.uab.edu/cdm/compoundobject/collection/faculty/id/161/rec/19.

Economist Intelligence Unit. 2012. "Competing across Borders: How Cultural and Communication Barriers Affect Business." https://www.eiuperspectives.economist.com/economic-development/competing-across-borders.

Fenstermacher, Hans. 2013. "The American Enterprise Language Advocacy: A New Voice Speaks for the US Language Industry." Ground Report, August 19. http://groundreport.com/the-american-enterprise-language-advocacy-a-new-voice-speaks-for-the-u-s-language-industry/.

Fryer, T. Bruce. 1986. "Proficiency-Guided Business Units in High School Foreign Language Classes." *Hispania* 69, no. 1: 101–9. http://files.eric.ed.gov/fulltext/ED336997.pdf.

Grosse, Christine Uber. 1988. "Foreign Languages for Business in the Secondary School Curriculum." *Hispania* 71, no. 1: 166–70. doi 10.2307/343237.

Klein, Carol E. 1988. "What's Happening in High School Spanish? Forces and Sources of Change." *Hispania* 71, no. 1: 171–75. doi: 10.2307/343238.

Language Flagship. 2009. *What Business Wants: Language Needs in the 21st Century*. Washington, DC: Language Flagship. www.thelanguageflagship.org/media/docs/reports/what_business_wants_report_final_7_09.pdf.

Lessard-Clouston, Michael. 1997. "Language Learning Strategies: An Overview for L2 Teachers." *Internet TESL Journal*, December. http://iteslj.org/Articles/Lessard-Clouston-Strategy.html.

Long, Mary. 2010. "Spanish for the Professions Degree Programs in the United States: History and Current Practice." In *How Globalizing Professions Deal with National Languages: Studies in Cultural Studies and Cooperation*, edited by Michel Gueldry. Lampeter, UK: Edwin Mellen Press. www.mellenpress.com/mellenpress.cfm?bookid=8197&pc=9.

Long, Mary K., and Isabel Uscinski. 2012. "Evolution of Languages for Specific Purposes Programs in the United States: 1990–2011." *Modern Language Journal* 96, no. s1: 173–89. doi: 10.1111/j.1540-4781.2012.01303.x.

Maxwell, John C. 1999. *Las 21 cualidades indispensables de un líder: Conviértase en una persona que los demás quieran seguir*. Nashville: Grupo Nelson.

Morrison, Nick. 2014. "Learning a Language Is for Life, Not Just for Business." *Forbes*

Education, April 17. www.forbes.com/sites/nickmorrison/2014/04/17/learning-a-language-is-for-life-not-just-for-business/#453c170046ad.

Mortiz-Saladino, Amanda. 2015. *Bilingualism across the US*. www.brainscape.com/blog/2012/05/bilingualism-in-america/.

Risner, Mary. 2006. "Integrating Business Language into the High School Curriculum." Paper presented at annual CIBER Business Language Conference. Georgia Technological University, Atlanta.

———. 2009a. *Design and Development of a Community of Practice of Business and Foreign Language Faculty*. E-Learn: World Conference on E-Learning in Corporate, Government, Healthcare, and Higher Education, October 9. www.editlib.org/p/32736/.

———. 2009b. "Network of Business Language Educators—NOBLE." Available at www.nble.org.

———. 2011. "A Community of Practice of Business and Foreign Language Faculty." In *Specialized Languages in the Global Village: A Multi-Perspective Approach*, edited by Carmen Pérez-Llantada and Maida Watson. Cambridge: Cambridge Scholars. www.cambridgescholars.com/download/sample/60511.

Risner, Mary, and Linda Markley. 2013. "The Business of Languages in the Classroom Today: A Model for K-12 Professional Development." *Global Business Languages* 18: 121–30. http://docs.lib.purdue.edu/gbl/vol18/iss1/10.

Singmaster, Heather. 2013. "Globally Competent Workforce: Why We Need One." *Education Week*, June 19. http://blogs.edweek.org/edweek/global_learning/2013/06/globally_competent_workforce_why_we_need_one.html.

Spaine Long, Sheri, Jean W. LeLoup, LeAnn Derby, and Ramsamooj J. Reyes. 2014. "Fusing Language Learning and Leadership Development: Initial Approaches and Strategies." In *Dimension 2014: Uniting the Corps: Uniting the Core.* http://scolt.org/images/PDFs/dimension/Dimension2014_FINAL.pdf.

Takami, Tomoko. 2010. "Infusing the National Standards into Business Language Curricula." *Global Business Languages* 15: 33–47. http://docs.lib.purdue.edu/cgi/viewcontent.cgi?article=1189&context=gbl.

Tinsely, Teresa. 2013. *Languages: State of the Nation: Demand and Supply of Language Skills in the UK*. Summary Report. London: British Academy. www.britac.ac.uk/policy/State_of_the_Nation_2013.cfm.

Workforce 20/20. 2011–13. *Job Service North Dakota: Helping Train Today's Workers for New Technologies.* www.jobsnd.com/sites/default/files/Workforce-2020-Biennium-Report.pdf.

Zich, Janet. 2003. "Don Quixote's Lessons for Leadership." Stanford Business Graduate School, May 1. www.gsb.stanford.edu/news/bmag/sbsm0305/leadership.shtml.

3 | Preparing Students for the Workplace

Heritage Learners' Experiences in Professional Community Internships

Carmen King de Ramírez

Courses on language for specific purposes (LSP) have gained popularity in the United States due to their focus on practical, skills-based approaches that help students meet language goals related to their advancement in a specific area of interest. Although a growing number of publications are concerned with methodology, vocabulary, assessment tools, and curriculum development in LSP programs (Basturkmen 2010; Douglas 2001; King de Ramírez and Lafford 2013), there has been little literature regarding heritage learners (HLs) in postsecondary LSP courses and even fewer studies regarding HLs' experiences in professional community internships (PCI).

The importance of investigating the appropriateness of LSP curricula for HLs is underscored by the fact that few university language programs take this population's linguistic goals into account (Petrov 2013). Although national standards committees have recognized the needs of HLs since the 1970s (Gaarder 1972), fewer than 18 percent of postsecondary language courses in the United States are designed specifically with HLs in mind (Ingold et al. 2002). The lack of suitable language course options for HLs forces these students to enroll in foreign language courses designed for L2s that often leave HLs feeling frustrated, self-conscious, and out of place (Valdés et al. 2008; Benjamin 1997; Potowski 2002).

The lack of HL-specific courses and the alienation that these students experience in traditional language courses challenge educators to establish curricula that both validates HLs' linguistic background and challenges them to strengthen academic and professional language skills; this chapter explores how LSP curricula with service learning (SL) components can help HLs enrolled in language programs meet their academic and professional goals. In an effort to offer important findings concerning the appropriateness of SL-infused LSP programs for Spanish-speaking HLs, the chapter provides an overview of studies that address how LSP curricula have been implemented in courses designed for HL populations, the importance of providing HLs with SL opportunities, and new research regarding HLs who completed a 135-hour PCI in order to obtain a minor in Spanish for the professions.

Review of the Literature

The limited number of studies on HLs' experiences in language programs makes it difficult to fully evaluate the appropriateness of specific pedagogical approaches for HL populations (Beaudrie, Ducar, and Releño-Pastor 2009); this is especially true in the case of LSP, an approach to teaching language that has steadily gained popularity in universities across the United States (Long and Uscinki 2012). The implementation of professions-based curricula in HL education has been supported by investigators such as Angelelli and Degueldre (2002), who argue that LSP courses allow HLs to develop their language abilities naturally, and Lynch (2008), who states that LSP programs are more likely to take an assets-based approach that builds on HLs' previously acquired cultural knowledge and linguistic proficiency.

The assets-based approach implemented in LSP courses provides HLs with instrumental motivation that may not be found in language courses that focus on skills already mastered by HLs (Ducar 2008). An example of an LSP course built around HLs' specific needs can be found in Pino's (2001) study that highlights professional gains made by HLs enrolled in a course on Spanish for business. Due to many HLs' lack of knowledge of Hispanic cultures outside the United States and Mexico, the course required students to research foreign business models, demonstrate culture competency, and practice professional linguistic registers.

The real-world outcomes promoted by LSP courses are best met through assignments that establish a relationship between preservice and practicing professionals; such relationships can be accomplished through SL initiatives. The field of SL, which was initially conceived as connecting community service to academic study (Sigmon 1979), has evolved during the past several decades and is now widely defined as a credit-bearing course that includes projects that meet an identified community need and provide subsequent self-reflection opportunities (Bringle, Hatcher, and McIntosh 2006). Service learning allows students the opportunity to observe authentic language usage, network with individuals outside academia, and become familiar with sociocultural issues that affect their immediate community.

Although several studies exist regarding language courses that position HL communities as recipients of SL projects conducted by L2 students (Tijunelis, Satterfield, and Benkí 2013; Tacelosky 2013), far fewer studies focus on community SL activities initiated by HLs. Those investigations regarding Spanish-language HLs who conduct SL within their communities that do exist, frequently focus on community building and cultural identity issues—thus, Bruno (2003) investigates SL as a means of helping HLs promote culturally diverse communities; Petrov (2013) explores how HLs' social identity is influenced through SL among Hispanics in Chicago communities; and Leeman, Rabin, and Román-Mendoza (2011) report on how HL students can use their language skills to promote social change.

Notable lacunae in these studies pertain to how community SL can increase professional language acquisition in HLs. Martínez and Schwartz (2012) published one of the few studies regarding this topic as they detailed HLs' participation in Spanish-language internships at local health centers. This study differs from other SL-based research in both the focus on language maintenance and the emphasis on internships. Professional community internships may be considered a subcategory of SL as they depend on relationships between academic and community partners; however, while professional SL activities incorporate community projects that complement content-based learning outcomes specific to a particular course (King de Ramírez 2015), PCIs support learning outcomes that are tailored to each student's goals and help students understand how academic preparation can be translated into marketable job skills in their specific field of interest (Carter 1998).

The current study seeks to contribute to research pertaining to HLs in PCIs by providing insights on the following questions:

- What are HLs' goals for PCIs?
- What linguistic and cultural skills are HLs required to demonstrate in professional community venues?
- How do PCIs prepare HLs to work with Hispanics in professional fields?

Methodology

In the spring of 2014, seven HLs enrolled in a PCI course were invited to participate in the current study. The internship was part of a minor in Spanish for the Professions at a large university in the Southwest. The minor consisted of five upper-division, professions-based Spanish courses followed by the 135-hour PCI course. Requirements for participation in the study were the completion of the 135-hour PCI, a pre-internship questionnaire, bimonthly self-reflections, weekly meetings with community mentors, and a postinternship survey.

Subjects

Of the seven interns invited to participate in this study, four HLs were chosen according to the diversity of their PCI venues and the completion of the required coursework. According to the pre-internship survey, all the participants were first-generation Americans in their senior year at the university, and their ages ranged from eighteen to twenty-five years. The survey also determined that all participants had learned Spanish at home and used the language frequently to communicate with family members.

Instruments

The two main instruments used to collect data for this study consist of an end-of-semester survey and bimonthly student reflections. The reflections (see appendix 3A) required students to record experiences regarding their progress in six categories: summary of activities, vocabulary/pragmatics, grammar/orthography, culture, professional skills, and goals.

The end-of-semester survey included twenty questions measured on a Likert scale (strongly agree, agree, disagree, strongly disagree) to determine HLs' perspectives regarding their linguistic and professional skills developed during the community internship. The survey was administered via Survey Monkey during the last week of the internship course.

Data Analysis

The data derived from the reflections were qualitatively analyzed to determine common HL experiences across all four community internship sites: social work, community advocacy, communication, and mass media. The findings from the data collected via surveys and reflections are represented in four tables that include summaries compiled by the professor as well as direct student quotations taken from HLs' reflections. The names of the community organizations for which the students volunteered have not been changed; however, the student participants were given pseudonyms to protect their identities.

Results and Discussion

In order to clearly connect the research questions expressed in this study to the data derived from the instruments, this section is divided into three subsections.

Professional Goals

In response to research question number one concerning HLs' PCI goals, table 3.1 contains excerpts from the first reflection regarding the academic and personal goals HLs wished to accomplish during the internship experience. Although all the participants in this study regularly speak Spanish at home, HLs' goals conveyed vulnerabilities associated with using Spanish in professional environments. For example, Clara and Karen hoped to use their internship

Table 3.1 Community Placements and Internship Goals

Student	Community Venue	Internship Goals
Karen	Mass media	1. Aprender más de marketing y promociones. (Learn more about marketing and advertisement.) 2. Tener mejor comunicación con mis compañeros de trabajo, profesores y amistades. (Have better communication with my colleagues, professors, and friends.)
Clara	Community advocacy	1. Mejorar mi español oral. (Improve my oral Spanish.) 2. Conocer las diferentes formas en que una organización puede ayudar a personas con problemas de inmigración. (Learn different ways in which an organization can help people with immigration problems.)
María	Communication	1. Poner mucho empeño en mejorar mi escritura en español y usarla en mi práctica profesional. (Work harder on improving my writing in Spanish and use this in my internship.) 2. Conocer a más gente profesional que algún día me podría contratar para su empresa. (Meet professional people who can someday hire me at their business.)
Julia	Social work	1. Quería experimentar un ambiente de hispanohablantes. (I wanted to experience a professional Spanish-speaking environment.) 2. Tener más contacto con la comunidad y los eventos sociales. (Have more contact with the community and social events.)

experience to improve their ability to communicate orally in formal settings, while Julia wished to have more contact with the Hispanic community.

Requiring students to express their academic and personal goals not only allowed the students to critically consider what they wanted to gain from the internship experience but also allowed the course instructor to work with professional mentors to ensure that the interns were allowed opportunities to work on the goals they had set forth.

Linguistic and Cultural Skills

In response to research question number 2 regarding the linguistic and cultural skills HLs are required to demonstrate in professional community venues, table 3.2 illustrates a summary of professional activities that HLs completed during their community internships. The activities listed in the table were compiled by the professor after reading the students' biweekly reflections.

Although the professional tasks completed varied according to the internship placement, there were similar expectations placed on HLs in all four internship

Table 3.2 Professional Activities

Student	Internship Site	Professional Activities Completed
Karen	Mass media	• Promoted the radio station • Attended community events such as swap meets, malls, car dealerships • Made flyers in Photoshop for local magazines • Helped with trade agreements • Sent e-mails • Edited audio recording for radio
Clara	Community advocacy	• Wrote tweets • Transcribed interviews • Interpreted for the media • Educated the community about staging protests and strikes • Added subtitles to video recordings • Updated internet site
María	Communication	• Translated press releases • Presented to professionals in the community • Spoke with organizations about Red Cross services • Was interviewed by Fox 10 news • Interpreted at events

venues: oral communication skills, translation skills, social networking abilities, and immigration knowledge. Julia wrote that she was asked to prepare PowerPoint presentations that represented the organizations' past initiatives. María, who was one of the only Spanish speakers at her internship venue, was continually called on to meet with Hispanic-serving organizations and the Spanish-language press.

Another skill that was required was the ability to interpret and translate. Although professional internship mentors were explicitly informed that interns were not trained in interpretation and translation, many community organizations could not afford to pay certified individuals for these services. As a result, three of four community placements asked interns to produce written documents that ranged from press releases to educational literature for Spanish speakers in the community; however, most of these documents were translations of an original English-language document.

Two internship sites, Community Advocacy and Social Work, required HLs to possess knowledge about local and national immigration issues. Interns at these community venues interacted firsthand with undocumented migrants regarding topics that ranged from immigration law to national initiatives such as Deferred Action for undocumented youth. Clara, whose internship was primarily based on working with undocumented community members, participated exclusively in immigration-based activities such as Conoce tus derechos (Know Your Rights) workshops and border excursions dedicated to creating a documentary on local immigration issues.

Professional Preparation

In response to research question number three regarding how community internships prepare HLs to work with Hispanics in professional fields, tables 3.3 and 3.4, as well as the comments pertaining to relationships with mentors, contain excerpts directly copied from student reflections regarding new skills acquired at their internship sites.

Most of the terms that HLs identified as new vocabulary were intimately related to the field in which they completed their PCI. It could be concluded that words such as "solidarity, hunger strike, donors, and trade agreement" were not high-frequency words in the home environments where these students learned Spanish. Clara and Julia noted that words they routinely used at home seemed unacceptable in their professional internship. Clara specifically mentioned her use of the widely spread regionalism "haiga" and explained that she was working on using "haya," a more grammatically correct and universal conjugation of the

Table 3.3 Grammar/Orthography/Vocabulary

Student	Vocabulary	Grammar/Orthography Points
Karen	Tradeagreement, radioton	En los correos electrónicos que mando yo tengo que poner los acentos y estar pendiente de que el correo se vea profesional, entonces necesito trabajar en eso. (In the e-mails that I send, I have to put accent marks and make sure that the e-mail looks professional, so I have to work on this.)
Clara	Solidaridad, manifestación, huelga de hambre, partidario, simpatizante, violación de propiedad privada, social media, upload, alquilar	Tengo la mala costumbre de usar "haiga" en vez de "haya" y cuando intento cambiarlo solo me causa más problemas. Conforme a los acentos, lo más difícil para mí es recordar ponerle los acentos a las palabras como "el, esta, esto, están, etc." (I have the bad habit of using "haiga" instead of "haya" and, when I try to change it, it only causes me problems. Regarding the accent marks, it's hard for me to remember to put accents on words like "el, esta, esto, están, etc.")
María	To keep an eye on someone, niño vs. hijo, when to leave a word in English	Creo que tal vez me falla la gramática en los acentos, pero he mejorado mucho desde que empecé las clases de español. (I think that maybe my grammar is weak regarding accent marks, but I have improved a lot since I started Spanish classes.)
Julia	Defensores, donantes, permiso de trabajo, actualizar los datos del sistema	Suelo usar algunos anglicismos desconocidos para el público general pero que se usan con frecuencia en los medios de comunicación. (I tend to use English-influenced words that the general public doesn't know but that are frequently used in the media.)

Table 3.4 Professionalism and Linguistic Growth

Question	Strongly Agree	Agree	Disagree	Strongly Disagree
1. I feel that my oral Spanish improved during my internship.	2 (50%)	2 (50%)		
2. I feel that my *written* Spanish improved during my internship.	4 (100%)			
3. My Spanish-language vocabulary has increases because of my internship experience.	3 (75%)	1 (25%)		
4. Because of my internship, I feel more confident about using Spanish in the workplace and-or with the community.	4 (100%)			

verb *haber*. Julia, conversely, noticed that certain terms she had learned as a mass media and journalism student were highly influenced by English and therefore were difficult to understand for many of the Spanish speakers with whom she was working. The vocabulary lists compiled, as well as the commentary provided in the student reflections, illustrated that PCIs encouraged HLs to begin to develop a more advanced linguistic register related to professional contexts.

Heritage learners were also prompted to reflect on grammar and orthography skills they wished to improve during their PCIs. Karen noted that she needed to work more on the proper use of accent marks. Though orthography had previously been identified by her Spanish instructors as an area for improvement, the immediate need to create professional e-mails and the feedback from her community mentor increased her motivation to work on her written skills.

The importance of community mentors has been underlined by both LSP and community service learning experts (Sánchez-López 2013; Lear and Abbott 2009; Gibb 1999) and was echoed by the students who participated in this study. The PCI mentors not only were the acting supervisors for the HL interns but also wrote their monthly performance evaluations and maintained contact with the course instructor. The following comments, which were directly copied from the postcourse survey, represent students' perspectives regarding their relationships with their professional mentors:

Karen: "En uno de los 'feedback's' que me dio mi primer mentor una de las cosas que me decía era que me tenía que mejorar en mi ortografía. Entonces eso a mí me ayudo [sic] porque a si [sic] yo me daba cuenta de 'en que' es lo que tengo que seguir trabajando para mejorarme." (In one of the feedbacks that my mentor gave me, one of the things that he said was that I had to improve my orthography. So that helped me because I realized what I have to keep working on to improve myself.)

Clara: "Ellos me ponían a intentar varias cosas que nunca había hecho y aunque tuve nervios al principio, terminé haciendo buen trabajo y aprendiendo cosas nuevas. Lo que más me ayudó fue ver que ellos apreciaban mi trabajo." (They had me try several things that I had never done before, and although I was nervous at the beginning, I ended up doing a good job and learning new things. What helped me the most was seeing that they appreciated my work.)

María: "Mi supervisora hizo muy buen trabajo en esto porque ella sabía que esta era mi meta y por eso me mandaba a eventos a representar el departamento de comunicaciones de la Cruz Roja, me mandaba a juntas para hablar de lo que hacemos y también me trataba de incluir en todos los demás eventos fuera del departamento de comunicación." (My supervisor did a good job on this [feedback] because she knew that this was my goal and that's why she used to send me to events to represent the Red Cross communications department. She sent me to meetings to talk about what we do and tried to include me in other events outside of the communication department.)

Julia: "Mi mentora me animaba mucho a practicar mi español escrito y hacer preguntas acerca de palabras o frases que no estaba segura en como traducir del inglés al español. Al principio me sentía poco insegura y avergonzada de cuánto tiempo me tomaba, pero estuve satisfecha de tener guía y apoyo incondicional." (My mentor encouraged me to practice my written Spanish and ask questions about words or phrases that I wasn't sure how to translate from English to Spanish. At first I felt a little insecure and ashamed of how long it took me but I was satisfied to have a guide and unconditional support.)

And

"Al principio sentí que estaba siendo criticada. [La mentora] Me hacía preguntas muy personales y me hacía sentir incomoda, pero después describí [*sic*] que lo hacía para conocerme más y para hacerme sentir como parte de ellos. (At first, I felt that I was being criticized. [The mentor] would ask me personal questions that made me feel uncomfortable, but afterward I figured out that she did it in order to get to know me better and make me feel part of the group.)

In the case of HLs, mentors from similar backgrounds can be especially helpful because they are able to identify and share common experiences with aspiring professionals (Burgess and Dyer 2009). In the current study, the fact that three of four community mentors were native Spanish speakers seemed to have a positive impact on the performance of Karen and Julia, who greatly valued the constructive criticism given by their bilingual Hispanic mentors. Clara, María, and Julia all noted that despite some difficulties faced during the internships, they continued their work because they felt appreciated and encouraged by their professional mentors.

Though the students' comments regarding their mentors were overwhelmingly positive, cultural differences did arise between native mentors and HL interns. Clara and Julia expressed feeling embarrassed or unsure of their abilities to fulfill certain tasks requested of them by their professional mentors. Furthermore, Julia remarked that her mentor sometimes made her feel uncomfortable when she would ask questions about her family and love life. A possible explanation for the uneasiness expressed by Julia could be differences in communication styles and organizational culture. Julia, who was born and raised in the United States and had previously completed several English-speaking internships, could have been more accustomed to an organizational culture in which personal questions are discouraged, whereas her mentor, who was born and raised in Mexico and has worked for more than fifteen years with Spanish-speaking communities, may have viewed these questions as a way to strengthen the relationship with her intern.

Julia had previously indicated in her reflections that she had noticed differences in the organizational culture of the Social Services venue, as compared with internships she had completed with organizations dominated by Anglophone culture:

> En el ambiente de trabajo he notado que casi todos son muy amables. Se gritan buenos días y se saludan con cariño. Por ejemplo, mi mentora, Maricela, siempre dice: "Buenos días alegría!" Antes de ponernos a trabajar le gusta charlar cada mañana. Creo en el mundo angloparlante somos más serios y conservados. No perdemos tiempo socializándonos. (In the work environment, I have noticed that almost everyone is very nice. They yell to each other "good morning" and welcome each other with warmth. For example, my mentor, Maricela, always says "Good morning, sunshine."

Before we begin to work, she likes to talk every morning. I think that in the English-speaking world we are more serious and reserved. We don't waste time socializing.)

Although Julia easily adapted to the salutatory hugs and morning chats, which may have been considered an intrusion of personal space in comparison with her past internships with Anglophone-dominant cultures, she struggled to answer the questions posed by her native Spanish-speaking mentor regarding her family situation and dating life. This anecdote supports the notion that though many HLs may possess a good command of the cultural practices used by their family and friends, they frequently lack experience using the same skills in professional environments (Angelelli and Kagan 2002; Pino 2001). In this particular case, Julia's lack of experience in Spanish-speaking workplaces left her unsure of the appropriate relationship boundaries she should establish with her professional mentor.

The last data provided regarding professional skills gained by students were taken from the postinternship survey completed by the HL interns. Table 3.4 above summarizes students' perspectives regarding the linguistic gains achieved through the community internship experience.

The data rendered from the postcourse survey and final self-reflection made it clear that all the HLs had experienced professional growth through the community internship experience. María, whose initial goal was to improve her written Spanish abilities, commented the following: "Al final pude mejorar mucho mi ortografía y mi gramática. Al realizar mis traducciones y mis reflexiones para esta clase me daba cuenta en los comentarios de la profesora que mi ortografía y mis acentos habían mejorado." (I could finally improve my orthography and grammar. Upon completing the translations and my reflections for this class, I realized in the professor's comment that my orthography and my accent marks had improved.) Although María was satisfied that she met the objective she had set at the beginning of the internship course, other students noted that aside from making progress on the goal they had set, they gained unexpected exposure to other topics that were pertinent to working with Hispanics in the local community.

In the postinternship reflection, Clara, who was initially preoccupied with improving her oral Spanish, noted that, although she grew up in a Mexican family in a border town, her internship heightened her awareness of issues currently affecting many immigrants: "Trabajar con Puente me abrió los ojos para entender lo que pasan, han pasado o están pasando muchas familias hispanas." (Working with Puente opened my eyes to what many Hispanic families have gone through and are currently experiencing.) Ultimately, she concludes that after working more closely with the immigrant community, she feels more prepared to work with the Hispanic community: "Ante todo, ahora me siento cómoda [con?en?] la comunidad hispana a un nivel mucho más alto de lo que empecé. Estoy contenta con lo que aprendí y estoy segura que me preparó para el mundo profesional si me toca trabajar con la comunidad hispana."(More than anything, I now feel more comfortable in the Hispanic community at a much higher level than I started. I am happy with what I learned, and I am sure that it prepared me for the professional world if I end up working with the Hispanic community.)

Finally, Karen, who reported less improvements than other HLs regarding Spanish vocabulary and oral skills, noted the following when asked what she valued the most about her internship with a Spanish-language Catholic radio station: "learning new faith vocabulary and being in a place where I am learning more about my religion and at the same time being at an internship." Karen's experience calls attention to the fact that the internship experience has significance for every HL; though some HLs, such as Karen, may begin their community internship with an advanced command of the Spanish language and thus do not note immense progress in their linguistic skills, there are still areas where they can experience personal growth as they interact with other Hispanics and local professionals.

Conclusions

Although HLs' motives for enrolling in PCIs were varied, some commonalities were found, such as the desire to improve written skills and increase familiarity with Spanish-speaking communities. Professional organizations that hosted bilingual interns specifically placed value on HLs' oral communication skills and their ability to make social connections with other Spanish speakers. The production of written documents was required less frequently than oral skills and mainly focused on the translation of documents from English into Spanish.

HL interns noted several gains from participating in the PCIs. Although they were often unaccustomed to the cultural differences they encountered in Spanish-language-dominant work environments, they learned to bridge cultural gaps with Hispanic coworkers and community members. Professional community internships also increased HLs' awareness of immigration policy and how it immediately affects Spanish-speaking communities, especially families with mixed immigration status. Finally, all the HL interns reported notable gains in specialized vocabulary, in oral and written language skills, and in their ability to interact with native professionals and community members.

Based on these findings, the author concludes that LSP courses with SL components, such as PCIs, serve the linguistic and social needs of HLs and may be an alternative to HL-specific language courses. In order to prepare HLs for expectations that will be placed on them as bilingual professionals, LSP courses should focus on the ability to render oral interpretations and written translations in formal and informal registers. Heritage learners must also be well versed in the socioeconomic and cultural realities of the communities where they will work; in the Southwestern United States, bilingual professionals are expected to be well versed in immigration policy and able to make interpersonal connections with other Spanish speakers.

Last, LSP courses must teach skills that help students manage the cultural differences they will encounter in the workplace; this is especially important for HLs who may assume that cultural practices learned at home are shared by all Hispanics in their community. In order to help students maneuver through cultural differences and ensure rewarding PCI experiences, LSP instructors should encourage relationships between professional mentors and student interns. Mentors with similar sociolinguistic backgrounds can be highly effective in helping HLs adapt to cultural differences as well as develop appropriate workplace conduct and prepare them for expectations that will be placed on them as bilingual professionals.

Appendix 3A

Pasantía Profesional Comunitaria: Reflexión Quincenal

I. Resumen de Actividades
Durante las últimas semanas ¿Qué hiciste, qué aprendiste, qué dificultades tuviste en la práctica profesional?

II. Vocabulario/Pragmática
¿Qué palabras aprendiste o usaste durante las últimas semanas? ¿Qué palabras o frases son comunes en tu sitio de trabajo? ¿Qué frases comunes se usan para ciertas situaciones?

III. Gramática/Ortografía
¿En qué puntos gramaticales u ortográficos necesitas trabajar? ¿Qué palabras o verbos te dan problemas? ¿Tienes problemas con los acentos ortográficos? ¿Qué estás haciendo para mejorar estos puntos débiles?

IV. Cultura Comunitaria
¿Qué prácticas culturales has notado entre los colegas y clientes en tu práctica profesional? ¿Cómo se observa la cultura en los clientes? ¿Qué hacen en tu prác-

tica profesional para respetar la cultura de los clientes? ¿Las prácticas culturales que has observado en la práctica profesional son similares o diferentes al mundo angloparlante?

V. Habilidades Profesionales y Cultura Organizativa
¿Qué has aprendido a hacer en tu práctica profesional que te puede ayudar en futuros trabajos? ¿Hay algo que hacen en tu práctica profesional que es diferente a otras experiencias de trabajo que has tenido? ¿Qué habilidades necesitas tener para tener éxito en este campo profesional?

VI. Metas Profesionales y Académicas
¿Qué metas profesionales o académicas tienes para mejorar tu uso del español o tu habilidad de trabajar con la comunidad hispana? ¿Qué harás para lograr estas metas?

References

Angelelli, Claudia, and Christian Degueldre. 2002. "Bridging the Gap between Language for General Purposes and Language for Work: An Intensive Superior-Level Language/Skill Course for Teachers, Translators, and Interpreters." In *Developing Professional Level Language Proficiency*, edited by Betty Lou Leaver and Boris Shekhtman. New York: Cambridge University Press.

Angelelli, Claudia, and Olga Kagan. 2002. "10 Heritage Speakers as Learners at the Superior Level: Differences and Similarities between Spanish and Russian Student Populations." In *Developing Professional Level Language Proficiency*, edited by Betty Lou Leaver and Boris Shekhtman. New York: Cambridge University Press.

Basturkmen, Helen. 2010. *Developing Courses in English for Specific Purposes*. New York: Palgrave Macmillan.

Beaudrie, Sara, Cynthia Ducar, and Ana María Relaño-Pastor. 2009. "Curricular Perspectives in the Heritage Language Context: Assessing Culture and Identity." *Language, Culture and Curriculum* 22, no. 2: 157–74.

Benjamin, Rebecca. 1997. "What Do Our Students Want? Some Reflections on Teaching Spanish as an Academic Subject to Bilingual Students." *ADFL Bulletin* 29: 44–47.

Bringle, Robert G., Julie A. Hatcher, and Rachel E. McIntosh. 2006. "Analyzing Morton's Typology of Service Paradigms and Integrity." *Michigan Journal of Community Service Learning* 13, no. 1: 5–15.

Bruno, Paula. 2003. "Nuestra comunidad: Service-Learning and Communities in Albuquerque, New Mexico." In *Juntos: Community Partnerships in Spanish and Portuguese*, edited by Josef Hellebrandt, Jonathan Arries, and Lucía T. Varona. Boston: Thomson/Heinle.

Burgess, John, and Sharlene Dyer. 2009. "Workplace Mentoring for Indigenous Australians: A Case Study." *Equal Opportunities International* 28, no. 6: 465–85.

Carter, Jennifer K. 1998. "College-Community Internship Program: Collaborative Efforts to Develop Local Opportunities." *Journal of Career Development* 25, no. 2: 135–40.

Ducar, Cynthia M. 2008. "Student Voices: The Missing Link in the Spanish Heritage Language Debate." *Foreign Language Annals* 41, no. 3: 415–33.

Douglas, Dan. 2001. "Language for Specific Purposes Assessment Criteria: Where Do They Come From?" *Language Testing* 18, no. 2: 171–85.

Gaarder, A. Bruce. 1972. "Teaching Spanish in School and College to Native Speakers of Spanish." *Hispania-Membership Issue* 55: 619–31.

Gibb, Stephen. 1999. "The Usefulness of Theory: A Case Study in Evaluating Formal Mentoring Schemes." *Human Relations* 52, no. 8: 1055–75.

Ingold, Catherine W., William Rivers, Carmen Chavez Tesser, and Erica Ashby. 2002. "Report on the NFLC/AATSP Survey of Spanish Language Programs for Native Speakers." *Hispania* 85, no. 2: 324–29. doi: 10.2307/4141093.

King de Ramírez, Carmen. 2015. "Strategy and Action: Assessing Student-Led Culture Workshops within the Professions." Foreign *Language Annals* 48, no. 1: 56–67.

King de Ramírez, Carmen, and Barbara A. Lafford. 2013. "Spanish for the Professions: Program Design and Assessment." In *Scholarship and Teaching on Languages for Specific Purposes*, edited by Lourdes Sánchez-López. University of Alabama at Birmingham: UAB Digital Collections. http://contentdm.mhsl.uab.edu/cdm/compoundobject/collection/faculty/id/161/rec/19.

Lear, Darcy, and Annie Abbott. 2009. "Aligning Expectations for Mutually Beneficial Community Service-Learning: The Case of Spanish Language Proficiency, Cultural Knowledge, and Professional Skills." *Hispania* 92, no. 2: 312–23. 0-www.jstor.org.libraries.colorado.edu/stable/40648364.

Leeman, Jennifer, Lisa Rabin, and Esperanza Román-Mendoza. 2011. "Identity and Activism in Heritage Language Education." *Modern Language Journal* 95, no. 4: 481–95.

Long, Mary K., and Isabella Uscinski. 2012. "Evolution of Languages for Specific Purposes Programs in the US: 1990–2011." *Modern Language Journal* 96, no. s1: 173–89. doi: 10.1111/j.1540-4781.2012.01303.x0026–7902/11/173–189.

Lynch, Brian K. 2008. "Locating and Utilizing Heritage Language Resources in the Community: An Asset-Based Approach to Program Design and Evaluation." In *Heritage Language Education: A New Field Emerging*, edited by Donna M. Brinton, Olga Kagan, and Susan Bauckus. New York: Routledge.

Martínez, Glenn, and Adam Schwartz. 2012. "Elevating." *Heritage Language Journal* 9, no. 2: 37–49.

Petrov, Lisa Amor. 2013. "A Pilot Study of Service-Learning in a Spanish Heritage Speaker Course: Community Engagement, Identity, and Language in the Chicago Area." *Hispania* 96, no. 2: 310–27. 0-www.jstor.org.libraries.colorado.edu/stable/23608329.

Pino, Frank. 2001. "A Pilot Project to Include Culture in the Spanish Business Language Curriculum for Heritage Speakers." In *Proceedings of the Annual Meeting of Hispanic and Latino Studies*. Westbrook, ME: National Association of African American Studies and Affiliates.

Potowski, Kim. 2002. "Experiences of Spanish Heritage Speakers in University Foreign Language Courses and Implications for Teacher Training." *ADFL Bulletin* 33, no. 3: 35–42.
Sánchez-López, Lourdes. 2013. "Service-Learning Course Design for Languages for Specific Purposes Programs." *Hispania* 96, no. 2: 383–96.
Sigmon, Robert. 1979. "Service-Learning: Three Principles." *Synergist* 8, no. 1: 9–11.
Tacelosky, Kathleen. 2013. "Community-Based Service-Learning as a Way to Meet the Linguistic Needs of Transnational Students in Mexico." *Hispania* 96, no. 2: 328–41. 0-www.jstor.org.libraries.colorado.edu/stable/23608330.
Tijunelis, Viktorija, Teresa Satterfield, and José R. Benkí. 2013. "Linking Service-Learning Opportunities and Domestic Immersion Experiences in US Latino Communities: A Case Study of the 'En Nuestra Lengua' Project." *Hispania* 96, no. 2: 264–82. 0-www.jstor.org.libraries.colorado.edu/stable/23608326.
Valdés, Guadalupe, Joshua A. Fishman, Rebecca Chávez, and William Pérez. 2008. "Maintaining Spanish in the United States: Steps toward the Effective Practice of Heritage Language Re-Acquisition/Development." *Hispania* 91, no. 1: 4–24. 0-www.jstor.org.libraries.colorado.edu/stable/20063620.

4 Developing Intercultural Competence and Leadership through LSP Curricula

LeAnn Derby, Jean W. LeLoup, James Rasmussen, and Ismênia Sales de Souza

More than a decade after the publication of the original document on national standards for foreign language (FL) learning—now retitled "World Readiness Standards for Learning Languages"—the American Council on the Teaching of Foreign Languages (ACTFL) published the *21st Century Skills Map* (2011), in which the word "leader" appears. The purpose of the skills map is to integrate more general skills within language and cultural education. The document includes explicit references to the role of global perspectives and global citizenship in twelve skill areas deemed critical for the future education of FL students. Of particular importance to the present chapter is the skill area titled "Leadership and Responsibility." The definition of this skill area states that "students as responsible leaders leverage their linguistic and cross-cultural skills to inspire others to be fair, accepting, open, and understanding within and beyond the local community" (ACTFL 2011). Certainly, these skills of leadership and responsibility are of use to all citizens who aim to participate successfully in a global society and demonstrate robust intercultural communication ability (Kramsch 2001).

Leadership studies as a multidisciplinary area of inquiry is still new, but it is gaining ground in tertiary education in the United States (Badaracco 2006; Brungardt et al. 1997; Committee for Economic Development 2006; Murphy and Riggio 2003). The presence of the leadership skill on the ACTFL map may be a strong indication that language learning and leadership education will be converging in mainstream FL curricula and classrooms in the future. It is also easily assimilated into ACTFL's already familiar "connections" category, bolstered by recent studies from interdisciplinary research with the neurosciences and education showing that fusion between disciplines can provide effective pathways to learning (Coyle, Hood, and Marsh 2010, 25). A foreign language course with a focus on leadership is currently probably most readily categorized among courses denominated as language for specific purposes (LSP), insofar as leadership is not currently fully integrated as one of the standard concerns of any FL course. What leadership studies can add to LSP is, first of all, a new focus, related in some ways to business courses but decidedly different. How leadership studies also might add to the field of LSP studies is as a topic readily integrated into hybrid courses that include more traditional elements as well as specifically LSP concerns. One might of course create a fully LSP-oriented course "Spanish for Leadership" along the lines of "Spanish for Business," which may often be a kind of "what's next" course after the more basic courses have been completed. One example of this is the "Spanish for Leadership" course created and taught in 2012 by a Colorado high school Spanish teacher, Cristin Bleess (see chapter 2 by Risner et al. in this volume; Crouse 2013). But there may also be flexibility to take a value-added approach in which already-existing courses add leadership studies to their goals without dramatically changing their basic orientation or design (Badaracco 2006). This could allow leadership studies to be integrated at all levels of the curriculum.

The area of leadership studies is particularly important to the vision of the US Air Force Academy, which as an institution is committed to producing new officers for the Air Force with strong moral character and leadership qualities. According to the US Air Force (2011), "Leadership is the art and science of motivating, influencing, and directing Airmen to understand and accomplish the Air Force mission in joint warfare." Students are required to participate in regular workshops organized by the Center for Character and Leadership Development, which also helps organize an annual National Character and Leadership Symposium that all students must attend and that features distinguished scholars, military leaders, and corporate executives from around the nation as guest speakers. In addition, individual departments are tasked with finding ways to incorporate leadership studies into their teaching, regardless of the subject matter.

The Air Force Academy's Department of Foreign Languages (DFF) focuses on helping to produce culturally adept and language-enabled emerging leaders capable of responding to the Air Force's needs in its global operations, which generally require close engagement and cooperation with allies and local populations. Students who are preparing to be leaders need to learn that certain traits, skills, and forms of behavior may be effective in certain cultural situations but not in others (Kramsch 2001), and that effective leaders and leadership styles vary across cultures (Long et al. 2015). Recognizing that there are different ways of conceptualizing leadership, and that there are many different types of leaders, is part of a process of leadership development and can be taught effectively through attention to culture and cultural difference (Long et al. 2014).

Leadership development can and should thus go hand-in-hand with the development of intercultural competence, and because intercultural competence has long been perceived as a central purpose of foreign language education (Kramsch 1993), the addition of leadership development to the goals of the foreign language classroom need not be something external or extraneous to the main content of the course. The notion of intercultural competence has of course been defined in various ways (Deardorff 2006). For purposes of its language and culture-related programs and institutions, the Air Force has defined it as "the ability to quickly and accurately comprehend, then appropriately and effectively act, to achieve the desired effect in a culturally complex environment" (US Air Force Culture and Language Center 2012). This definition bears many similarities with the "desired external outcome" in Deardorff's pyramid model of intercultural competence: "Behaving and communicating effectively and appropriately (based on one's intercultural knowledge, skills, and attitudes) to achieve one's goals to some degree" (Deardorff 2006, 254), though its stronger language reflects a military context in which one's goals or desired effects are assumed to involve issues of national security and the personal safety of one's subordinates. The Air Force's definition also implies many of the same types of knowledge Deardorff identifies as necessary to such an outcome: "cultural self-awareness; deep understanding and knowledge of culture (including contexts, role and impact of culture & others' world views); culture-specific information; sociolinguistic awareness" (254).

Although the Air Force Academy's DFF has long perceived intercultural competence as an important outcome and has sought ways to integrate it into the foreign language classroom, the DFF has only recently begun to develop explicit and methodical ways of incorporating leadership development. In 2012, several faculty members began a study under the aegis of the Center for Scholarship of Teaching and Learning (SoTL) in order to better understand the current state of leadership development within DFF courses. They also participated in a Faculty Learning Community (FLC), exchanging possible activities and strategies that could be incorporated in DFF courses in order to more explicitly develop leadership in a discipline-specific manner.

That phase I study, conducted in the fall semester of 2012, revealed several perspectives and ideas for classroom activities. Student focus groups revealed that cadets wanted more integration of leadership and FL learning but preferred this to be accomplished through culture-related activities rather than through lessons about leadership per se (Long and Derby 2013). During the spring of 2013, members of the FLC in DFF explored the concept of leadership development within the context of the institution, shared numerous cultural scenarios that had leadership embedded in the learning of languages and cultures, and examined and exchanged ideas about informal and formal experimentation that took place during spring 2013 classes (Long et al. 2014).

The DFF's investigation of ways to incorporate leadership-oriented teaching entered a second phase, also carried out during the spring semester of 2013, which specifically targeted advanced-level Spanish and German courses with readings, discussions, and written comparisons of leaders within the target culture and between the two target cultures. The idea that knowing foreign languages and cultures helps produce good leaders became an explicit part of many cadets' thinking, and considerations of how leadership and leadership styles may vary across cultures was fully integrated into literature and culture seminars that focused on the experience and representations of war in German- and Spanish-language texts. Cadets also indicated that the joint discussion sessions, which provided a forum for reflection on relations between German, Hispanic, and American notions and practices of leadership, broadened their perspective in enjoyable and profitable ways, and they suggested that there be more such sessions (Long and Rasmussen 2014).

The present study, phase III of the SoTL suite of investigations, builds on the research findings from phase I, phase II, and the interactions throughout the meetings of the FLC, and continues to consider the relationship between the development of leadership and language/cultural expertise by focusing on the use of cultural scenarios with students studying four different languages in first-, third-, and fifth-semester language courses. According to Shrum and Glisan (2010, 58), the classroom environment should foster a sociocultural community of learners engaged in meaning making and acquiring knowledge through the foreign language, and at the same time enable learners to develop more relevant cultural insights in the target culture and their own. The implication is that leadership development can be intentionally, explicitly, and systematically embedded in FL learning to enhance relevancy and overall development. Research also shows that making things real for students by using authentic situations makes them more motivated to learn (Peterson and Coltrane 2003). The purpose of this study, therefore, was to determine the impact of having cadets respond to cultural scenarios that would try to approximate authentic situations in the classroom and that would be explicitly related to cadets' future career and leadership opportunities.

Research Questions and Design

The focus of the present project was to experiment with and assess the effectiveness of melding leadership content and certain aspects of language instruction by way of carefully crafted cultural scenarios involving both cultural practices and issues related to leadership studies. Most, but not all, scenarios contained a military component in order to focus students' attention on the potential effect of these scenarios on their future occupations. The main objective was to better understand the overall impact of incorporating these scenarios with respect to cadets making cultural comparisons, understanding culturally appropriate behaviors, and appreciating the relevance of intercultural competence to their future careers as Air Force officers. These cultural scenarios cover all four of the DFF language standards—cultures, careers, communication, and connections (see Long et al. 2014)—which are closely aligned with, although not completely parallel to, the ACTFL-sponsored national standards for foreign language learning (NSFLEP 2006). This adaptation of the standards was realized in order to reflect our particular institutional context. The specific research questions addressed by this study were:

1. How effective are scenarios in facilitating cadets' understanding of appropriate behavior in other cultures? Why are they effective (or not) for this outcome?
2. How effective are scenarios in facilitating cadets' appreciation of the relevance of cultural understanding to their careers as officers? Why are they effective (or not) for this outcome?

The study systematically focused on four different language courses from elementary to advanced: Beginning French, Intermediate Spanish, Intermediate German, and Advanced Portuguese. Although all the instructors involved included cultural scenarios, the scenarios were incorporated in slightly different ways in each course. Because our goal was to experiment with integrating leadership as a value-added element of a course already being taught, rather than with designing a completely new course centered entirely on leadership, we decided that it would be best for each instructor to integrate the scenarios in ways that seemed least disruptive to what he or she was already planning to do in the course. Thus, first-semester French (135 cadets) incorporated three different cultural scenarios during class sessions across the semester, and each scenario presentation included paired conversation followed by a class discussion about how the scenario could best be handled to maximize intercultural sensibility. Third-semester Spanish (185 cadets) presented the scenarios in a similar way—small group dialogue followed by a class discussion about how the scenario may possibly be handled to reveal intercultural understanding and exhibit appropriate cultural comportment—but included seven different cultural scenarios rather than three. Fifth-semester Portuguese (30 cadets) had student groups prepare to enact five different cultural scenarios in class (in the target language), and after each presentation, the class discussed how the scenario might best be handled to demonstrate intercultural awareness. Third-semester German (75 cadets) did not include direct discussion of the scenarios but rather included presentation and discussion of specific cultural differences linked to the cultural content of each chapter unit. In the assessment essay, a scenario was presented and students were asked to indicate not only how they would respond but also their rationale, which would reveal their understanding of the cultural norms at issue.

Despite such differences, the scenarios themselves were quite similar, often involving interpersonal relations in social settings the cadets would likely encounter as Air Force officers visiting or working in a foreign culture. Many of these scenarios required students to demonstrate a familiarity with cultural practices and perspectives and necessitated explicit reflection on issues relating to leadership. This cultural knowledge is necessary in order to interact appropriately and successfully with counterparts in the target culture while concomitantly providing an example or leadership model for one's subordinates. (See appendix 4A, available online at press.georgetown.edu, for two examples of scenarios used in the study.)

Assessments

Measures of impact included embedded questions in quizzes, graded reviews (tests), and finals as well as self-reported responses from cadets. The embedded assessments varied somewhat in each course, as explained in the following subsections.

French 131

An essay question was included in the graded review and final exam of the French 131 course, dealing with the military cultural scenarios discussed in class. On the exams, cadets wrote about their reaction, as an officer, to the specific military cultural scenario, displaying their understanding of the need for appropriate behavior in specific circumstances. Answers were in English unless they included greetings or responses in French learned in class. A subset of 50 cadets was analyzed using only part 2 of the scoring rubric (see appendix 4B, part 2, available online at press.georgetown.edu).

Spanish 221

In Spanish 221, an essay question was included in both the midterm and final exams dealing with military cultural scenarios discussed in class. In the essay, cadets described a specific cultural scenario that presented a potential problem, offered a culturally appropriate solution, and then connected this action to their leadership position as an officer. Answers were written in Spanish; however, they were graded for content and not for grammar. A three-part scoring rubric was used for grading (see appendix 4B, available online at press.georgetown.edu).

Portuguese 321

In Portuguese 321, a scenario was included on both the midterm and final exams dealing with military cultural situations discussed in class. In the scenario, cadets described a potential cultural or leadership problem, offered an actionable solution, and then connected this action to their leadership position as an officer. Answers were written in Portuguese or English; however, they were graded for content and not for grammar. A three-part scoring rubric was used for grading (see appendix 4B, available online at press.georgetown.edu).

German 221

In German 221, an essay question was included in each of four chapter exams, and the final exam dealt with the cultural scenarios in the context of the specific German-American cultural differences discussed in class. In the essay, cadets explained how they would react to the scenario and provided a detailed response about why, given the cultural norms discussed in class, they would react in that way. Answers could be written in either German or English. Extra points were available if they wrote in German; German responses were graded for content and not for grammar. A 10-point scoring rubric was used for grading (see appendix 4C, available online at press.georgetown.edu).

Additionally, we gathered subjective data on the impact of incorporating said scenarios on cadets' thinking via a two-item questionnaire that was exactly the same for all the courses involved (see appendix 4D, available online at press.georgetown.edu). It was available online (via SharePoint) for cadets to access during the last week of class. Each item incorporated both a Likert-scale section and an open-ended portion that cadets could use to expound on their scale selection and thus to better reveal cadet reasoning.

Research Findings

Research data were collected from two sources: embedded assessments in each of the four courses, and a student questionnaire. Each set of data is discussed in turn.

Essay Data

The data from the assessments embedded in the four different language courses were analyzed using rubrics (see appendixes 4B and 4C, available online at

Table 4.1 Spanish 221 Results, by Instructor

Instructor	Number of Sections	Average Score (%)
A	3	83.0
B	3	73.0
C	2	70.5
D	2	80.0
E	1	85.0

press.georgetown.edu), with the goal of assessing how well cadets understood the appropriate behavior given the culture they were in and the relevance of that understanding to their career as an officer. In three of the four languages, all cadets were graded by only one faculty member to avoid inter-rater reliability errors.

The French course included 135 cadets in nine sections, with five instructors. A random sample of 50 cadets was selected. One instructor graded all 50 cadets in order to calculate the scores on the four cultural scenarios on the final exam, based on the 10-point rubric (see appendix 4B, part 2, available online at press.georgetown.edu). Their overall score was 80 percent.

The Spanish course included 181 cadets in eleven sections with five instructors. Only one instructor graded all 181 cadets, with an overall average of 78.5 percent based on the 30-point rubric (see appendix 4B, available online at press.georgetown.edu). However, there were notable score inconsistencies among sections by instructor, as shown in table 4.1. Discrepancies were also evident in cadet comments, suggesting that some classes did not discuss the scenarios in as much depth or detail as did others.

The Portuguese course included 30 cadets in two sections with only one instructor. The overall average was 89 percent for both the midterm and the final exams based on the 30-point rubric (see appendix 4B, available online at press.georgetown.edu).

The German course included 74 cadets in five sections with three instructors. Each instructor graded their own four scenarios with the 10-point rubric (see appendix 4C, available online at press.georgetown.edu), and the overall average was 86.5 percent. However, scores on each of the four scenarios varied, with the first scenario's 79 percent average being the lowest. After subsequent instructional adjustments were made, the scenarios that followed had higher averages.

Questionnaire Data

On the cadet questionnaire, 306 cadets responded to the first research question, "How effective are scenarios in facilitating cadets' understanding of appropriate

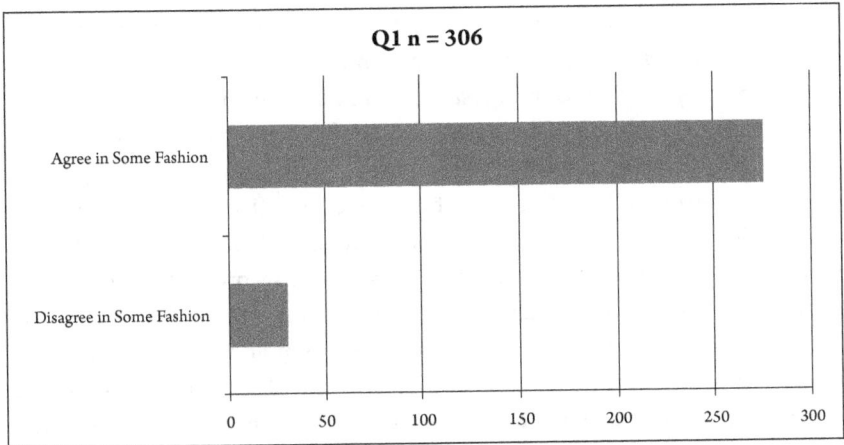

Figure 4.1 Q1: The Scenarios Increased My Understanding of Appropriate Behaviors in the Other Cultures

Note: 276 / 306 agree in some fashion = 90%

behavior in other cultures?" Ninety percent agreed in some fashion (by choosing ratings 4–6 on the Likert scale) that the scenarios *increased their understanding of appropriate behaviors in the other cultures* (see figure 4.1). The proportions differed slightly by language: French, 88 percent; German, 98 percent; Portuguese, 93 percent; and Spanish, 88 percent. Most interesting were the open-ended explanations from cadets as to the reason(s) for their individual response. (Not all cadets offered this optional explanation.)

In French, of the 74 cadets who gave an explanation, the data were categorized into four themes. The first theme, "new ideas provided understanding," made up 49 percent of responses. The second theme, "new ideas were useful for an Air Force career," accounted for 29 percent of the responses. The third theme, with 16 percent of the comments, suggested that the "cadets needed more scenarios for understanding." And, the fourth theme, with only 6 percent of the comments, was "the scenarios made no sense or were common sense."

In Spanish, of the 167 cadets who gave an explanation, the data were also categorized into four themes. The first theme, "intercultural competence is important," made up 49 percent of the responses. The second theme, with 18 percent of responses, included comments like "unknown" or "common sense." The third theme, with 10 percent of comments, suggested that the "scenarios were instructor dependent" (see table 4.1). And the fourth theme, with only 8 percent of the comments, pertained to the scenarios underscoring an "important effect on an Air Force career."

In Portuguese, of the 14 cadets who gave an explanation, the data were categorized into three themes. The first theme, "intercultural competence is important," encompassed 46 percent of responses. The second and third themes, each accounting for 32 percent of the responses, were "cultural scenarios involved critical thinking" and the "cadets appreciated the cultural scenarios."

In German, of the 51 cadets who offered an explanation, five distinct themes were evident. The first theme recognized cognition—"sparked new thinking / new awareness," with 35 percent of responses. The second theme recognized relevance—"applicable/useful for future engagements with other cultures," with 30 percent of responses. The third theme involved sensation—the cadets found the "scenarios interesting and/or enjoyable," with 10.5 percent of responses. The fourth theme, "not enough scenarios and/or time spent," had 14 percent of responses. The fifth theme included comments like "common sense, or already knew, or otherwise unhelpful" and had 10.5 percent of responses.

All four languages had similarities in their responses from cadets regarding their "understanding of appropriate behaviors" in the other cultures. One student comment that could be considered representative is "I want to be able to connect with people as a future officer, and I can't do that if I don't know the most basic things about their culture."

The second research question was "How effective are scenarios in facilitating cadets' appreciation of the relevance of cultural understanding to their careers as officers?" The synopsis of the 306 cadets' responses to this item on the questionnaire—about the cultural scenarios used in French 131, Spanish 221, German 221, and Portuguese 321—follows: 87.6 percent agreed in some fashion (ratings 4–6 on the Likert scale) that "the scenarios increased their appreciation of the relevance of cultural understanding to their career as an officer" (see figure 4.2).

Again, the proportions differed slightly by language: French, 93 percent; German, 92 percent; Portuguese, 86 percent; Spanish, 85 percent. Once again, the open-ended explanations from cadets provided further insight into the reasons for their response(s).

In French, of the 74 cadets who gave an explanation, the data were categorized into three themes. The first theme, "intercultural competence is important," made up 60 percent of responses. The second theme, "cultural learning has implications for an Air Force career," included 36 percent of the responses. The third theme, with only 4 percent of the comments, suggested that the "cadets needed more scenarios for understanding."

In Spanish, of the 167 cadets who gave an explanation, the data were classified

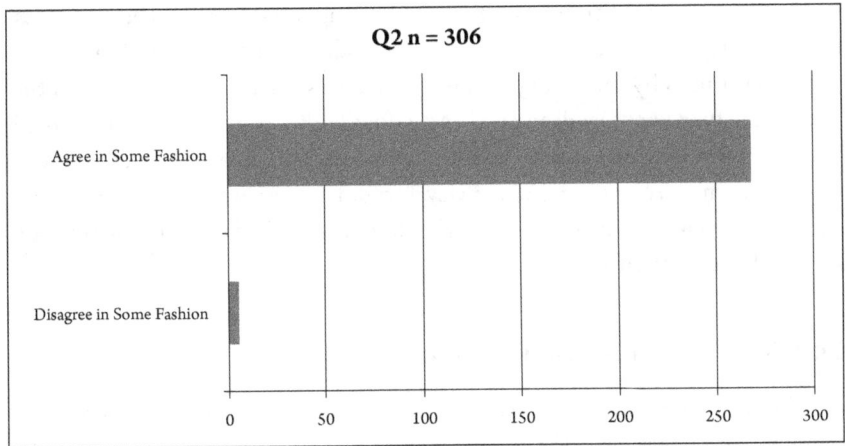

Figure 4.2 Q2: The Scenarios Increased My Appreciation of the Relevance of Cultural Understanding to My Career as an Officer
Note: 268 / 306 agree in some fashion = 87.6%

into four themes. The first theme, "effect on their Air Force career," encompassed 45 percent of responses. The second theme, "the importance of intercultural competence," included 28 percent of the responses. The third theme, with 6 percent of comments, suggested that the "scenarios were not covered or only slightly touched upon in class." And, the fourth theme, "the scenarios were either realistic or common sense," included only 4 percent of the comments.

In Portuguese, 100 percent of the 14 cadets who gave an explanation to the question about the relevance of cultural understanding to their career as an officer fell into the theme "cultural learning has implications for an Air Force career."

In German, of the 51 cadets who offered an explanation, four distinct themes emerged. The first theme recognized "a greater sense of the importance of intercultural competence," with 42 percent of responses. The second theme, with 21 percent of responses, was "new thought or awareness of what is needed for a future career." The third theme was cadets found "the scenarios interesting and/ or enjoyable," with 16 percent of responses. The fourth theme, titled "Actual experience needed; scenarios can't help or are otherwise unhelpful," had 13 percent of responses. A fifth category included comments like "common sense," or "already knew," and made up 8 percent of responses.

All four languages had similarities in their responses from cadets regarding the relevance of cultural understanding to their career as an officer. One student comment was particularly illustrative and indicated that the purposeful integration of leadership and culture in the language classroom had been successful: "I personally believe that the only way to handle a situation properly and make wise decisions is by practicing in similar scenarios. That is what we did in this class. More than likely, I will end up in situations fairly close to the ones presented. Perhaps it will be while I am in an official capacity in the Air Force, or it may be while I am on a personal trip. Either way, I would have no way of dealing with the situation if I was unaware of the cultural differences and had never thought of how I would handle the situation."

Conclusion and Future Directions

On the basis of our research, we put forward the following conclusions and thoughts for further directions of research:

- Cultural scenarios—approximations of authentic situations and settings, in which students need to draw on intercultural knowledge to respond in an appropriate way—can be powerful tools to reinforce and expand student learning not only about the L2 culture but also about leadership and what it can mean or look like in a variety of settings.
- The idea of incorporating leadership development with language and culture study can be successfully implemented in FL classes at all levels of language ability as a value-added element and not necessarily just as an advanced LSP course. This kind of hybrid course, with a topic of such broad interest as "leadership," can help integrate the interests and value of the LSP movement into other, long-standing goals of FL education such as intercultural competence. One does not necessarily need very advanced students or an entirely new course in order to incorporate the teaching of leadership into the FL classroom.
- Our project, focusing on the inclusion of cultural scenarios but allowing variations in scenario design, presentation, and assessment, may prove useful to others because of its adaptability and flexibility. Individual instructors who are interested in the idea of using cultural scenarios can and should experiment with different ways of incorporating them (e.g., acting them out, discussing them in detail, discussing only the required cultural knowledge, and requiring the students to engage with a particular scenario on their own before discussing together) and with different scenarios.
- One further direction our research could go is to look carefully at whether particular ways of presenting the scenarios produce better results.
- Another possible variation would be to construct different types of cul-

tural scenarios, perhaps tailored to one's particular student body and its concomitant characteristics.

Linking leadership and language is important to our DFF mission: to develop leaders of character with a global perspective. Cultural scenarios that include a leadership component can be constructed and presented in a variety of ways and are viable strategies to cover all four of the DFF language standards—cultures, careers, communication, and connections. Because leadership as an educational notion is rising in importance throughout academe and, in particular, in FL instruction, it behooves us to find creative ways to incorporate this key concept into FL curricula as often and as effectively as possible. The present study demonstrates one way to do so with positive results at varying language levels and in different language contexts. Scant evidence exists in the literature of efforts to explicitly relate the fields of FL and leadership. Future research endeavors should aim to meld these two concepts and then measure the success of doing so in order to integrate leadership as a core value in FL education. In this way, we will be helping to develop future citizens who achieve solid intercultural competence and, indeed, lead in a global society.

References

ACTFL (American Council on the Teaching of Foreign Languages). 2011. *21st Century Skills Map*. www.actfl.org/sites/default/files/pdfs/21stCenturySkillsMap/p21_world languagesmap.pdf.

Badaracco, Joseph L. 2006. *Questions of Character: Illuminating the Heart of Leadership through Literature*. Boston: Harvard Business Review Press.

Brungardt, Curtis L., Lawrence V. Gould, Rock Moore, and Joe Potts. 1997. "The Emergence of Leadership Studies: Linking the Traditional Outcomes of Liberal Education with Leadership Development." *Journal of Leadership Studies* 4, no. 3: 53–67.

Committee for Economic Development. 2006. *Education for Global Leadership: The Importance of International Studies and Foreign Language Education for US Economic and National Security*. Washington, DC: Committee for Economic Development.

Coyle, Do, Philip Hood, and David Marsh. 2010. *Content and Language Integrated Learning*. Cambridge: Cambridge University Press.

Crouse, Douglass. 2013. "Languages for Specific Purposes in the 21st Century." *Language Educator* 8, no. 3: 32–35.

Deardorff, Darla K. 2006. "Identification and Assessment of Intercultural Competence as a Student Outcome of Internationalization." *Journal of Studies in International Education* 10, no. 3: 241–66.

Kramsch, Claire J. 1993. *Context and Culture in Language Teaching*. Oxford: Oxford University Press.

———. 2001. "Intercultural Communication." In *The Cambridge Guide to Teaching English to Speakers of Other Languages*, edited by Ronald Carter and David Nunan. Cambridge: Cambridge University Press.

Long, Sheri S., and LeAnn Derby. 2013. "Linking Leadership and Language Development: Data and Implementation Strategies." Paper presented at Annual Conference of American Council on the Teaching of Foreign Languages, Orlando, November.

Long, Sheri S., LeAnn Derby, Lauren Scharff, Jean W. LeLoup, and Daniel Uribe. 2015. "Leadership Development and Language Learning: A Foundational Framework." In *Dimension 2015: All That Glitters Is SCOLT: 50 Years of Language Teaching and Learning*, edited by Pete Swanson. Valdosta, GA: Southern Conference on Language Teaching.

Long, Sheri S., Jean W. LeLoup, LeAnn Derby, and Ramsamooj J. Reyes. 2014. "Fusing Language Learning and Leadership Development: Initial Approaches and Strategies." In *Dimension 2014: Uniting the Corps: Uniting the Core*, edited by Kristin Hoyt and Pete Swanson. Valdosta, GA: Southern Conference on Language Teaching.

Long, Sheri S., and James Rasmussen. 2014. "Integrating Leadership Development and Literary Studies: Towards a Sustainable Model of Advanced Foreign-Language Literary Instruction." Special session and papers presented at Annual Conference of the South Atlantic Modern Language Association, Atlanta, November.

Murphy, Susan E., and Ronald E. Riggio, eds. 2003. *The Future of Leadership Development*. Mahwah, NJ: Lawrence Erlbaum Associates.

NSFLEP (National Standards in Foreign Language Education Project). 2006. *Standards for Foreign Language Learning in the 21st Century (SFLL)*, 3rd ed. Lawrence, KS: Allen Press.

Peterson, Elizabeth, and Bronwyn Coltrane. 2003. "Culture in Second Language Teaching." Eric Digest, EDO-FL-03-09. www.cal.org/resource-center/briefs-digests/digests.

Shrum, Judith L., and Eileen W. Glisan. 2010. *Teacher's Handbook: Contextualized Language Instruction*, 4th ed. Boston: Heinle.

US Air Force Academy. 2011. *United States Air Force Academy Curriculum Handbook 2011–2012*. USAF Academy, CO: Academy Board.

US Air Force Culture and Language Center. 2012. "Culture Department: Background." http://culture.af.mil/culture_background.aspx.

5 Developing a More Efficient Conversation Paradigm for Learning Foreign Languages

Lessons on Asking and Answering Questions in an LSP Context

Robert A. Quinn

During the past forty years, language educators have greatly improved the delivery and evaluation of language instruction. The proficiency movement, national standards, performance-based assessment, better curriculum design, and more emphasis on culture are now established as major factors, and technological support has advanced at a rapid pace. Textbook authors have not, however, made commensurate progress in revising and improving instructional materials, even though the success of delivery depends to a great extent on the effectiveness of content.

The grammar diagrams and explanations in language textbooks and ancillary materials, for instance, are still much the same as those published decades before the proficiency movement. A prime example is the information provided to learners about how to answer questions. Using the traditional verb chart, many students still struggle with the verb changes involved in conversation, when being able to understand and answer questions is crucial for developing communicative proficiency.

The way instructors teach question/answer techniques must be as helpful and effective as possible for all language learners, particularly for students of language for specific purposes (LSP). Medical and legal students learning career-related skills, for example, are often already working in their profession and are pressed for time, so it is even more important to make their learning experiences as time-saving, useful, and productive as possible.

In the medical field, nurses comment that they can pronounce questions yet have difficulty understanding patients' replies. Nurses can form questions that elicit a "yes" or "no," a choice from a list, or a fill-in, but such questions frustrate patients who want to add or request information beyond that restricted scope. In the legal profession, attorneys consulting with clients must understand them and respond accurately. Therefore, especially in courses for medical and legal professionals—but also in courses for engineers, business personnel, and other learners—LSP instructors need to strengthen their teaching of an essential methodological element: question/answer processes.

Accordingly, when English-speaking college students eighteen to thirty-two years old who were enrolled in Spanish courses cited difficulty with answering questions as one of their main concerns, the researcher asked them what teaching strategies would help. Those in introductory, intermediate, and LSP courses wanted better diagrams and explanations. They were especially puzzled about how the verbs change from questions to answers.

As a result, the author composed a unit titled "Asking and Answering Questions," which included interrogative words, the traditional verb chart, types of questions and replies, and exercises. After the researcher helped the participants understand and correct their mistakes on formative written and oral work, he assessed their progress through summative evaluations. Then the researcher revised the lessons, discussed them with students and teachers to obtain feedback for improvement, and modified the chart to provide a more practical conversation model. The focus of this chapter is the principal product of those efforts—the design of the new paradigm—and its implications.

Five considerations guided the development of the new paradigm. The first two pertained to needs analysis: (1) Why do students need to know how verb forms function in questions and answers? and (2) why do learners need a new verb paradigm? The next two focused on the model: (3) Why use an input/output processing design? and (4) how do processing paradigms help learners more readily understand question/answer verb changes? The last consideration was (5) what are the implications for further research? The remainder of this chapter concentrates in turn on each of these considerations.

Why Do Students Need to Know How Verb Forms Function in Questions and Answers?

A careful reading of the Five Cs of the National Standards for Foreign Language Education in the United States (ACTFL 2016) shows that the ability to communicate—to ask and answer questions in the second language—is essential for every standard. In addition, teachers evaluate curricula as well as student performance by the criteria for the standards.

Student evaluations, in large part, depend on how well learners understand questions and formulate appropriate responses. For instance, teachers have long depended on questions at the ends of readings to assess comprehension and the ability to answer adequately, and the Oral Proficiency Examination provides a similar appraisal. Perhaps even more important is how, after graduation, the students' professional counterparts will judge their ability to communicate in the second language.

Why Do Learners Need a New Verb Paradigm?

Language learners need a better paradigm for several reasons. First, when engaging in conversations, students must move beyond memorizing and recognizing. They have to recall and apply, whenever needed, processes as well as content. As Lee and VanPatten (2003, 118–19) state: "What is common to all advanced learners of a language is exposure to lots of communicative or meaning-bearing input. In addition these persons were probably engaged in quite a bit of conversational interaction with others." In other words, because both input and output—listening and understanding, plus recalling and speaking—are involved in conversation, acquisition depends on understanding questions, attempting to formulate acceptable responses, and learning from errors.

Lee and VanPatten's statement brings out the differences between pedagogy (teaching youngsters), andragogy (instructing adults), and synergogy (a blend of the two) (Clardy 2005, 557). Adults prefer to acquire information and skills through clearly explained, logically sequenced material that is related to their personal and career interests. They like to discover ways to solve problems, use their own learning styles, work toward specific goals, and reinforce, through performance, what they are studying (Colorado Christian University 2011). Thus, because adults learn through far more than memorizing and practicing memorized content, they need learning materials that go beyond such memory aids as the traditional verb chart. In addition, first language speakers do not try to remember charts when they converse in their own language. Instead they seem to subconsciously recall the processes and information needed for expressing their ideas (Lee and VanPatten 2003, 127). In other words, they recall their performance experiences, which is similar to the way that adults prefer to learn through performance. Of course, communicative proficiency depends on knowing and understanding grammar forms, as displayed in the traditional model, but it also involves combining content with processes like those shown in the new paradigm.

We often hear beginners comment, "I understand more than I can speak." This problem may plausibly result from the use of the old model, which only lists forms and thereby does not help students grasp how the forms change during conversation. Phrased differently, the traditional verb chart does not promote communicative proficiency, because it was not designed to foster application. Using it, students can recognize forms in questions but have difficulty changing them to give a response. Thus, at present, learners understand more than they can speak until they experience multiple conversations, attempt to engage in those, and struggle through how to apply the forms.

Unfortunately, because many novices still have difficulty applying what they study by using current textbooks and ancillary materials, the traditional charts and explanations may actually somewhat impede rather than promote progress toward proficiency. If the goal of LSP instructors is for students to be able to use the second language, then it is important to seek the instructional content that is the most helpful for fostering application and, thereby, the most effective for promoting communicative skills.

Second, the updated model consolidates the verb forms, their translations, and the question/answer changes in one paradigm. It also offers a way for learners to begin seeing relationships between grammar topics. In contrast, textbooks usually present translations separately from verb diagrams, spread verb information over several chapters, and do not relate the changes to other grammar transformations. In addition, when students receive instruction about interrogative words and how to form questions, textbooks seldom explain how to give answers to those types of questions (Spinelli, García, and Galvin Flood 2013, 22). Consequently, learners who are pressed for time and not especially talented in acquiring a second language have to discover—virtually on their own—meanings, how the verbs change, and how to form answers. Their problem is compounded when questions involve indirect objects (as with the verb "gustar") or other complications. In contrast, besides fostering retention and application, the new paradigm can serve as the centerpiece for a unit that brings together essential question/answer information.

Third, language instructors have come to take the traditional chart for granted. Although students cite question/answer verb changes as a challenging aspect of learning conversational skills, and the old model does not promote oral proficiency by addressing the changes, textbook authors continue to use it in the most recent, proficiency-oriented textbooks and grammars, even when an improved, updated verb paradigm is warranted. Many teachers accept the traditional verb chart as a fait accompli and do not realize that the traditional chart has been used without significant revision for more than a century in American textbooks. For example, in the early twentieth century, Ramsey's grammar and exercise book (Ramsey 1902, 451) and Hills and Ford's grammar (Hills and Ford 1904, 186) displayed charts of the same type employed for teaching Latin (*Allen and Greenough's Latin Grammar* 1898, 98). Subsequently, numerous others—such as Tarr and Centero (1933, 237); Bolinger, Ciruti, and Montero (1960, 23, 62); Turk,

Espinosa, and Solé (1985, 16, 29, 42); and Kattan-Ibarra and Pountain (1997, 64)—included the same verb model in their textbooks and grammar books. In the twenty-first century, authors like the following continue using the traditional chart, which is inadequate for promoting proficiency: Butt and Benjamin (2011, 196); Zayas-Bazán, Bacon, and Nibert (2012, 62, 64); VanPatten, Leeser, and Ketting (2012, 23, 50); Kearon and Di Lorenzo-Kearon (2000, 53, 70, 75, 111, 211); and Spinelli, García, and Galvin Flood (2013, 11, A-19).

Why Use an Input/Output Processing Design?

Input-Processing Theory focuses on the comprehension (input) side of conversation. Lee and VanPatten, two major proponents of this theory, claim that traditional grammar teaching already focuses on the production (output) side of communication. As a result, VanPatten and his coauthors devised improved formulas and exercises only for the input phase and used traditional verb charts for the output phase in their textbook *Sol y Viento* (VanPatten, Leeser, and Keating 2012, 23, 50).

Lee and VanPatten, however, also contend that the traditional charts are inadequate for language teaching (Lee and VanPatten 2003, 128). If, as they posit—and the practical experience of many teachers and students indicates—the old charts are indeed insufficient, researchers are compelled to improve them. Providing a realistic depiction of the back and forth of conversation, both input and output, is essential for helping learners more readily understand question/answer verb changes and for facilitating their development of communicative proficiency. This researcher, therefore, chose an input/output design.

Using this design also further corroborates the practical value of the innovative paradigm. A key tenet of educational psychology is that learning occurs at the application level and beyond (Yuly 2010). This statement is linked to Bloom's Taxonomy, which served as the basis for the Defense Language Institute's proficiency scale, was later adapted to become the foundation for the US national standards, and is now often called the Taxonomy of Education. The traditional Spanish verb chart addresses only the two lowest levels of that classification system: knowing and comprehending, or, in other words, memorizing and recognizing. Conversely, the revised model promotes application, which is the gateway to the higher levels: analyzing, evaluating, and creating. Because modern courses emphasize practical application, or transcending just memorizing and recognizing, and because lasting learning occurs at the application level and beyond, the innovative paradigm is more suitable for proficiency-oriented courses.

The new model is also more appropriate because, as indicated above, it reduces the time and effort required for grasping how to understand and answer questions, brings together the essentials of conversational verb changes in one place, and is in harmony with modern developments such as Input-Processing Theory, Skill Acquisition Theory (Ortega 2008, 227, 230), and the Taxonomy of Education. The innovative paradigm, with its input/output design, thereby offers a more practical substitute for the traditional verb chart.

How Do Processing Paradigms Help Learners Understand Question/Answer Verb Changes?

By comparing and contrasting the traditional chart with the new processing paradigm, the reader can see how the two differ and how the latter is more helpful. Before examining the two models, keep in mind three caveats. First, processing paradigms are just depictions. They are not actual conversations any more than a photograph of a tree is a real tree. Second, the give-and-take in dialogues comprises more than what can be portrayed on paper because they include factors such as body language, tone of voice, speaking distance, and social level. Third, a realistic depiction must include both the understanding and the answering phases because for communication to occur, production usually needs to be followed by comprehension and then comprehension is followed by production, in a continuing cycle as the conversation proceeds. During communication, of course, one person typically speaks or writes and another listens or reads; then the listener or reader speaks or writes in response to the person who initiated the conversation.

Table 5.1 represents the traditional verb chart. Textbook writers typically present a separate chart for each of the three Spanish conjugations (Spinelli and

Table 5.1 The Traditional Verb Chart, Present Tense

Subject	Hablar	Comer	Vivir
yo	hablo	como	vivo
tú	hablas	comes	vives
él/ella/usted	habla	come	vive
nosotros/-as	hablamos	comemos	vivimos
vosotors/-as	habláis	coméis	vivís
ellos/-as, ustedes	hablan	comen	viven

Note: This is a composite of the traditional verb model. Typically, textbooks provide a separate chart for each of the three Spanish conjugations, which are shown here in the vertical columns. The three are combined here to conserve space. The symbol "/" indicates other subject endings that are possible for the same form. This model is merely a list and does not portray the dynamic nature of conversation, in which the verb forms change from questions to answers.

Rosso-O'Laughlin 2001, 34, 69, 75). All three follow the same format, so they are combined in table 5.1 to conserve space. Sometimes textbooks offer a translation for each form only in the –ar chart (Ríos and Fernández Torres 2004, 45). Occasionally, authors combine the charts for the –er and –ir conjugations because the two are quite similar (Zayas-Bazán, Bacon, and Nibert 2012, 64).

Tables 5.2 through 5.4 depict the innovative conversation paradigm with a separate version for each conjugation. All three follow the same organization, but because they show the changes from asking to answering plus a translation for each verb form, they require more space and are presented separately in tables 5.2, 5.3, and 5.4. Although these charts for the old model and the new one illustrate forms only in the present indicative, comparable charts can, of course, be designed for other tenses and the subjunctive.

What does the traditional chart (table 5.1) show learners? On the left are the subject pronouns for I, you (familiar singular), he, she, and you (formal); we, you (familiar plural); and they, you (formal plural). To the right and above the three columns, an infinitive for each conjugation appears, with the forms that correspond to each pronoun listed below the infinitives. This model gives students no information about how verbs change during conversation. Using the traditional chart (table 5.1), some learners mistakenly infer that subject pronouns must be included with Spanish verbs, just as they often accompany English ones. Such learners tend to overuse the pronouns, which can result in social blunders. Repeating "yo" frequently seems egotistical. Saying "tú" (you, familiar) over and over sounds demeaning.

In comparison, the revised paradigm (table 5.2) provides a different arrangement of subject pronouns to reflect the question/answer changes in verb forms. It shows the verbs in questions (the input) on the left side, while it displays their corresponding forms in answers (the output) on the right side, thereby giving a more realistic schema of conversation. Spanish verb endings designate the subject, so the matching pronouns do not accompany verbs unless they are needed to clarify or emphasize the subject. Therefore, unlike the traditional chart, the new paradigm does not display the Spanish pronouns unless they are needed to avoid ambiguity when using the third person singular or plural. To avoid cognitive overload and focus on the forms that learners will hear most often, such as "usted" and "ustedes" when living or working in Latin America, the revised models do not include the "vos" or "vosotros" forms. The teacher discussed these pronouns later, as necessary. Similarly, he introduced more ways of translating each verb form into English (the progressive, emphatic, and historical present; and the use of the present to indicate the future) only after students had become accustomed to making the question/answer changes.

Table 5.2 An Innovative Paradigm for –ar Conjugation, Present Tense

Change these verb forms from questions to answers, as illustrated:			
¿Necesit**as** (tú)?	Do **you** need?	Necesit**o**	**I** need
¿Necesit**a**(usted)?	Do **you** need?	Necesit**o**	**I** need
¿Necesit**an** (ustedes)?	Do **you** (plural) need?	Necesit**amos**	**We** need
Notice that the following forms do not change from question to answer:			
¿Necesita (ella)?	Does **she** need?	Necesita	**She** needs
¿Necesita (él)?	Does **he** need?	Necesita	**He** needs
¿Necesitan (ellos)?	Do **they** need?	Necesitan	**They** need

Note: This new model shows how forms change from questions to answers. It includes English translations. It also displays Spanish and English subject correspondences, which are in boldface. The Spanish subject pronouns are enclosed in parentheses to indicate that they are needed only for emphasis or to avoid ambiguity. This paradigm is original work by the author and may be reproduced, transmitted, copied, or adapted only by crediting the author and receiving written permission from him.

Table 5.3 An Innovative Paradigm for –er Conjugation, Present Tense

Change these verb forms from questions to answers, as illustrated:			
¿Beb**es** (tú)?	Do **you** drink?	Beb**o**	**I** drink
¿Beb**e** (usted)?	Do **you** drink?	Beb**o**	**I** drink
¿Beb**en** (ustedes)?	Do **you** (plural) drink?	Beb**emos**	**We** drink
Notice that the following forms do not change from question to answer:			
¿Bebe (ella)?	Does **she** drink?	Bebe	**She** drinks
¿Bebe (él)?	Does **he** drink?	Bebe	**He** drinks
¿Beben (ellos)?	Do **they** drink?	Beben	**They** drink

Note: See the note for table 5.2, including the statement about proprietary information.

Tables 5.3 and 5.4 follow the same format as table 5.2. Because learners have asked for the clarity provided by having a separate chart for each conjugation, 5.2 illustrates the –ar group, 5.3. the –er conjugation, and 5.4 the –ir verbs. To facilitate comprehension, the new paradigm shows only the translation most closely revealing the relationship between the Spanish and English forms (the simple present). In these tables the subject marker at the end of each Spanish verb and the subject pronouns at the beginning of every English verb are emphasized in bold type to draw attention to the correspondences between how subjects are expressed. This new emphasis helps students more readily recognize where

Table 5.4 An Innovative Paradigm for -ir Conjugation, Present Tense

Change these verb forms from questions to answers, as illustrated:			
¿Escri**bes** (tú)?	Do **you** write?	Escri**bo**	**I** write
¿Escri**be** (usted)?	Do **you** write?	Escri**bo**	**I** write
¿Escri**ben** (ustedes)?	Do **you** (plural) write?	Escri**bimos**	**We** write
Notice that the following forms do not change from question to answer:			
¿Escri**be** (ella)?	Does **she** write?	Escri**be**	**She** writes
¿Escri**be** (él)?	Does **he** write?	Escri**be**	**He** writes
¿Escri**ben** (ellos)?	Do **they** write?	Escri**ben**	**They** write

Note: See the note for table 5.2, including the statement about proprietary information.

changes occur and where they do not. No such clarifying emphasis appears in the traditional chart.

Maintaining focus on where the verb transformations occur is strengthened not only by the novel arrangement and use of boldface type in the new paradigm but also by having the top half of each new model display a set of second person–to–first person forms and showing how they change from question to answer, while the bottom half shows the third person forms and indicates that they do not change. This more practical design greatly simplifies the question/answer process and makes it more obvious—either the learners hear "you" (you familiar singular, you formal singular, you familiar plural, or you formal plural) and they have to change the verb form that is in the question, or they do not hear "you" and do not change the form. Even for questions like "Do I need bread?" or "Can we (inclusive) go?" the same dichotomy prevails. Because "you" is not in either question, no change occurs in the answer.

By revealing that simplified duality—change or do not change—the new model is more immediately useful because it points out exactly what students need to pay attention to, thus significantly reducing the time required for learning how to apply the verb forms. This simplification has not been emphasized during all the years the traditional chart has been used. During this research, however, the researcher found that more than fifty years ago, this dichotomy was included in a few exercises in a textbook (Bolinger, Ciruti, and Montero 1960, 24, 25). Even so, as far as he has been able to discover, until now it has never been stated explicitly, incorporated into verb charts, or presented as a teaching strategy.

Teaching with the new paradigm differs from that with the traditional chart. Conceptualized as a summary rather than an introduction, the new one is presented gradually, section by section, by the researcher. This guided, inductive approach complies with discovery techniques, like those in the professional development modules taught at the University of Texas, Austin (Salaberry 2010, lessons 3 and 4 and conclusion). After students became familiar with question/answer changes in English, the teacher showed them the English columns of the paradigm. When they had become accustomed to similar changes in Spanish, he presented the Spanish columns. Subsequently, the researcher had learners cover the paradigm and try to sketch it or explain the changes in their own words. Next, they worked in groups of three to fill in questions or answers with the correct verb forms in a career-oriented cloze dialogue. Then they took quizzes individually. Thereby, students gained a keener awareness of both the input and output processes, were allowed to use their preferred learning styles, moved beyond mere memorizing and recognizing to apply their newly acquired communicative skills, and were studying in the way adults prefer to learn. As the students performed the group exercises and took unannounced self-checking quizzes, noticeable improvement in completion time and performance was evident.

Afterward, when the participants in this action research studied indirect objects, possessive pronouns, and reflexive pronouns, the teacher used a peripatetic approach to extend and expand what they had learned from the processing paradigm. Because the students had become familiar with changing "you?" to "I," they quickly understood that when they saw or heard "for you?" in a question, they had to give "for me" in the answer, but "to her?" did not change and was "to her" in the reply. Likewise, "your?" changed to "mine," while "theirs?" stayed "theirs." "Yourself?" became "myself," but "himself?" did not change. In addition, when learning other tenses, the students noticed that verbs in answers are usually in the same tense as they are in questions. Learners were thus able to recognize connections between grammar topics and apply what they had learned from the processing paradigm in a wider range of ways than was possible with the traditional chart.

This compare-and-contrast section has shown that the traditional chart is just a memory aid, whereas the updated and revised paradigm strengthens teaching in several ways. It helps students realize that subject pronouns are usually omitted before Spanish verbs, saves them time because they do not need to search for translations in various parts of a textbook or technological ancillary materials, provides a simplified dichotomy, and frees them from having to struggle through extensive conversations before understanding how the verb forms change from questions to answers. The improved model especially benefits those pursuing careers such as medicine and law. The processing paradigm empowers students not only by presenting a clearer, simplified approach to question/answer changes and helping them apply the forms, but also by making them aware of connections between verb changes and transformations in other parts of speech. These benefits—which facilitate progress toward communicative proficiency—did not accrue to students during all the years learners used the traditional chart.

What Are the Implications for Future Research?

Due to the growing demand for professionals who communicate well in a second language, the need for improved learning materials is becoming increasingly compelling. Learners in LSP courses must achieve communicative proficiency while mastering career skills; therefore, they face constraints that make it all the more important for textbooks and ancillary materials to provide the most up-to-date and time-saving content possible. Researchers need to do more "beyond-the-frame" thinking to design additional, innovative paradigms that will facilitate student progress and possibly reveal other simplifications, such as the "change-or-do-not-change" duality resulting from this research.

Along with understanding and answering questions, other problems merit attention. As Pinto and Rex (2006, 620, 621) point out, the way we teach "por" and "para" needs improvement. Researchers should also focus on the use of "ser," "estar," "hacer," and "tener," in related expressions, the preterit contrasted with the imperfect, the indicative versus the subjunctive, and sentences such as those with "gustar." These grammar topics have been discussed in books and professional journals since at least the 1960s (Stockwell, Bowen, and Martin 1965, 285–87), yet the explanations and diagrams in our textbooks, as exemplified by those cited above, have remained basically the same.

A critical reading of the grammar sections in the scope-and-sequence sections of textbooks shows that authors still compartmentalize grammar presentations according to the parts of speech. Due to this type of organization, the topics that are difficult for students seem disparate, possible simplifications remain hidden, and functional relationships are obscured. By creatively studying problems and designing paradigms in harmony with advances in linguistics and second language acquisition, researchers may be able to discern overarching relationships between grammatical categories like those revealed by this research between the subject markers of verbs and the transformations required from questions to answers for indirect, personal, and reflexive pronouns. Eventually, such insights may enable textbook authors to integrate the teaching of grammar into a more cogent, cohesive whole.

In the past forty years, researchers, authors, and instructors have promoted significant progress in the delivery of content and the evaluation of student performance. Equivalent headway, however, has not been made in upgrading the content of lessons. After more than a hundred years of using the traditional verb charts, now is the opportune moment for similar efforts to improve paradigms, watch for simplifications, update explanations, and explore innovative approaches that will better meet the practical needs of modern language learners.

References

ACTFL (American Council on the Teaching of Foreign Languages). "Standards Summary." Alexandria, VA. www.actfl.org/publications/all/world-readiness-standards-learning-languages/standards-summary.

Allen and Greenough's Latin Grammar. 1898. Revised and Enlarged by James Bradstreet Greenough and George L. Kittredge. Boston: Ginn.

Bolinger, Dwight L., Joan E. Ciruti, and Hugo H. Montero. 1960. *Modern Spanish.* New York: Harcourt, Brace & World.

Butt, John, and Carmen Benjamin. 2011. *A New Reference Grammar of Modern Spanish.* London: Hodder Education.

Clardy, Alan. 2005. "Andragogy: Adult Learning and Education at Its Best?" *Journal of Educational Psychology* 91: 549–63.

Colorado Christian University. 2011. "How Adults Learn Compared to Younger Learners." College of Adult and Graduate Studies Blog. www.ccu.edu/blogs/cags/2011/10/how-adults-learn-compared-to-younger-learners/.

Hills, E. C., and J. D. M. Ford. 1904. *A Spanish Grammar with Alternative Exercises.* Boston: D. C. Heath.

Kattán-Ibarra, Juan, and Christopher J. Pountain. 1997. *Modern Spanish Grammar: A Practical Guide.* London: Routledge.

Kearon, Thomas P., and Maria Antonia Di Lorenzo-Kearon. 2000. *Medical Spanish: A Conversational Approach.* Fort Worth: Holt, Rinehart & Winston.

Lee, James F., and Bill VanPatten. 2003. *Making Communicative Language Teaching Happen.* Boston: McGraw-Hill.

Ortega, Lourdes. 2008. "Second Language Learning Explained? SLA across Nine Contemporary Theories." In *Theories in Second Language Acquisition,* edited by Bill VanPatten and Jessica Williams. New York: Routledge.

Pinto, Derrin, and Scott Rex. 2006. "The Acquisition of the Spanish Prepositions Por and Para in a Classroom Setting." *Hispania* 84, no. 3: 611–22.

Ramsey, William Montrose. 1902. *A Spanish Grammar with Exercises.* New York: Henry Holt.

Ríos, Joanna, and José Fernández Torres. 2004. *Complete Medical Spanish.* New York: McGraw-Hill.

Salaberry, Rafael. 2010. "Foreign Language Teaching Methods: Grammar." Texas Language Technology Center, University of Texas, Austin. http://coerll.utexas.edu/methods/modules/grammar/.

Spinelli, Emily, Carmen García, and Carol E. Galvin Flood. 2013. *Interacciones.* Boston: Heinle Cenage Learning.

Spinelli, Emily, and Marta Rosso-O'Laughlin. 2001. *Encuentros*. Fort Worth: Harcourt College.

Stockwell, Robert P., J. Donald Bowen, and John W. Martin. 1965. *The Grammatical Structures of English and Spanish*. Contrastive Analysis Series of Center for Applied Linguistics. Chicago: University of Chicago Press.

Tarr, F. Courtney, and Augusto Centero. 1933. *A Graded Spanish Review Grammar with Composition*. New York: Appleton-Century-Crofts.

Turk, Laurel H., Aurelio M. Espinosa Jr., and Carlos A. Solé. 1985. *Foundation Course in Spanish*. Lexington, MA: D. C. Heath.

VanPatten, Bill, Michael J. Leeser, and Gregory D. Keating. 2012. *Sol y Viento: Beginning Spanish*. New York: McGraw-Hill.

Yuly (pseudonym). 2010. "The Art of Instructional Design and E-Learning." https://instructionaldesignblog.wordpress.com.

Zayas-Bazán, Eduardo, Susan M. Bacon, and Holly J. Nibert. 2012. *¡Arriba!: Comunicación y cultura*. Upper Saddle River, NJ: Prentice Hall.

6 | Integrating Project-Based Learning into English for Specific-Purposes Classrooms

A Case Study of Engineering

Tatiana Nekrasova-Beker and Anthony Becker

Overview of Project-Based Learning

With an increasing number of international students entering US universities each year, educators are faced with the need to customize language instruction to provide specialized support to groups of students studying a specific discipline. In a situation when a one-size-fits-all English-language curriculum does not seem to meet the specific needs of students preparing to study engineering, business, or medicine, among other fields, language instructors are pushed to consider and incorporate the content that is relevant to the students and will help them succeed in their academic careers. As a result, many intensive English programs at US universities have adopted the principles of content-based instruction (CBI) to work on the development of students' linguistic skills in the target language while, at the same time, advancing their content knowledge of a specific subject.

Typically referred to as learning language through content, CBI can be conceptualized in a number of ways. Initially, CBI was associated with the immersion programs that emerged in Canada in the 1960s. In the early origins of CBI, students were concurrently taught the subject matter and the language skills. Later, CBI was extended to the contexts with nonacademic content that focused on topics that were of interest or importance to students (i.e., American history, cultural stereotypes, technology in the twenty-first century) as well as to workplace language programs that were helping employees gain proficiency in a second language (L2) in order to perform their jobs. Today, one of the most typical realizations of CBI that is directly related to its original application is teaching a second or foreign language for specific purposes (LSP), particularly English for specific purposes (ESP), a pedagogical context featured in the present study. As applied in LSP/ESP contexts, CBI is generally perceived as "an approach to language instruction that integrates the presentation of topics or tasks from subject matter classes (e.g., math, social studies) within the context of teaching a second or foreign language" (Crandall and Tucker 1990, 187).

Researchers are generally in agreement about the effectiveness of CBI for teaching LSP/ESP by drawing support from current language acquisition theories as well as analyzing the results from empirical studies. Specifically, Grabe and Stoller (1997) have discussed four main research-based findings that help strengthen the face validity of CBI for language educators: (1) Students are immersed in a context in which they acquire a language naturally while engaged in meaningful interactions and simultaneously learning the form and the meaning of language constructions; (2) students have ample opportunities to be exposed to comprehensible input and to negotiate meaning during interactions, two conditions that were found to have an effect on L2 acquisition; (3) while studying new content, students are challenged to develop cognitively and to use language to express more complex ideas and to complete authentic tasks; and (4) by working on coherent and meaningful content, students can make better connections to other related information, which promotes better learning overall.

Although research on language acquisition and educational and cognitive psychology provides support for the use of CBI in LSP/ESP classrooms, practitioners often find it challenging to organize classroom teaching that incorporates the five features described by Grabe and Stoller (1997) and provides students with adequate learning opportunities. Specifically, procedural questions about how to best balance the content and the language and to what extent the subject matter expertise that is required to keep students motivated and learning might become overwhelming for a language instructor. To partially alleviate these concerns and to give a framework for planning and implementing sequences of meaningful classroom activities, many LSP/ESP educators have looked to project-based learning (PBL) as a means of integrating discipline-specific content and L2 learning.

In general, PBL as a method calls for students to learn concepts via collaborative work that continues over an extended period of time and motivates the students by engaging them in real-world tasks. When applied to an LSP/ESP context specifically, PBL is viewed as a way to teach both language and content in a student-centered activity that helps them establish "a direct link between learning and its application" (Legutke and Thomas 1991, 214). Besides the integration of language and content, Stoller (1997, 2002, 2006) lists three additional features of PBL that make it promising for improving students' learning outcomes:

- PBL fosters L2 learning by engaging students in important, authentic projects that require students to use their L1 and L2 knowledge and skills in order to complete the project.

- Students are pushed to practice all four skills—listening, speaking, reading, and writing—in their L2 at different levels of complexity, both inside and outside the classroom.
- Students work collaboratively and construct knowledge through exploration and interaction with others, which promotes their autonomy and socialization as well as the development of cognitive skills and competencies.

With a large number of resources available for planning and implementing a project activity in an LSP course, practitioners have been reporting successes with using PBL to attain the goals of the Standards for Foreign Language Learning (Mills 2009) and discipline-specific standards (e.g., for a discussion of PBL in geography education, see Hardwick and Davis 2009) as well as to promote cross-disciplinary collaboration among subject and language instructors that benefits students and promotes learner autonomy (Tatzl et al. 2012).

At the same time, studies that have investigated student perceptions of project work and its impact on L2 development have yielded mixed results. For example, Beckett (2002) and Beckett and Slater (2005) collected L2 students' evaluations of projects conducted in academic ESL courses and noted three main reasons for students' negative perceptions of project work. First, students felt that projects required too much work and, thus, were perceived as too hard to accomplish. Second, students reported frustration over the seemingly unstructured nature of projects that required them to take responsibility for their own learning instead of relying on their teachers. And third, it was difficult for the students to see how some of the tasks they had completed as a part of a project were related to language learning.

As Beckett and Slater (2005) concluded, L2 learners and instructors may have had different goals for student learning in general and for PBL in particular. The differences in goals and, consequently, in expected outcomes, may cause major conflicts and need to be addressed in order for PBL to be successful. As a solution to this problem, Beckett and Slater (2005) suggested keeping students informed about the goals of the project activity and the resources that might be useful for the students. Furthermore, engaging students in the process by raising their awareness about how their language skills develop as they complete the project tasks might also be beneficial.

In order for PBL to be successful, ESP researchers have conceptualized it as a series of implementable steps that scaffold the whole process into manageable objectives and tasks, from identifying a theme to project evaluation. Specifically, the framework developed by Stoller and colleagues includes seven steps: (1) identifying a relevant theme from the subject curriculum, (2) determining the final outcomes, (3) structuring the project, (4) gathering information, (5) compiling and analyzing information, (6) reporting information, and (7) evaluating the project (Sheppard and Stoller 1995; Stoller 1997, 2010).

The project activity described here was conducted in an introductory engineering course offered to international students in a Pathway program at a large public university in the United States. One of the authors cotaught the course with a faculty member in the Engineering Department. Although the course incorporated a substantial amount of language-focused practice (which was provided by one of the authors) to support students during a project activity, its main purpose was to develop students' knowledge of engineering concepts and their ability to carry out discipline-specific tasks. The project activity, therefore, was a unique solution to address the lack of students' discipline-specific language by introducing language-focused practice into the course. The following sections provide a detailed description of how this project activity was planned and implemented, beginning with procedures taken to conduct a needs analysis that resulted in determining the focus of the project and its final outcomes (i.e., steps 1 through 3 in Stoller's framework).

Introductory Engineering Course: Needs Analysis

According to Long (2005), the purpose of a needs analysis (NA) is to determine what specific needs students have in order to customize classroom instruction and, at the same time, to be selective in choosing the topics, skills, discourse practices, and tasks that are to be taught. In the LSP literature, students' needs are often described in performance terms—that is, with respect to what students can do with the content knowledge and the language they learned in a course.

After 90 percent of the students who had enrolled in the initial offering of a basic (non-ESP) engineering course for international students failed the course, the Engineering Department administrators concluded that the course needed to be revised. Several faculty members from the university's graduate program to teach English to speakers of other languages were consulted, and a semester-long NA was carried out by one of the authors to collect information about the content and language needs of international students in the above-mentioned (non-ESP) engineering course (see appendix 6A for possible methods to collect data during an NA).

A triangulation approach to data collection was adopted (Long 2005; Richards 2001). As shown in table 6.1, information was collected from the literature on engineering, education, and applied linguistics as well as from administrators, domain experts, and students via classroom observations, interviews, and informal discussions.

Table 6.1 Description of Data Collected during an NA

Data Collection	Description
1. Literature	1a. Publications regarding basic skills and tasks in engineering
	1b. Publications regarding ESP course design and instructional support for international students
2. Classroom observations	2a. Five 50-minute lectures
	2b. Two 50-minute labs in engineering building
3. Interviews	3a. Face-to-face interview with the associate dean for academic and student affairs (College of Engineering) and the interim dean (College of Engineering)
	3b. E-mail correspondence with course instructor 1
	3c. Face-to-face interviews with students enrolled in the course—three students on two occasions during the semester (middle and end of the semester) and two students on one occasion (end of the semester)
4. Informal discussions	4. Three 60-minute informal discussions with course instructor 2

Many questions were worth considering during this initial stage of the NA. Some questions were more general (e.g., "What are the pedagogical practices that students have been mostly exposed to in their different cultures?" Or "Have students been accustomed to conducting projects in their previous schooling?"). Others were more detail-oriented (e.g., "What is the relative difficulty level of a certain discipline-specific text, and does it match students' current ability?"). However, several questions in particular guided the initial analysis. These questions included (but were not limited to) the following:

- What types of tasks do students perform in engineering fields?
- What types of texts do students engage with in engineering fields?
- What is students' current level of ability to perform discipline-specific tasks and comprehend and-or produce discipline-specific texts?
- What types of linguistic support might students need in order to work with discipline-specific content (i.e., perform the tasks and engage with the texts)?
- Is collaboration with a content specialist possible? If yes, is there a clear understanding of how the efforts of the language and content specialists should be distributed throughout the project activity?

Based on the information collected during the initial NA, students' needs were identified with specific recommendations for the types of support that could be provided as a part of the language-focused engineering course, including:

- Development of language of basic terminology and concepts in engineering;
- Inclusion of a course textbook, with introductory chapters;
- Inclusion of task-based activities;
- Writing assignments that focus on different text types found in engineering;
- Support for students in their classroom acculturation experiences; and
- Preparation for situating oneself within the engineering profession.

Because of the task-based, problem-solving nature of activities in the field of engineering, it was decided that project-based instruction offered an ideal approach to incorporate many of these recommendations. Several projects were considered; however, only one integrative, semester-long project was included for the course. The remainder of this chapter is devoted to describing this project.

Project-Based Learning in an Introductory Engineering Course

The engineering course was taught by both a content instructor and a linguist with experience teaching ESP to engineers. The semester-long project—"Preparing for an Engineering Interview, Job, and Career" (Vermeulen 2012)—was divided into individual subtasks allowing for various forms of content/language support throughout the semester.

As Long (2005) argues, *tasks* are particularly important to consider in course design because they can be sequenced coherently to provide contextualized language experiences, and they naturally lend themselves to promoting student-centered learning. Furthermore, tasks can also vary in terms of their complexity, which makes them appealing units of instruction for engaging learners at different levels of language proficiency and with varying degrees of expertise in the subject matter. Therefore, before the implementation of the semester-long project, a list of possible tasks specific to the project was identified by the content instructor. From that list, a number of tasks were chosen for both content and language instruction.

It is important to choose tasks that provide a reasonable balance between authenticity, relevance, and practicality. In the next section we discuss how standard procedures employed in language assessment—defining target language

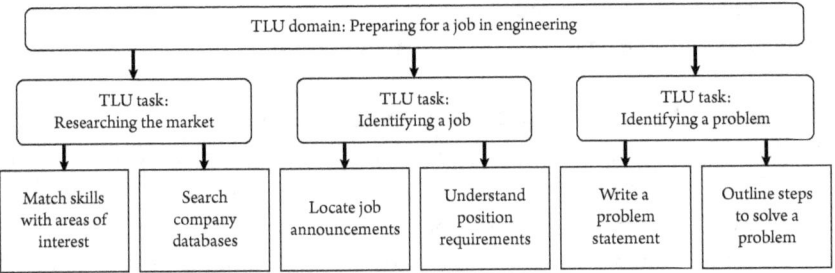

Figure 6.1 An Engineering ESP Course: Sample TLU Tasks

use (TLU) domains and TLU tasks, and analyzing task characteristics—were adapted to inform the project employed in the engineering classroom.

Analysis of a TLU Domain and Tasks

The analysis of the tasks associated with the project expanded on the framework presented by Bachman and Palmer (1996), who focus on the identification of TLU task characteristics and their correspondence to the characteristics of a given language ability assessment. In their framework, they introduce two specific concepts: *TLU domain* and *TLU task*. The "TLU domain" refers to "a specific setting outside of the test itself that requires the test taker to perform language use tasks" (Bachman and Palmer 1996, 60). Meanwhile, "TLU task" is used to refer to the tasks that belong to a specific TLU domain. Applying these two concepts to LSP instruction, TLU domain is used to describe authentic contexts in which students are expected to carry out specific TLU tasks.

Based on feedback from several engineers in the industry, the content instructor identified a number of TLU tasks that corresponded to the TLU domain— preparing for a job in engineering (for a sample of tasks identified for the project activity, see figure 6.1).

Then, the list of potential tasks was narrowed down to the most relevant as well as the most feasible to cover within one semester at the university. Overall, a series of eight main tasks were defined:

- Selecting a job description;
- Justifying a particular job choice;
- Identifying relevant educational experiences;
- Researching companies in the industry;
- Researching the job market;
- Identifying and solving a technical problem;

- Preparing a résumé; and
- Preparing a cover letter.

Collaboration between Language and Content Instructor

The involvement of a content instructor in planning a PBL activity solidifies the identification of the appropriate learning goals as well as students' perception of the relevance and learning potential of the activity. Both collaboration between language and content instructors as coteachers of an entire course, or targeted visits by a subject matter expert to a stand-alone LSP course, are beneficial for students and enable them to complete the project.

Following the identification of tasks for the project activity described in this chapter, the content instructor and one of the authors, who also served as the language instructor for the course, met to clarify their team-teaching roles for the project activity. Both instructors agreed that they wanted their collaboration to reflect the type of work-related relationship that students will need to develop and sustain in their professional careers. As Tatzl and others (2012, 299) contend, collaboration is "a fact at universities and in industry," and it "mirrors the future professional reality for . . . students." Therefore, the content instructor and language instructor felt that it was crucial to establish a cooperative teaching relationship early on in the course.

In addition, before the implementation of the project (see appendix 6B for a description of the project), the content instructor and language instructor also discussed the project tasks to determine the language instruction that could be provided to the students at certain points throughout the semester-long activity. Based on this information, the language instructor was able to establish the language objectives and outcomes for all the tasks associated with the project, as well as the discipline-specific language (i.e., vocabulary, linguistic patterns) that students would need to comprehend and produce when carrying out the tasks.

What follows is a discussion of the main types of linguistic support provided to the students throughout the project (and typically embedded in content-focused tasks), including sample pedagogical activities carried out to guide students' work throughout the entire project.

Preparing for the Project

To prepare for the demands of the project, the language and the content requirements of the project were analyzed by the language instructor, including discipline-specific vocabulary and tasks. Based on the outcomes of these analyses, a series of comprehension tasks were developed, which served two main purposes. First, the tasks diagnosed students' current level of understanding of the discipline-specific vocabulary used in the project description. Second, the tasks aimed to help students identify and understand the specific subtasks included at each step and to raise awareness of the requirements for completing each of the subtasks. To analyze discipline-specific vocabulary, we utilized a corpus-based software program. The following subsections give a detailed discussion of how corpus methodology can be employed to analyze discipline-specific texts so as to extract relevant vocabulary items that can be targeted during instruction.

Analysis of Discipline-Specific Language
With an objective to target authentic, discipline-specific language in LSP instruction, an increasing number of researchers and material developers look to corpus analysis techniques to identify relevant linguistic units. A *corpus* is typically defined as a collection of electronic texts of specific genres and types, different features of which (e.g., the frequency of certain keywords, contexts in which specific words occur, and word distributions) can be analyzed using computer software. The use of corpus data provides a quick and reliable means for collecting and analyzing actual language use. In L2 teaching, corpus software has been used to examine the vocabulary demands of commercial textbooks and research articles (Hsu 2011) as well as to compile discipline-specific word lists to use in syllabus design and classroom instruction (Ward 2009). A set of free computational tools that LSP instructors might find useful for analyzing discipline-specific language, as well as for creating a variety of corpus-based pedagogical materials, is available from Tom Cobb's (2015a) Complete Lexical Tutor website (for an overview of these tools, see Cobb 2010).

The two tools we used in the present analysis were Web Vocabprofile (Cobb 2015c) and KeyWords Extractor (Cobb 2015b). Web Vocabprofile is a corpus-based software program that scans text files and develops a vocabulary profile of a target text in terms of the vocabulary frequency identified in a language in general (available in English and French). The program is based on Laufer and Nation's (1995) Lexical Frequency Profile, which classifies all vocabulary into four frequency bands: the first thousand (1K) and second thousand (2K) frequently used words in the vocabulary (West 1953); the Academic Word List (AWL), which includes 570 additional word families identified in four sections of the Academic Corpus—including art, commerce, law, and science (Coxhead 2000)—and the off list, which includes all the remaining vocabulary. KeyWords Extractor is another corpus tool that enables the user to perform a keyword analysis so as to show which words are unusually frequent or infrequent in a specialized text by comparing their frequency in a more general corpus, also referred to as a reference corpus.

Based on the outcome of the Web Vocabprofile analysis, 62.25 percent of the vocabulary of the scanned text belonged to 1K (e.g., ability, continuous, determine, familiarity, manufacturing, preventative, recognized, supplier, vessels); 8.9 percent of the words were from 2K (e.g., avoid, behavioral, composite, essential, immediate, preferences, pumps, qualifications, responsible, treatments); 15.63 percent came from the AWL (e.g., allocation, benefits, contractors, cycle, enhance, guidelines, implement, maintenance, regulatory, requirements, vehicles), and 13.22 percent were identified as off-list. With the first three word lists (i.e., 1K, 2K, and AWL) accounting for only 86.78 percent of the text vocabulary, we expected that the students would require additional assistance with less-frequent and, likely, more specialized vocabulary identified in the off-list. Therefore, we further examined the off-list with the purpose of identifying lexical units that students might find difficult in order to target them in the comprehension activity.

Because the off-list included a variety of words not recognized under the first three word lists—such as proper nouns (e.g., Egypt, Africa, Cairo, and Asia); misspellings; abbreviations (e.g., CO for Colorado, cc'd, ENGR for engineering, pdf); vocabulary that entered the lexicon relatively recently, such as technology; computer-related terms (e.g., interface, laser, mobile, movies, online, software, technologies, update, videos, wirelessly, worldwide, YouTube); and specialized vocabulary—we manually scanned the list to eliminate all irrelevant units and words with which students would most likely be familiar. Using frequency information (i.e., the number of times each word occurred in a text) for each of the specialized vocabulary items, with the most frequent words receiving the priority, we identified a list of potential targets.

Next, we performed the Keywords analysis to identify any vocabulary items that, compared with the reference corpus, were unusually frequent in our material, indicating their special status and, therefore, their potential as instructional targets. The reference corpus selected for this analysis was one of the default corpora available in the tool—the 14-million-word, mixed written–spoken, US–UK corpus developed by Paul Nation. The program identified every word that was at least twenty-five times more numerous (and thus more key) in the analyzed text compared with the reference corpus. Following Chung and Nation (2004), we adopted a more conservative criterion of keyness of fifty and above to identify truly meaningful key words, which resulted in forty-four items in the output file that met this criterion. Next, we eliminated all proper nouns (e.g., Aspen, Korea, Arab) and frequent academic vocabulary that students were likely to know (e.g., program, meaning, folder, software), with the final list including thirteen items. These items were then cross-listed with a list of words generated in the Web Vocabprofile analysis, and a final set of thirty-six words was identified to be targeted in the comprehension activity (see table 6.2).

Table 6.2 Discipline-Specific Vocabulary Identified in Corpus-Based Analyses

Acceleration	Composites	Hazard	Procurement
Aerospace	Dimensioning	Hybrid	Robust
Adhesives	Drainage	Installations	Satellites
Alignment	Equip	Interface	Simulations
Assemble	Fabricate	Interpersonal	Spreadsheet
Assets	Facility	Manufacturability	Troubleshooting
Benchmarking	Fixtures	Mechatronics	Utility
Calibrate/calibration	Glucose	Multivariable	Vehicle
Compliance	Groundwater	Pipeline	Wastewater

Our overall goal in utilizing corpus tools to identify specialized vocabulary was to adopt a more comprehensive approach to the linguistic analysis of discipline-specific texts. Rather than relying on our linguistic intuition, the corpus-based analyses provided more objective criteria for selection of the vocabulary based on the frequency counts in a specialized text as well as in the language in general (the reference corpora). Although in our analyses we worked primarily with the off-list words, because they accounted for a considerable percentage of all words included in the text, it might be useful to examine the vocabulary items included in other word lists, such as AWL, to ensure that students have a good grasp of general-purpose vocabulary. A sample diagnostic activity targeting fifteen (out of the original thirty) vocabulary items from the AWL, along with a few nonwords to establish the reliability of students' self-reports of their knowledge of the target vocabulary, is included in appendix 6C (available online at press.georgetown.edu).

Analysis of Project Tasks

Once the vocabulary requirements for the project had been determined, we analyzed each project task in order to outline the specific subtasks and the types of knowledge, skills, and abilities that students needed to utilize in order to be able to complete each task (see table 6.3).

Based on the results of the language and content analyses, we developed three comprehension tasks to introduce the project requirements to the students and to collect diagnostic information about the aspects of the project that might be potentially challenging to the students. The three comprehension activities (see appendixes 6D through 6F, available online at press.georgetown.edu) administered over several class sessions (or as homework assignments) scaffolded the project content by engaging students in progressively more complex processing of the tasks, from understanding the language in the project description (appendix

Table 6.3 Knowledge and Abilities Targeted in Project Tasks

Step	Project Task	Knowledge, Skills, Abilities
1	Select a job description	• Understand the format of a job announcement • Understand general job requirements in engineering
2	Explain why you selected a specific job	• Identify reasons to explain the selection of a job • Informative writing: Compose a 200-word paragraph
3	Identify university courses that will prepare you for the job	• Identify key skills and responsibilities in a job announcement • Identify key knowledge and skills taught in relevant engineering courses • Match key skills and responsibilities in a job announcement with relevant knowledge and skills in engineering courses • Develop short (one-sentence) descriptions of relevant courses and how they apply to the chosen job • Computer literacy skills: Navigate a school website to identify necessary information
4	Research three companies that offer similar jobs	• Research job search engines and company databases to look for jobs in engineering • Identify keywords and phrases to search for jobs • Understand general job requirements of identified jobs • Computer literacy skills: Navigate job search engines / company websites to identify relevant information • Descriptive writing: Develop a brief description of a job
5	Research the current state of the field and predict how the job market will change by the time you graduate	• Identify three to five relevant sources to elicit statistical information about the job and the current status of the respective field of engineering, using the criteria of currency, reliability, accuracy, appropriateness • Summarize information from each relevant source

		- Cite sources appropriately (for visuals, data, quotations)
- Synthesis/argumentative writing: develop a paragraph of 200–250 words to present an argument and synthesize information from relevant sources to provide support for the argument
- Computer literacy skills: Use university (academic) databases to identify relevant sources
6	Identify and solve a technical problem typical for your selected job	- Understand the types of technical problems that are typical for different fields of engineering
- Identify a relevant engineering problem that matches the job requirements selected for the project
- Understand the seven-step problem presentation procedure and the type of information required in each step
- Demonstrate appropriate (fundamental) level of theoretical knowledge in various aspects of engineering (e.g., mechanics, material balance, thermodynamics, electrical theory)
- Computer literacy skills: Use university (academic) databases to identify relevant sources for the report
- Computer literacy skills: Use software to develop visuals and carry out calculations for the project report (as needed)
- Cite sources appropriately (for visuals, data, quotations)
- Discipline-specific (descriptive) writing: Develop a technical report that follows the seven-step problem presentation format established in engineering
7	Prepare a pro forma résumé	- Understand the content and format requirements of résumé statements in engineering
- Determine a list of relevant skills, qualifications, and (educational) experiences that match the position description
- Select and use an appropriate template to prepare the résumé
8	Prepare a pro forma cover letter	- Understand the content and format requirements of cover letter statements in engineering
- Descriptive/argumentative writing: Develop a cohesive letter of two to three paragraphs

6D, available online at press.georgetown.edu) to critically analyzing the samples (appendix 6E, available online at press.georgetown.edu) to reflecting on their own knowledge and skills with respect to the requirements of the project (appendix 6F, available online at press.georgetown.edu). At the same time, all three activities included a diagnostic component, asking students to self-report on both their perceived strengths and weaknesses regarding the project tasks as well as their knowledge of specific content (e.g., discipline-specific vocabulary). Collecting diagnostic information at the very beginning of the project helped the language instructor develop more individualized support for the students throughout the project that targeted their specific linguistic (and general academic) needs. The next subsection includes a detailed discussion of the support provided during the project activities.

Supporting Students during the Project

Analyzing each project task in terms of its components and the types of knowledge, skills, and abilities necessary for its completion (refer to table 6.3 above) helped us to determine

1. The linguistic competencies embedded in each task;
2. The general academic and discipline-specific competencies targeted in each task; and
3. The characteristics that can be adapted and-or revised in pedagogical tasks to make them more practical and transparent to the students.

During the development of the pedagogical tasks to support students throughout the project, we also considered the characteristics of the input and the output of the project tasks, which in turn reflected the characteristics of the authentic tasks identified in the TLU. The input refers to the material contained in a project or task that students need to process in order to formulate a response. Meanwhile, the output refers to the response that is elicited by way of the instructions, task design, and the kind of input that is provided. Both the input and output of the project or task can be described in terms of the same set of characteristics: format, language, and topic (see table 6.4). *Format*, which has to do with the way in which information is presented or produced, consists of six different components (channel, form, language, length, degree of speediness, and vehicle). *Language* describes the nature of the linguistic features that are used. Here, language can be considered in terms of the organizational and pragmatic components of communication. Finally, *topic* refers to a student's real-world knowledge of the issue and includes personal, cultural, academic, and technical aspects of this knowledge.

Table 6.4 Considerations for Project Task Characteristics (for Input and Output)

Characteristic	Description of Components
Format	• Channel (aural, visual) • Form (language, nonlanguage, both) • Language (native, target, both) • Length (short, moderate, long) • Degree of speed (slow, moderate, fast) • Vehicle (live, reproduced, both)
Language	• Organizational (grammatical—vocabulary, syntax, phonology, graphology; textual—cohesion, rhetorical/conversational organization) • Pragmatic (functional—ideational, manipulative, heuristic, imaginative; sociolinguistic—variety, register, naturalness, cultural references)
Topic	• Personal • Cultural • Academic • Technical

Having identified the required competencies to complete each project task as well as task input and output characteristics, we developed a series of scaffolding activities for each project step. Here we discuss several activities that focused on the most challenging tasks (based on information collected from the students at the beginning of the project, see table 6.3), which included:

Step 6: Identify and solve a technical problem typical for your selected job; and
Step 7: Prepare a pro forma résumé.

The scaffolding activities developed for these steps (see appendixes 6G through 6H, available online at press.georgetown.edu) required students to engage with authentic language and promoted their noticing of and engagement with specific linguistic and textual features, including identification of specialized/key vocabulary, syntactic patterns and discourse structures that are used in different types of texts, visual representation of ideas in a text, and critical content and language analysis of samples. Furthermore, a variety of learning formats were used in the activities to involve students in peer group and small group work, allowing them to rely on their peers as additional sources of information and to incorporate additional opportunities for feedback. These activities were used both in class and as homework assignments to provide students with guidance and help them identify gaps in their knowledge and skills, in order to seek more individualized assistance from the language instructor during weekly office hours and tutoring sessions. In addition to scaffolding activities, several assessments were developed to track students' progress with project activities, as discussed in the following subsection.

Assessing Project-Based Learning

As discussed by Becker and Nekrasova-Beker (2013), assessments for PBL can be viewed in terms of two facets: formative/summative assessment, and direct/indirect assessment. Formative assessment is used to collect information about learning progress, whereas summative assessment is used for determining achievement at the end of instruction. In addition, PBL can also be assessed directly or indirectly; that is, students' knowledge, skills, and abilities can be directly observed against learning objectives (i.e., direct assessment), or students' attitudes and values can be obtained through self-reflection (i.e., indirect assessment). However, as Miller, Linn, and Gronlund (2009) note, the most effective assessment plan for project-based activities is one that integrates a variety of assessments to evaluate student learning and inform the instructional process. In what follows, we present several examples of assessments that were implemented by the instructors throughout the semester-long project activity.

Assessments during the Project

At various points throughout the project, the instructors included different assessments that were used to evaluate progress. The first assessment, an individual presentation that was formative/direct in nature, required students to create a presentation in English that illustrated their progress with steps 1 through 5. Using a scoring rubric (see appendix 6I, available online at press.georgetown.edu), each student was evaluated by the two instructors. Although scores were not assigned for this particular assessment, the instructors used the scoring rubric to provide specific feedback to each student.

Preceding step 6 of the project, a mid-project survey that was formative/indirect in nature (see appendix 6J, available online at press.georgetown.edu) required students to reflect on their experiences with the project activity to that point in the semester. Students reported on their attitudes, self-confidence levels, and abilities to perform the necessary project-related tasks. Upon the completion of the survey, the instructors reviewed the responses and used the results to address specific content- and language-related gaps in the course instruction.

Assessments at the End of the Project
Finally, students' mastery of the content and language learning objectives was evaluated. The first assessment, a peer evaluation rubric that was formative/direct in nature (see appendix 6K, available online at press.georgetown.edu), was used to evaluate the performance of fellow students with respect to the final report that they were to submit at the end of the project. It was believed that the information from this peer review form could be used by students to make final revisions before submitting their final report to the course instructors.

Once the final project report was completed, students were also asked to complete a self-assessment survey (adapted from Becker and Nekrasova-Beker 2013). The survey (see appendix 6L, available online at press.georgetown.edu), which was summative/indirect in nature, gave students a final opportunity to reflect on their own learning experiences and to consider the progress that they had made since the beginning of the project. The results of this survey, though helpful for students for monitoring their own achievement, were not included as part of students' final project grade.

Final Considerations for Teachers

Overall, there are many possible things for teachers to consider when carrying out project-based learning projects. In this section we discuss several important considerations when doing such work.

Collaboration between Instructors

To develop trustworthy and equitable relationships with a content instructor, LSP instructors should involve subject matter experts early on in the process as one of the information sources while conducting an NA. The input from the content instructor can be used to inform your decisions for the inclusion of tasks and linguistic units later on during the planning stage. Once the overall activity has been conceptualized in terms of the principal steps and the goals and outcomes associated with each step, it might be useful to clearly define the roles of both contributors during each step. For example, Tatzl and others (2012) discussed the specific responsibilities of content and language instructors as part of their proposed model for Project-Based Collaborative Technical Writing Instruction, focusing on the overlapping tasks and procedures (e.g., agreeing on educational objectives, assessing final project reports) as well as the specialized tasks and procedures (e.g., assigning subject-specific project topics, meeting regularly with project groups to assess progress and troubleshoot) that instructors carried out. As Tatzl and others (2012, 299) concluded, their model "demonstrated that the cooperation among content and language instructors yielded fruitful results and encouraging prospects for future team work in engineering education." Overall, discussing the results of the NA and the overall conception and structure of the project with a subject matter expert will help to ensure that the planned activity is relevant for the students and is truly interdisciplinary.

Preparing Students for Projects

Beckett and Slater (2005) call for making the learning objectives of the project activity and the resources associated with it transparent to the students to help them buy in to the activity and recognize its pedagogical value. They developed a tool—the Project Framework, as they called it—that should help LSP instructors raise students' awareness of the multifaceted nature of a project activity that is used to promote development of content knowledge, linguistic units, and skills. According to Beckett and Slater (2005, 110), the framework "provides a bridge to new ways for students to think about language learning, and the new learning activities being carried out in the new institutional context."

The framework includes two key components—*the planning graphic* and *the project diary*. The authors suggest that the planning graphic, which can either be created by a teacher or co-constructed with students, helps categorize different linguistic units, content themes and topics, and skills that are considered important learning targets in the project so that it is easier for students to recognize the progress they are making on different aspects of the activity. Meanwhile, the project diary is seen as a tool for the students to articulate their progress on a regular basis. The diary incorporates questions about the same three aspects of the project activity—language, content, and skills—that are targeted in the planning graphic, and it creates learning objectives (in the form of a to-do list) for students for the upcoming week. Beckett and Slater (2005) contend that the framework makes various components of project work explicit, and thus promotes a more valuable experience for students.

Addressing Diverse Needs

According to Strevens (1988), the underlying principles of ESP courses are that they should be (1) designed to meet the specified needs of the learner; (2) related in content, such as having themes and topics keyed to particular disciplines, occupations, and activities; and (3) centered on the language used in these activities. In addition to these principles, Hyland (2002) also argues that ESP courses should be designed for students targeting one particular professional or academic environment discipline. However, the reality is that many ESP courses include students from various disciplines (e.g., business, computer science, and engineering). Thus, the content and language needs, as well as the expectations, of the students might be quite different within the same classroom.

In a situation where a course includes L2 students with varying academic interests, PBL can help to establish a middle ground for LSP instructors. Although an instructor can target general academic competencies by incorporating a wide-angled design (Basturkmen 2003, 48), at the same time, he or she can also implement PBL to target content that is specific to a student's particular discipline. For instance, an LSP instructor can focus on semitechnical vocabulary (i.e., general academic vocabulary) when working with students as a whole but can also expose individual students to technical (i.e., discipline-specific) vocabulary through the use of authentic materials that are used in particular disciplines. Furthermore, LSP instructors can collaborate with content-area specialists to identify databases, professional journals, and so on that students can use throughout their own project. In this way, students can gain access to relevant content and discourse features that they are likely to encounter later on in their academic and professional endeavors. Finally, using a similar step-by-step PBL framework described in this chapter, LSP instructors can integrate various aspects of language knowledge, content knowledge, and analytic skills in a similar manner, regardless of the academic discipline of interest.

Conclusion

The purpose of this chapter has been to discuss the steps that an LSP instructor can take to plan and implement a successful project-based learning activity that promotes students' development of language skills as they engage in learning discipline-specific content. The planning steps are ordered sequentially to help an LSP instructor approach the very challenging task of determining what specific content and language should be targeted in scaffolding activities.

We have provided a comprehensive overview of the planning procedures and specific scaffolding activities carried out during a semester-long project that helped enhance the project activity and made it a more enjoyable experience for both the instructors and the students. However, our list of the included procedures is far from exhaustive. Practitioners can benefit from further discussions of this topic featuring other challenging aspects of the project activity, such as integrating language and content objectives in PBL by, for example, considering the difference between content-obligatory and content-compatible language objectives (Snow, Met, and Genesee 1989) and by discussing how both types of objectives can be reflected in the module content and assessment tasks (see Hoare, Kong, and Bell 2008). Regardless of which challenging aspect of a project activity is discussed next, it is important to keep the conversation flowing because similarly to our LSP/ESP students who are often overwhelmed by the complexity of language–content interactions in their respective disciplines, as language specialists, we are pushing ourselves outside our comfort zone by learning how to look at this interaction holistically—as one complex learning system.

Appendix 6A

Possible Methods for Collecting Data for Needs Analysis and Their Main Characteristics

Questionnaires
- can be distributed to large numbers of people,
- can be administered anonymously, and
- may bring about superficial or imprecise responses.

Interviews
- enable in-depth coverage of an issue,
- can be structured or open-ended, and
- are time consuming to conduct.

Observation
- allows collection of data in natural environment,
- helps to capture people's attitudes and perceptions, and
- typically requires specialized training.

Learner samples
- provide a direct source of information,
- can be collected in the context of the learning environment, and
- can result in an overwhelming amount of data.

Self-ratings
- promote self-awareness of learners,
- encourage learners' participation in the process, and
- provide only impressionistic information.

Diaries and journals
- can be done quickly and regularly,
- promote a learner-centered curriculum, and
- require significant time to write and analyze.

Ethnography
- provides an "insider" perspective,
- minimizes preconceived categories and bias, and
- can require lengthy immersion in target setting.

Appendix 6B

Project: Preparing for an Engineering Interview, Job, and Career

This project was inspired by a student (let us call him "Frank") who asked the instructor for help in 2005.[1] Frank was a university senior with below-average grades and four years of skiing experience. He would soon graduate and still did not know how to be hired as an engineer. This project is designed to help you avoid Frank's situation. Here are the things you must complete and submit:

1. Choose one of the job descriptions in the appendix or find another job description online for a job that requires an engineering degree. You will be applying for this job as if you were an engineering student in the senior year. Copy this entire job description into your project report. (1 point)
2. Explain why you chose this job. This explanation should be about 50–200 words in length and include at least two reasons. (4 points)
3. List the CSU undergraduate courses that would prepare you for this job, and complete the information below for each course you identify:
    - Course 1 number and title
        - What is learned in the course
        - How this applies to the chosen job.

For maximum credit, you must list no more than eight courses and no fewer than five courses. Points will be deducted if you forgot to list the three most important courses for this job based on what is written in the job description. To complete this section, (1) Research the courses for the relevant engineering major, (2) select the courses that are most relevant, (3) write (20 words maximum) what is learned in this course, and (4) write (20 words maximum) how this course applies to your chosen job (10 points):

4. Find three more companies that hire engineers to do jobs similar to your chosen job description. These companies can be anywhere in the world. Determine where these companies and jobs are located and how you might contact someone who would hire engineers at this firm. Provide a list of these companies and include the following information in your list (10 points):

- Company/organization name
- Company/organization address and phone number
- Brief description of the engineering jobs available

5. Research whether jobs similar to your chosen job description, between now and the time you graduate, are likely to increase, decrease, or stay the same. Make sure that you include references that show where you found your information. Also provide a quantitative logical analysis that justifies your conclusion. (10 points)

6. Identify a typical technical problem that you would need to solve if you were hired to do this job. Solve this problem and prepare a description of the problem and the process you used to solve it. That description needs to include all the steps identified using one of the problem solution processes we will be discussing in class. This step is the most important part of this project assignment. Make sure that you present your information in a professional manner—clear, detailed, well-illustrated, and well organized. We do not expect you to be able to solve all the complex engineering problems from a quantitative standpoint (you are not a senior yet), but we expect you to be able to have good diagrams, a clear understanding of any forces, vectors, and the like, and to give a clear qualitative visual overview of the problem and how one would solve it. If you put your mind to it and work on it week by week, you should be able to amaze us (and yourself) with your ability to communicate engineering problems and their solutions. (50 points)

7. Prepare a one-page "pro forma résumé" that shows the skills and experience you expect to have by you senior year if you were to enroll as an undergraduate engineer at the university. A pro forma résumé means a résumé that is dated November 15, 2017, and written as if you are a senior, having taken the courses listed in item 3 above. The résumé should list other significant things you plan to accomplish in your college years (i.e., between August 1, 2013, and November 15, 2017). You will be making up this information, but it should be realistic, given what you plan to do between now and the time you might start looking for full-time postgraduation employment. You are writing this résumé so you can have a clearer plan for your next four years. (10 points)

8. Prepare a "pro forma cover letter" that can be used to send with your résumé and the problem and solution. Your cover letter should describe why you are interested in this job and why you believe you are qualified to do this job well. It should describe why you chose the problem that you solved and what this demonstrates about your abilities and motivation

as an engineer. The cover letter cannot be longer than one page, it must be dated November 15, 2017, and it must be addressed to the hiring manager, Engineering Company, and the city and-or country in the job description. (5 points)

This report is due in two parts, and you should be working on it throughout the semester.

Job Descriptions
Note: For this project, students choose a job description that they find online or select from a list that is provided to them in class.

Note
1. The project requirements have been revised to remove sensitive information.

References
Bachman, Lyle, and Adrian Palmer. 1996. *Language Testing in Practice: Designing and Developing Useful Language Tests.* Oxford: Oxford University Press.
Basturkmen, Helen. 2003. "Specificity and ESP Course Design." *RELC Journal* 34: 48–63.
Becker, Anthony, and Tatiana Nekrasova-Beker. 2013. "Evaluating a Project-Based Activity: Suggestions for CLIL Courses." In *The Language Resource: Crossroads in the Classroom.* Washington, DC: National Capital Language Resource Center. www.nclrc.org/newsletter.html.
Beckett, Gulbahar H. 2002. "Teacher and Student Evaluations of Project-Based Instruction." *TESL Canada Journal* 19, no. 2: 52–66.
Beckett, Gulbahar H., and Tammy Slater. 2005. "The Project Framework: A Tool for Language, Content, and Skills Integration." *ELT Journal* 59, no. 2: 108–16.
Chung, Teresa M., and Paul I. S. Nation. 2004. "Identifying Technical Vocabulary." *System* 32, no. 2: 251–63.
Cobb, Tom. 2010. "Instructional Uses of Linguistic Technologies." *Procedia Social and Behavioral Sciences* 3: 14–23.
———. 2015a. *Complete Lexical Tutor.* Available at www.lextutor.ca.
———. 2015b. *KeyWords Extractor.* www.lextutor.ca/key/.
———. 2015c. *Web Vocabprofile.* www.lextutor.ca/vp/.
Coxhead, Avril. 2000. "A New Academic Word List." *TESOL Quarterly* 34, no. 2: 213–38.
Crandall, JoAnn, and Richard G. Tucker. 1990. "Content-Based Instruction in Second and Foreign Languages." In *Foreign Language Education: Issues and Strategies,* edited by Amado M. Padilla, Halford H. Fairchild, and Concepcion M. Valadez. Newbury Park, CA: Sage.
Grabe, William, and Fredricka L. Stoller. 1997. "Content-Based Instruction: Research

Foundations." In *The Content-Based Classroom: Perspectives on Integrating Language and Content*, edited by Marguerite A. Snow and Donna M. Brinton. New York: Longman.

Hardwick, Susan W., and Robert L. Davis. 2009. "Content-Based Language Instruction: A New Window of Opportunity in Geography Education." *Journal of Geography* 108, nos. 4–5: 163–73.

Hoare, Philip, Stella Kong, and Jill Bell. 2008. "Using Language Objectives to Integrate Language and Content Instruction: A Case History of Planning and Implementing Challenges." *Language and Education* 22, no. 3: 187–205.

Hsu, Wenhua. 2011. "The Vocabulary Thresholds of Business Textbooks and Business Research Articles for EFL Learners." *English for Specific Purposes* 30: 247–57.

Hyland, Ken. 2002. "Specificity Revisited: How Far Should We Go Now?" *English for Specific Purposes* 21: 385–95.

Laufer, Batia, and Paul I. S. Nation. 1995. "Vocabulary Size and Use: Lexical Richness in L2 Written Production." *Applied Linguistics* 16: 307–22.

Legutke, Michael, and Howard Thomas. 1991. *Process and Experience in the Language Classroom*. Harlow: Longman.

Long, Michael. 2005. *Second Language Needs Analysis*. Cambridge: Cambridge University Press.

Miller, David M., Robert L. Linn, and Norman E. Gronlund. 2009. *Measurement and Assessment in Teaching*. Upper Saddle River, NJ: Pearson Education.

Mills, Nicole. 2009. "A *Guide du Routard* Simulation: Increasing Self-Efficacy in the Standards through Project-Based Learning." *Foreign Language Annals* 42, no. 4: 607–39.

Richards, Jack C. 2001. *Curriculum Development in Language Teaching*. Cambridge: Cambridge University Press.

Sheppard, Ken, and Fredricka L. Stoller. 1995. "Guidelines for the Integration of Student Projects in ESP Classrooms." *English Teaching Forum* 33, no. 2: 10–15.

Snow, Marguerite A., Myriam Met, and Fred Genesee. 1989. "A Conceptual Framework for the Integration of Language and Content in Second/Foreign Language Instruction." *TESOL Quarterly* 23: 37–53.

Stoller, Fredricka L. 1997. "Project Work: A Means to Promote Language Content." *English Teaching Forum* 35, no. 4: 29–37. http://dosfan.lib.uic.edu/usia/E-USIA/forum/vols/vol35/no4/p2.htm.

———. 2002. "Project Work: A Means to Promote Language and Content." In *Methodology in Language Teaching: An Anthology of Current Practice*, edited by Jack C. Richards and Willy A. Renandya. Cambridge: Cambridge University Press.

———. 2006. "Establishing a Theoretical Foundation for Project-based Learning in Second and Foreign Language Contexts." In *Project-Based Second and Foreign Language Education: Past, Present, and Future*, edited by Gulbahar H. Beckett and Paul C. Miller. Greenwich, CT: Information Age.

———. 2010. "Promoting Purposeful Language Learning with Project Work." Paper presented at the annual meeting of the Institute of English Language Education, Tokyo.

Strevens, Peter. 1988. "ESP after Twenty Years: A Re-appraisal." In *ESP: State of the Art*, edited by Makhan L. Tickoo. Singapore: SEAMEO Regional Language Center.

Tatzl, Dietmar, Wolfgang Hassler, Bernd Messnarz, and Holger Flühr. 2012. "The Development of a Project-Based Collaborative Technical Writing Model Founded on Learner Feedback in a Tertiary Aeronautical Engineering Program." *Journal of Technical Writing and Communication* 42, no. 3: 279–304.

Vermeulen, Bert. 2012. "Preparing for an Engineering Interview, Job, and Career." Department of Engineering, Colorado State University, Fort Collins.

Ward, Jeremy. 2009. "A Basic Engineering English Word List for Less Proficient Foundation Engineering Undergraduates." *English for Specific Purposes* 28: 170–82.

West, Michael. 1953. *A General Service List of English Words*. London: Longman.

PART II
Rethinking Instructor Roles

7 | The Instructor's and Learner's Roles in Learning Arabic for Specific Purposes

El-Hussein Aly

This chapter describes a study that aims to investigate the roles of the instructor and learner in courses on Arabic for specific purposes (ASP). The study attempts to fill a gap in the literature on language teaching and learning. Although there is a huge literature on English for specific purposes (ESP), little attention has been paid to other languages used for specific purposes. Nevertheless, studies on languages other than English may attract attention to hidden aspects that may contribute positively to language teaching and learning in general, and may also contribute positively to our understanding of ESP. Furthermore, although the role of the instructor has been the focus of some studies (e.g., Carver 1983), little attention has been paid to the contributions of learners to language learning and teaching in a course on language for specific purposes.

Due to the gap in the literature on ASP, models of ESP have been adapted to serve the purpose of this study. Widdowson (1998, 3) states that "the S of ESP links language with purpose and establishes the association." In an answer to his question "But what exactly is the nature of that specificity?" Widdowson claims, as a start, that "*all* uses of English, as of any other language, are specific. All uses of the language serve particular purposes" (Widdowson 1998, 3; emphasis in the original). The existence of a particular purpose is in fact a precondition for effective communication, and the more specific the purpose, the more effective a communicator can be to the insiders of a specific discourse community and less effective to the outsiders of that discourse community—that is, "the more communicatively effective we are, the more exclusive we become. This is because we count on the sharing of common assumptions, beliefs and values" (Widdowson 1998, 13).

Widdowson (1998) gives the example of a bradawl as an example of restricted language that is communicative to the insiders and less communicative to the outsiders of a certain community. A bradawl is a tool that is well known to the do-it-yourself community. For a person who is an outsider to that community and does not know the name of the tool, being communicative enough for that community may be a difficult task, as the following statement shows: "I am looking for a sort of thingumajig, a whatsit, a sort of metal thing that has a sharp pointed end, which you use for making holes in wood so that you can put a screw in without it falling out when you reach for the screwdriver" (Widdowson 1998, 6).

If this person who is an outsider wants to join an English-language session on woodworking tools, the session will be classified as ESP. This is mainly because (1) the session addresses a specific need—to learn about woodworking tools; (2) the session is related to a specific field; and (3) the session is centered on the language used in that specific field. According to Strevens (1988), courses can be classified as ESP on the basis of four absolute characteristics:

- ESP is designed to meet specific learners' needs;
- ESP is related to particular disciplines, occupations, and activities;
- ESP is centered on language appropriate to those activities; and
- ESP is used in contrast with general English.

Strevens (1988) also notes that ESP courses have two variable characteristics:

- ESP may be restricted to the skills to be learned, and
- ESP may not follow any preordained methodology.

Dudley-Evans and St. John (1998) modified Strevens's (1988) models so as to include only three absolute characteristics and two variable characteristics. The three absolute characteristics are:

- ESP is designed to meet specific learners' needs.
- ESP makes use of the methodology and activities of the disciplines it serves.
- ESP is centered on language appropriate to those activities.

The two variable characteristics are:

- ESP may be designed for a specific discipline.
- ESP may use a different methodology from that of general English.

Robinson (1991) defines ESP courses according to two criteria and a number of characteristics. The two criteria are:

- ESP is goal-oriented.
- ESP is based on needs analysis.

The characteristics include:

- ESP is characterized by a limited number of hours, for example, 60 hours of English for academic writing.
- ESP is studied by adult learners.
- ESP is characterized by homogeneous learners in terms of work or specialization.

The first most common characteristic of all the definitions of ESP courses given above is that they are designed to meet the learner's needs. ESP courses are specific because they address specific needs. However, some specific needs can still be the focus of general language courses. For example, the need to communicate effectively with middle-class, middle-aged, Cairene female coworkers is specific; but the material for that course can be general, in the sense that it is not based on any specific discipline. Hence, the second most common characteristic is that LSP courses are designed for specific disciplines. Thus, an English-speaking employer who needs to learn how to carry out tasks in a human resources department—where he works with middle-class, middle-aged, Cairene female coworkers—may join a tutorial on Arabic for HR Purposes, which is also oriented toward communication with Cairene female coworkers.

Toward a Definition of ASP

This study adopts an eclectic approach to defining ASP. The model combines all the common features of the above-noted definitions of ESP (Dudley-Evans and St. John 1998; Robinson 1991; Strevens 1988). The three definitions are based on absolute characteristics or criteria that must be present in all ESP courses, in addition to variable characteristics that may be present in many but not in all ESP courses. Accordingly, an Arabic course is considered ASP if it has two absolute characteristics and a number of variable characteristics. The absolute characteristics are:

- ASP must meet specified learners' needs.
- ASP must be oriented toward certain disciplines, occupations, and-or activities.

The variable characteristics include:

- ASP may use a methodology different from general Arabic.
- ASP is usually designed to serve for forums for a limited period of time.
- ASP is usually designed for adult learners.
- ASP is usually restricted to the skills to be learned.

Research Questions

The study raises the following research questions:

1. Do instructors of ASP play other roles than teaching the language; and if yes, what are they?
2. Do learners of ASP play other roles than learning the language; and if yes, what are they?

Methodology

This study aims to explore the roles of instructors and learners in ASP courses. The definition of ASP given above was used to identify the ASP courses. Accordingly, four courses were identified as ASP, as table 7.1 indicates.

Participants

The participants were one male and three female instructors with experience from five to more than twenty years in teaching Arabic as a foreign language. All the instructors were Egyptians specialized in teaching Arabic. There were a total

Table 7.1 Courses on Arabic for Specific Purposes

Serial	Course Title	Level	Number of Hours	Number of Learners
1	Arabic for Political Science	Advanced	30	1
2	Arabic for Media	Advanced	30	1
3	Egyptian Arabic for Family Meetings	Elementary	30	1
4	Arabic for the Egyptian Lifestyle	Beginner	15	8

of eleven learners, both male and female. They belonged to different nationalities, although the majority of learners were from the United States. With the exception of one learner, who was a university professor in his early fifties, all the learners were recent graduates who had just started their careers.

Tools and Procedures

A methodological triangulation consisting of observations, questionnaires, and interviews was used to cross-examine the data. All observation sessions were of activities taking place in the normal setting of the classroom. They were all unstructured, as I noted down whatever I thought appropriate for the purpose of the study. When the learner or instructor was carrying out tasks with their language—for example, giving advice—I simply quoted them; otherwise, I described whole activities. Some of the observation was indirect—that is, through video recordings that were prepared as part of quality assurance evaluations. Observation time ranged from 20 to 90 minutes. The input from observations was used to design a questionnaire administered for instructors and learners (see appendix 7A for the list of statements and response options). To further validate the data from observations and questionnaires, interviews with both instructors and learners were used to cross-examine the data. The interviews were semistructured, with both close- and open-ended questions.

Limitations of the Study

The study is based on 200 minutes of classroom observation, individual and group interviews, and a small-scale questionnaire, which targeted four instructors and eleven learners in four ASP courses at the American University in Cairo (however, the actual responses received were from four instructors and seven learners from four classes). Although the sample group is small, the results provide unique information about questions not traditionally considered within the field of ASP. It is hoped that others will replicate the design of this study to add further data in the future.

Results and Discussion

Observation of the four classes indicated the existence of various roles for both the instructors and learners. Table 7.2 includes the roles of instructors (in addition to explicit teaching) and their frequency in the four classes.

The instructor carries out needs identification when he or she realizes that a learner(s) needs more training on a certain component. For example, in my notes,

Table 7.2 Roles of Instructors Identified through Classroom Observation

Serial	Role	Number of Occurrences				Total	%
		Class 1	Class 2	Class 3	Class 4		
1	Needs identifier	0	1	0	2	3	7.9
2	Needs assessor	2	1	1	2	6	15.8
3	Material provider	2	3	3	1	9	23.7
4	Information elicitor	4	5	1	3	13	34.2
5	Adviser	1	1	1	0	3	7.9
6	Evaluator	1	1	1	1	4	10.5
	Total occurrence of other roles of instructors than teaching	10	12	7	9	38	

I quoted one of the instructors saying "You still need training on writing from right to left." I took this statement as identification of the need to have more training on Arabic graphology. That was followed by a needs assessment, as the instructor wanted to assess to what extent the need was recurrent for the whole class. So she asked (while going around the class and having a look at the copybooks on the desks), "Anyone still have a problem writing from right to left?" Receiving no response, she sat down next to the learner who had a writing problem and started teaching her some techniques. In the interview, I asked her what she would do if the whole class had a problem in writing Arabic, and she said that she would give them handouts with a few activities. In that case, she would fulfill the role of material provider. In another class, the instructor identified the need of the learner to listen more to Arabic. She advised him to watch movies and promised to bring him a few clips of family gatherings from Arabic films.

The learners also performed other roles along with learning. Table 7.3 includes the roles of learners and their frequency in the four classes.

In the observation sessions, it was clear that learners serve as needs identifiers. For example, one of the learners said in Arabic, "I will read more, but I need simpler texts [i.e., simpler than the ones he has already had in the course]." This statement indicated that the learner identified his need to improve his language through reading. At the same time, he provided the instructor with feedback on the course material. Clearly, he wanted the course to include more texts that would be simpler in language. The instructor wanted to elicit more information on what the learner meant by "simpler." So she brought a few texts from her folder and showed them to the learner, asking which one he would consider simpler. Given the texts, the learner picked one of them as a model. By picking one of the

Table 7.3 Roles of Learners Identified through Classroom Observation

Serial	Role	Number of Occurrences				Total	%
		Class 1	Class 2	Class 3	Class 4		
1	Needs identifier	1	2	1	3	7	28
2	Feedback provider	3	2	2	11	18	72
	Total occurrence of other roles of learners than learning					25	

texts and expressing satisfaction, the learner provided feedback to the instructor. On the basis of that positive feedback, the instructor would provide the learner with more similar texts. Data from the questionnaires and interviews support the results of the observations.

The Instructor's Roles

This study indicates that instructors play more roles than just teaching. For example, they identify learners' needs, assess and elicit information on these needs, provide material, evaluate learning, and advise learners. The implications are clear: Instructors need to be trained and empowered to play other roles besides teaching that would contribute positively to the learning process.

The Instructor as a Needs Identifier

Statements one and two of the questionnaire pertain to the role of the instructor as a needs identifier. In response to the statement "The instructor identified the specific needs of the learner and invited the learner to the course," all eleven participants (100 percent) responded "disagree." In contrast, all eleven participants (100 percent) responded "strongly agree" to the second statement: "The learner identified his needs and asked for the course."

These responses indicate that the role of needs identification was performed by the learner rather than the instructor. It was the learner who felt the need to study a certain course and asked for it. This is particularly true for two reasons: First, all the courses included in this study were tailor-made according to the needs identified and expressed by the learner. And second, the language needs identified by the instructor were different in nature from those identified by the learner; the latter identified needs that were global and constituted language functions, whereas the former identified needs that constituted subfunctions such as grammar and pronunciation.

For example, observation indicated that sometimes the instructor identified some shortcoming in some skill, and so he designed some activity to deal with that shortcoming. That is to say, although it was the learner who initially identified the need for a certain course, the instructor could still draw attention to subneeds within the course. In order to make sure that the role of needs identification was sometimes performed by the instructor, a yes/no question and an open-ended question focused on that point in the interview. The participants were asked if the instructor sometimes found a need to deal with something that was not originally included in the course, and the responses were positive (ten of eleven interviewees answered yes). The participants were then asked to give examples of needs identifications. The examples included mistakes in pronunciation that required pronunciation activities and audio material.

Needless to say, some language courses for specific purposes are designed when some learning needs are identified by an institution (e.g., see Cutting 2012 and Lockwood 2012). This is particularly true in continuing education. In this case, the continuing education institution identifies and assesses the needs, designs the course, and invites the learners to the course. But even in this case, it is the learner who identifies his or her specific needs and decides to join the course.

The Instructor as an Information Elicitor

More than two-thirds of the participants responded with "very often" (55 percent) and "often" (20 percent) to the questionnaire statement "The instructor asked questions to elicit information on the learners' needs." The role of the instructor as an information elicitor reflected the attitude of the instructor to cooperate with the learner. Because the instructor was keen on assessing the needs of the learner, he asked questions to make sure of those needs. Many of the questions asked were yes/no questions, which were used to verify the learner's needs. An interesting conversation, which was reproduced from my notes taken while observing class 3, included the following questions:

- So, you think if you can pronounce the sounds more like Egyptians, you will feel more confident in the family meetings?
- So, there is no problem in talking English, but you want to insert some Egyptian Arabic slang expressions and phrases in your speech?

I was told during the interview with the instructor of class 3 that she asked the learner at the beginning of the course to describe a typical family gathering in terms of place, time, family members, topics to talk about, and so on. After that, she continued to elicit information, using yes/no questions like the ones above.

In fact, the success of the instructor in performing this role depends on his or her ability to find the appropriate questions, listen carefully to the learner, and ask for and receive feedback on what was understood of the learner's answers. In addition, the more details the instructor can find out about the learner's needs, the more he will be able to design the course and provide material (Day and Krzanowski 2011). Indeed, the collaboration between the instructor and learner right from the beginning of the course is a key factor in the success of LSP courses.

The Instructor as a Needs Assessor

Data analysis for questionnaire statements four and five indicates that it is the instructor who mainly assesses the needs of the learner. However, three (27 percent) and five (45 percent) participants responded with "undecided" to statements four and five, respectively. The eight "undecided" responses resulted from a lack of clarity about a needs assessment. In the interview, I explained that a needs assessment includes arranging the needs according to their importance and dependability. Therefore, after needs identification, someone needs to decide which need to start with and how much time each need should take. The eight people agreed in the interview that it was the instructor who performed this role.

Without accurate needs assessment, language courses for specific purposes can hardly be successful. Accordingly, needs assessment and goal orientation are viewed as the defining characteristic of ESP (e.g., see Belcher 2009; Kennedy and Bolitho 1984; Schmidt 1981; Strevens 1988; Widdowson 1981). This is because courses for specific purposes are based on "the need [of the learner] to use language as a tool in facilitating success in professional life" (Sierocka 2008, 33; see also Chostelidou 2010; Deepika, Devardhi, and Adinew 2012). Hence, "all decisions as to content and method are based on the learner's reason for learning" (Hutchinson and Waters 1987, 19).

The Instructor as a Material Provider

The questionnaire statements number six and seven focus on the role of the instructor as a material provider. All the participants "strongly agreed" that the instructor provided material that met the learners' needs. This high proportion (100 percent) of agreement resulted from the fact that there was no textbook for these courses, and the instructor prepared all the material. In fact, the experience of the instructor in the field of teaching foreign languages in general and language courses for specific purposes in particular is pivotal when it comes to material provision. The instructor relies on his or her experience when deciding which material is suitable for which level.

The Instructor as an Evaluator

The questionnaire statements eight and nine deal with the role of the instructor as an evaluator. All the participants responded with "never" to the statement

"The instructor asked the learner if the material provided has met his/her needs." In the interview, they also confirmed the responses to the statement. However, they clarified that whereas direct questions like the ones implied in the questionnaire statement were rarely used, indirect indicators were highly respected. For example, one of the instructors told me that she stopped an activity when she found out that the type font was too difficult for the learner to read.

Although the participants indicated that the instructor never asked the learner for feedback on the material, I think this is a good tool for quality control. Many institutions include one or more questions on the quality of the course material in their postprogram evaluation surveys, but I think it is a good idea if the instructor asks the question early in the course. This would give room for improvement, even though it might be difficult to substitute the course book, in which case the instructor could still enrich the course with supplementary material to meet the expectations of the learner.

The Instructor as an Adviser

The questionnaire statements ten and eleven deal with the instructor as an adviser. Although 55 percent of the participants responded with "never" to statement number ten, I was told in the interview that identifying a new need and integrating it in the course was the key factor in the success of class 3. In class 3, the instructor told the learner that he or she needs to understand the differences between men and women in speaking Egyptian Arabic in family gatherings, which the learner found very interesting. Unfortunately, at the time of the study, there was no evidence that the learner's behavioral pattern changed as a result of the instructor's advice.

As for statement eleven, 45 percent of the participants believed that the instructor often advised the learners on extracurricular activities. This may be explained in light of the fact that the course was given in an Arabic-speaking country, and so the instructors advised the learners to make use of that context. In my observation of class 4, the instructor suggested that during the break the whole class, together with the instructor, would go to the campus market and buy some food and drinks; she advised them to use Arabic with the shopkeeper and ask him where they would find a product if they could not find it on the shelf.

The Learner's Roles

This study indicates that learners play more roles than just learning. They serve as needs identifiers and providers of feedback. The implications are clear: Learners are active partners in the learning process and are responsible for their own learning.

The Learner as a Needs Identifier
Statements twelve and thirteen in the questionnaire state that the learner plays the role of a needs identifier; 81 percent and 72 percent of the participants strongly agree to the two statements, respectively. The role of the learner as a needs identifier is essential for language courses for specific purposes because it gives the course designer the basis on which to build the course.

The Learner as a Feedback Provider
Data analysis of statements fourteen and fifteen indicated that the learner performed the role of feedback provider. However, it was not clear from the questionnaire whether or not that role contributed positively to the classroom—that is, whether the instructor respected that feedback and reacted accordingly. In the interview, I asked the instructors and learners how the feedback provided by the learner affected the classroom. The answers indicated that negative feedback was usually dealt with as a request for change, which was usually respected by the instructor. As Knowles (1990, 1996) states, adult learners expect their opinions to be respected. Therefore, it is important for the instructor to take any feedback seriously, discuss it with the learner, and carry out any necessary modifications accordingly.

As an example of how instructors respected learners' feedback, the instructor for class 2 told me that he was teaching some texts on Arabs in *The Guinness Book of World Records*, and it seemed that the learner wanted to focus more on Arabic for the media. So the learner seized the opportunity of a transition from one text to another and expressed her interest in current political issues in the media. Although the feedback in this case was not direct, the instructor stopped the activity smoothly but immediately and brought a handout from his folder on vocabulary in the media. It is noteworthy that the role of the instructor as a material provider requires a great deal of flexibility on the part of the instructor. It also requires a great deal of skill to change the material without negatively affecting the learning outcomes.

Concluding Remarks

This study has clear implications for the instructor's professional development. What this study tries to say is that instructors play more roles than teaching, although they might not be aware of those roles. Therefore, it is necessary for instructors to understand and be trained for the roles they need to take on.

A crucial factor in any instructor's professional development is learning to help instructors think about what they are doing (Bubb and Earley 2011). In order to achieve this in terms of instructors' roles, observation can be used as a tool for instructor training. Observation is important because the more instructors observe their colleagues and seniors, the more they reflect on their own teaching and practices (Lovett and Andrews 2011). That is, observing one another teaching may attract attention to and increase awareness of the various roles of instructors.

In addition, sometimes the success of the whole course is dependent on the instructor's skill in playing other roles besides teaching. This is particularly true for customized, one-to-one classes, but it applies as well to any LSP course. One such role is needs identification. The ability of the instructor to identify the learners' needs increases the learners' satisfaction and reflects a perception of the course as a truly learner-centered experience.

And finally, this study stresses the fact that learners are responsible for their own learning. They are not passive receivers of knowledge, and the roles they play can affect even those areas that we think of as under the sole authority of instructors. These other roles, like needs identification and providing feedback on the material, can be a good source of information during the process of designing a course and selecting material.

In capsule form, this study indicates that instructors and learners play more roles than just teaching and learning. In a learning process that takes the form of a partnership between instructors and learners, both parties need to be aware of and exercise their various roles. In addition, instructors can promote their success not only by playing their roles but also by taking into account the varied roles played by learners in the two-way exchange that characterizes the ASP classroom.

Appendix 7A

Questionnaire

Heading: This questionnaire is designed for the instructors and learners of ASP. It is part of a study that aims at exploring the role(s) of instructors and learners in courses on Arabic for specific purposes.

Please indicate: Name (optional)   Sex   Years of Experience

Format: The statements were presented in a chart, and for each statement participants were asked to mark one column, with the following options as responses:

- For statements 1–5, 7, 9, 12, and 13: strongly agree, agree, undecided, disagree, strongly disagree

- For statements 6, 8, 10, 11, 14, and 15: very often, often, sometimes, occasionally, never

The Statements:
1. The instructor identified the specific needs of the learner and invited the learner to the course.
2. The learner identified his needs and asked for the course.
3. The instructor asked questions to elicit information on the learner's needs.
4. The instructor gave a needs assessment all the time it required.
5. The learner assessed his needs and gave a full report to the instructor.
6. The instructor provided the learner with material that met his/her needs.
7. The instructor provided the learner with lots of supplementary material.
8. The instructor asked the learner if the material provided has met his or her needs.
9. The instructor evaluated the development of learning and proceeded accordingly.
10. The instructor advised the learner on how to enrich the course by including other needs.
11. The instructor advised the learner on extracurricular activities that could help satisfy the learner's needs.
12. The learner was clear about his needs in the course.
13. The learner expressed his needs in the course.
14. The learner expressed his satisfaction or dissatisfaction with the course.
15. The learner provided feedback on the classroom activities.

References

Belcher, Diane. 2009. "Introduction." In *English for Specific Purposes in Theory and Practice*, edited by Diane Belcher. Ann Arbor: University of Michigan Press.

Bubb, Sara, and Peter Earley. 2011. "Ensuring Staff Development Impacts on Learning." In *International Handbook of Leadership for Learning, Part 1*, edited by Tony Townsend and John MacBeath. London: Springer.

Carver, David. 1983. "Some Propositions About ESP." *ESP Journal* 2, no. 2: 131–37.

Chostelidou, Dora. 2010. "A Needs Analysis Approach to ESP Syllabus Design in Greek Tertiary Education: A Descriptive Account of Students' Needs." *Procedia Social and Behavioral Sciences* 2: 4507–12.

Cutting, Joan. 2012. "English for Airport Ground Staff." *English for Specific Purposes* 31, no. 1: 3–13.
Day, Jeremy, and Mark Krzanowski. 2011. *Teaching English for Specific Purposes: An Introduction*. Cambridge: Cambridge University Press.
Deepika, Nelson, Devardhi Julia, and Tadesse Adinew. 2012. "The Issues Involved in ESP Course Design." *Language in India* 12, no. 9: 126–39.
Dudley-Evans, Tony, and Maggie Jo St. John. 1998. *Development in ESP: A Multi-Disciplinary Approach*. Cambridge: Cambridge University Press.
Hutchinson, Tom, and Alan Waters. 1987. *English for Specific Purposes: A Learning-Centered Approach*. Cambridge: Cambridge University Press.
Kennedy, Chris, and Rod Bolitho. 1984. *English for Specific Purposes*. London: Macmillan.
Knowles, Malcolm, S. 1990. *The Adult Learner: A Neglected Species*, 4th ed. Houston: Gulf Publishing.
———. 1996. "Adult Learning." In *The ASTD Training and Development Handbook*, edited by Robert L. Craig. New York: McGraw-Hill.
Lockwood, Jane. 2012. "Developing an English for Specific Purposes Curriculum for Asian Call Centres: How Theory Can Inform Practice." *English for Specific Purposes* 31, no. 1: 14–24.
Lovett, Susan, and Dorothy Andrews. 2011. "Leadership for Learning: What It Means for Teachers." In *International Handbook of Leadership for Learning, Part 1*, edited by Tony Townsend and John MacBeath. London: Springer.
Robinson, Pauline. 1991. *ESP Today: A Practitioner's Guide*. New York: Prentice Hall.
Schmidt, Maxine. 1981. "Needs Assessment in English for Specific Purposes: The Case Study." In *English for Academic and Technical Purposes*, edited by Larry Selinker, Elaine Tarone, and Victor Hanzeli. Rowley, MA: Newbury House.
Sierocka, Halina. 2008. "The Role of the ESP Teacher." www.jezykangielski.org/theroleoftheespteacher.pdf.
Strevens, Peter. 1988. "ESP after Twenty Years: A Re-appraisal." In *ESP: State of the Art*, edited by Makhan Lal Tickoo. Singapore: SEAMEO Regional Centre.
Widdowson, Henry. G. 1981. "English for Specific Purposes: Criteria for Course Design." In *English for Academic and Technical Purposes*, edited by Larry Selinker, Elaine Tarone, and Victor Hanzeli. Rowley, MA: Newbury House.
———. 1998. "Communication and Community: The Pragmatics of ESP." *English for Specific Purposes* 17: 3–14.

8 | LSP Educators as Informal Career Counselors

Annie Abbott

In a 2012 issue of the *Publications of the Modern Language Association of America* (*PMLA*) dedicated to the special topic of work, Margaret Ferguson (2012) contributed a brief essay titled "The Letter of Recommendation as Strange Work." Although she focused on letters for graduate students, her essay points to the growing length expected in letters of recommendation and the concomitant work required by faculty members to produce them, which also applies to such letters for undergraduate students seeking jobs. In addition to requests for letters of recommendation, faculty members who teach languages for specific purposes (LSP) receive student requests for various types of career assistance, such as conducting mock job interviews, critiquing cover letters, and suggesting job leads. This is not surprising given that the content of LSP courses centers on professional contexts, such as businesses, health professions, legal professions, education, and human services.

One apparently obvious solution is to send students to the campus career service center. However, these centers are undergoing serious transformations as they struggle to keep up with changing university curricula, evolving employer expectations, and increased demands to help students prepare for careers (Supiano 2013). Thus it is little wonder that students want LSP faculty members' expertise to help them highlight their linguistic and cultural experiences in their job search materials in ways that are often missed by a more generalized, campus-level approach. LSP faculty members are also much more familiar with students' coursework, and thus also can help to present it in professional terms and to incorporate preliminary job search preparation into the classroom itself (Abbott and Lear 2010). A recent report shows that among college graduates who studied the liberal arts, foreign language majors end up in higher-paying jobs (Weber 2014); so for students, it can literally pay to have informal career counseling from their LSP professor.

For students, rising tuition costs, burdensome student debt (College Board 2016), and a job market that continues to be challenging (Malcolm 2014) fuel their desire to graduate with a good job in hand. However, students are not the only ones who position LSP educators as informal career counselors. Universities, sensitive to criticisms about rising tuition rates, feel the need to justify these high prices with evidence of successful job placement for graduates (Jaschik 2014). And this directive gets pushed down to the level of particular academic departments. In addition to these top-down pressures to connect academic programs to career success, foreign language departments, facing downward enrollment trends, sometimes position LSP faculty members as informal career counselors in their efforts to recruit students to study a foreign language through a career-focused message. In sum, LSP faculty members can feel pushed by their university, their department, and their students to provide informal career services on an extracurricular basis in ways that have heretofore been the sole domain of the campus career center.

Taking on this informal role of career counselor means that LSP educators carry an invisible workload (Massé and Hogan 2010) that is not shared by colleagues whose interactions with students do not involve this counseling. To mitigate the burden of this invisible workload, it must be made visible while also being streamlined, so that as much work as possible can be done only once and then reused with each cohort of students. Because the value of the field of LSP is not fully recognized in some higher education environments (Grosse and Voght 2012; Fryer 2012), and because about half of LSP educators in US higher education are non-tenure-track faculty members (Long and Uscinski 2012) with high undergraduate teaching loads (MLA 2011), technological platforms provide an ideal venue for providing informal career counseling for LSP students that will achieve a high impact without requiring massive amounts of group or individual time with students.

LSP educators who accept the role of informal career counselor must find an efficient and streamlined way to accommodate the additional workload. Furthermore, it should be a process that can be easily adapted by any and all LSP instructors and incorporated into LSP instructor training. The rest of this chapter provides possible solutions for LSP educators and anyone training future LSP educators who assumes the role of informal career counselor. In particular, the chapter emphasizes how this work can be done efficiently with online tools.

Curated Content

One option available to LSP educators is to carefully curate language-specific career advice that already exists online instead of creating new content. Pinterest is a powerful platform for organizing existing Web content into visual "bulletin boards" that students can peruse at any time. An instructor of business Spanish can create Pinterest boards organized by different types of careers within business. For example, after creating a board titled "Management," one can go to the University of Texas at Austin's website with cultural interviews (2016) and create pins for each of the pertinent videos. Furthermore, a simple search for "redes sociales" within Pinterest yields many pins that have already been created and that could be sorted into a board titled "Social Media Marketing." Infographics about professional etiquette abound within Pinterest, and an LSP educator for any language or culture could collect pins about table etiquette, greetings, gift-giving, and so on. Finally, for students who are interested in creating their own jobs, a Pinterest board on "Entrepreneurship" could include the YouTube series in Spanish titled "Emprendimiento para principiantes."

On YouTube itself, LSP educators can curate video content about students' career preparation efforts and job searches. Certainly, LSP educators have a wealth of information they can make into their own videos (as described in the following section), but you can also easily create your own YouTube channel and populate it solely with videos produced and shared by others. After creating a YouTube channel, create playlists of pertinent topics (e.g., "Résumé Writing," "Job Interviews," "Cover Letters," and "Alumni Advice"), then add relevant videos on YouTube to these playlists by clicking on the "Add to" link that appears at the bottom of every video on YouTube. A search for "cómo prepararse para una entrevista de trabajo" will yield page after page of videos produced in Spanish that you can add to your playlists. Students can also benefit from similar information in their first language, such as the "before and after" job interview videos on darcylear .com's YouTube channel and the "Alumni Interviews" playlist on my own channel (AnnieAbbottPhD).

Although Pinterest, YouTube, Facebook, and many other online platforms can all be used to effectively curate existing online content that provides career counseling to LSP students, the following sections focus on online tools that will help you create original content. Ideally, LSP educators can use these tools to most efficiently share their career-related knowledge with their students, without becoming overburdened.

Blogs

Blogging has been popular among educators for several years. Blogs have been used to enhance student learning in the classroom in general (Richardson 2009) and in foreign language classrooms specifically (Blake 2013), as well as to provide professional development resources for educators. Blogs are also a logical platform for LSP career advice because they provide a permanent and searchable record whose information can be shared through other social media. Although blog posts do go further down the page as more posts are added, they are less ephemeral than other social media posts. Furthermore, blog posts show up in search engine results, whereas tweets, for example, do not. Additionally, each blog post has a unique link that can be shared on other social media platforms to increase its readership, an advantage not all other social media platforms offer. For example, one can share a blog post link within a Facebook post, but it is impossible to share the link to a particular Facebook post (as of the time of this writing). Finally, blog posts can be longer than posts in most other social media, allowing the blogger to go into more detail and provide links to more resources. In this way, LSP educators can use their time just once to create a blog post with career advice and resources, yet the information will be available to multiple students at multiple times.

LSP educators do not need to shoulder the responsibility of creating blog posts alone. In fact, involving students in the blogging strategy and in content creation will give them valuable preprofessional experience in the growing field of social media marketing. One strategy is to pay student bloggers. For example, in the Office of Undergraduate Admissions of the University of Illinois at Urbana-Champaign, students who want to be bloggers must apply for the job, are then required to write one to three blog posts each week, and were paid $10 per post during the 2014–15 academic year (Undergraduate Admissions, e-mail communication). Departments or programs that have the funds can invest in one or more student bloggers who post on a consistent basis. In order to write content that focuses on career advice for both current and prospective students, their task could be conceived in a number of ways: interview alumni about their current positions; research and share job ads that are pertinent to foreign language students; contact local businesspeople to inquire about internship possibilities or general career advice; visit campus job fairs and report on the firms in attendance and qualities they are looking for in students; and interview faculty members about how their courses connect to career success. If students are hired to blog, the LSP educator then takes on an advisory and editorial role.

Another strategy is to incorporate student blogging opportunities into the curriculum itself. Certain courses might assign blog posts for course credit. For example, honors students who each semester must transform one or more of their regular courses into an honors course by completing an additional innovative project can write a series of blog posts about their work in professional settings in the local Latino community. Although not the traditional academic essay, the reflective writing in students' posts strengthens their critical thinking in ways that an essay based on secondary sources and written in a distant, impersonal style does not. In terms of career advising, these posts also alert the students who read them to the kinds of preprofessional training that LSP service learning courses offer and that can be highlighted on their résumés.

It is also possible to incorporate student blogging into an LSP course itself. Students in a medical French course, for example, could blog at all three steps of the project. First, students could research census data about French speakers in the United States and present the results. (The results can be surprising, such as the sizable community of French-speaking refugees and immigrants from the Democratic Republic of the Congo who reside in small Midwestern cities.) Second, students could then find out and blog about the health services that are provided in French in these areas. And third, students could find related job ads from the area and practice writing cover letters that highlight their abilities to communicate and build ties with local French-speaking patients. Exercises such as these tie together multiple elements: the course content of French for medicine, an assessment of student learning through the information conveyed in their blog posts, and career training through practice job search materials.

Incorporating student posts into a blog does require some logistical forethought. For example, successful blog posts often incorporate both an image and text. Students utilize a critical thinking process as they search for creative ways to reflect the message of their post through a visual element, but they must also follow some basic rules. The image must be a file type that can be uploaded to a blog, such as a JPG or PNG file, not a PDF. If they use an existing image, they must respect the creator's copyright; and if they create their own image, they must obtain written permission from anyone who appears in the image. Although such rules may seem complex, a straightforward list of rules can guide students through the process of submitting blog posts. First, students sign a talent release form (UIUC 2016) and are alerted that anyone who appears in their images must sign the same talent release form. Second, students e-mail their blog posts to the LSP educator, who then uploads them to the blog; this allows the faculty member to check for quality and do any necessary editing. And though it is essential that the faculty member quickly proofread for factual errors, cultural misinformation, and minor copyediting, the students' bylines make it clear that the blog posts are 100 percent student work and do not necessarily represent the views of the university or its faculty. Third, any image should be attached to the e-mail, and videos should either be very brief video files or the embedded code of a video already on the Web. Fourth, the LSP educator can then consistently title and tag students' posts to make the content searchable, both within the blog itself and also with other search engines (e.g., careers, career advice, languages, health professions, legal professions, business). This can be accomplished by making a list of keywords that are then consistently used in titles and the tag fields that exist within the user-friendly online interface of any blog platform.

Former students can also create content. Alumni are often invited back to campus to speak to current students, but they could instead be recruited to write a brief blog post about their career path and advice for current students. Furthermore, when former students request a letter of recommendation and provide an update on their work since graduation, this information, with their permission, can be posted on the blog for current students' benefit. Stories from recent graduates often resonate with current students. For example, a former student sent me a message that I then posted on my blog. She provided specific job details (the name of the company, the job title, and precise duties) that current students can use for their own job searches. She also encouraged current students to continue with their LSP coursework:

> I love my new job and the best part is, I get to use my Spanish on a daily basis.... My bilingual skills have been a big help since we have such an international staff, with most of our employees coming from Spanish speaking countries.... I also wanted to encourage all your current students, because I know that the job market is very competitive right now. The ability to communicate in Spanish, along with the volunteer work I have done over the years, gave me a huge advantage in my job search. Your classes gave me the skills I needed to successfully land a new job, even though it was in a field outside of my degree. (Abbott 2013)

Involving students in the task of blogging about career preparedness does not make the task easy, but it does allow LSP faculty members to share the load with those who are most invested in receiving this information: students themselves. With careful planning, this service can also be an opportunity to further LSP educators' efforts to teach all students about critical, reflective writing for an audience of their peers who are eager to connect their LSP coursework to a career.

Screencasts

An important trend in education in recent years is the flipped classroom, "a pedagogical approach in which direct instruction moves from the group learning space to the individual learning space, and the resulting group space is transformed into a dynamic, interactive learning environment where the educator guides students as they apply concepts and engage creatively in the subject matter" (FLN

2014). Hybrid language learning, which possesses similar characteristics, has become increasingly popular in language departments (Rubio and Thoms 2014). Although the flipped classroom takes advantage of many technological tools to provide direct instruction and practice outside the classroom, videos are often the central medium for conveying information. These videos can be created in a variety of ways. Some instructors record themselves speaking directly into the camera, either through a Web camera or a camera application on a smartphone or tablet computer; these videos can be edited or not. Others record a Google Hangout on Air, which is automatically saved as a YouTube video that can be used for later reference. Even PowerPoint slides can contain audio and be saved as a video to share with students. To increase the production value of the videos, some faculty members work with the information technology experts on their campus to record and edit high-quality video and audio.

Using videos—and, in particular, screencasts—LSP educators can do the same: flip their informal career counseling. Screencasts are videos that capture what is displayed on the computer screen along with a voice-over narration. There are several specific screencast tools, and many of them are free. Jing (www.techsmith.com/jing.html) is one screencast tool that is both free and easy to use. In his book *Blogs, Wikis, Podcasts, and Other Powerful Web Tools for Classrooms*, Will Richardson (2009) thoroughly explains Jing and suggests a variety of educational uses for screencasts. Jing's website also offers useful tutorials that are examples themselves of screencasts. Jing's limitation can also be considered its advantage: The screencasts can be only 5 minutes long. Since research on massive, open online courses has shown that students tend to disengage from an instructional video after 6 minutes (Fowler 2013), 5-minute screencasts can be more effective than longer videos.

As with all educational technology, the tool itself is secondary to the information that is conveyed and its purpose. The question for LSP educators, then, is what content to share in these videos. Screencasts provide an ideal platform on which LSP educators can reuse and repurpose information they have already developed in other formats, such as presentations, lesson plans, and workshops. This way, at least half the work of producing a 5-minute screencast is already complete, and the career advice can then be viewed at any time by any student. Furthermore, just as the flipped classroom allows the instructor to give more direct feedback and selective instruction in the group learning space, asking students to view pertinent screencasts before any individual career counseling meetings or classroom activities allows the students' time with the LSP educator to be more focused on in-depth work and personalized advice. Screencasts, then, can be an efficient use of LSP educators' time as they seek to provide general career counseling to a broad audience of students as well as individualized and in-depth advice to specific students. The rest of this section presents several resources that LSP educators can use in finding the content for screencasts.

In many LSP courses, students write a cover letter as an in-class activity, assignment, or examination. LSP educators who have already prepared materials and tips to help their students complete this task in their course can use that existing information and transform it into screencasts. For example, if Spanish LSP students have to find a real ad for a nonprofit job in the Spanish-speaking world or a United States–based organization that serves Spanish speakers and write a cover letter for that job, then instructions and resources related to that assignment (appendix 8A) could be the basis of a screencast. Although such a screencast could be used by LSP instructors in their courses, it serves primarily as a free-standing example for students or former students to follow when they are actually applying for jobs. Furthermore, a short list of common cover letter mistakes and their solutions could be effective feedback for the LSP students working on a cover letter class assignment as well as for any student who watches the screencast.

Textbooks are another source of potential screencast content. *Éxito comercial* (Doyle and Fryer 2015) includes information about job interviews in its appendix, including a list of common interview questions. Selecting a few of those questions and suggesting answers that highlight students' linguistic knowledge and experiences in the LSP course would make a valuable screencast that any student could use in preparation for job interviews. *Spanish for Veterinarians: A Practical Introduction* (Frederick, Mosqueda, and García Ángeles 2000) contains two chapters that will be useful to students who are interested in any health profession: "Taking a Clinical History" and "The Diagnostic Exam." Although the precise vocabulary used by veterinarians will obviously be different than that of other health professionals, a screencast that highlights typical questions, common communication problems, and strategies for eliciting simple and easily understood answers would be helpful for many students interested in a career in the health fields.

Conference presentations can also be mined for helpful information to include in a screencast. Although these presentations are designed for an audience of fellow professionals, they often contain information that is also pertinent to language students. For example, at the 2014 Business Languages Conference of the Centers for International Business Education and Research, Deb Reisinger of Duke University presented a social entrepreneurship module she created within her course on French for business. One activity required students to fail, to fail often, and to fail in public as a lesson in the tolerance for failures that entrepreneurs must develop. During the conference presentation, Reisinger detailed the activity, students' learning outcomes, the broader implications for entrepreneurs, and the inherent role of mistakes and failures within entrepreneurship. A screencast that explains the role of failures in the professional world and provides a few examples can conclude with explicit advice on how current and former students can take more (calculated) risks in their job searches and in their careers.

Requests for letters of recommendation can lead to blog posts, as mentioned above, and also to screencasts. After a prudent amount of time has passed, the LSP educator can research the company to which the student was applying, note the job vacancies for which recent foreign language graduates could apply, make a phone call to the company to ask questions about their hiring priorities, and put this all together in a 5-minute screencast. In fact, student requests for job leads can be both the most urgent yet most difficult needs for LSP educators to meet, especially for those firmly planted in academia, not the business world. With just a little follow-up on the LSP educator's part, students' requests for letters of recommendation provide insights into jobs leads with companies and job sectors that need LSP students' language skills and experience.

Anyone who does face-to-face professional development workshops for students can either videotape the workshop and post it to the Web or use the information as the basis for a screencast or series of screencasts. In both cases, the valuable information shared in the workshop will be available to students who were unable to attend as well as future students. For example, a few years ago I gave a talk to Spanish majors titled "How to Maximize Your Major." I then created a screencast on one section of that workshop, using the same slides I had prepared for the face-to-face event and adding more detail in places where students showed the most interest or had the most questions (Abbott n.d.). This kind of career counseling encourages students to begin connecting their college experiences to their professional aspirations before they actually start job hunting.

Single, in-depth screencasts can also be combined to create a series. This is particularly useful for topics that require substantive instruction and multiple examples—for example, how to create a professional digital profile (Abbott 2009). Individual screencasts can convey important information, but a series of 5-minute screencasts allows LSP educators to address broad topics while respecting students' tendency to watch online educational videos for only a few minutes. This particular series on digital profiles alternates between direct instruction and activities in which students apply what they have learned. It also exemplifies other characteristics that LSP educators might consider in their own screencasts. The screencasts show both PowerPoint slides and websites; and anything that you can show on the screen, except videos, can be shared on a Jing screencast. They include written content that is then expanded on through the analysis of examples. To maximize the information conveyed within 5 minutes, the speaker can direct the listener to pause the screencast to read the screen, look at another website, and jot down an answer or any other type of instruction that helps the listener actively interact with the information. Although this series of screencasts is presented in Spanish and uses examples from Spanish-speaking countries, there is no imperative to use the target language in informal career counseling. Finally, this series also demonstrates that screencasts can be imperfect yet still impart helpful information.

Conclusions

LSP educators complement the work of career counseling professionals; they do not replace them. LSP educators' specialized expertise in languages, cultures, and careers can be extremely valuable to foreign language students, who often struggle to integrate their career path with their passion for the language. By blogging and pinning or creating screencasts and playlists, LSP educators can provide detailed advice and specific examples that are tailored to language students' skills, interests, and experiences.

The focus of this chapter has been on recognizing the additional work involved in providing students with expert career counseling and suggesting ways to make these efforts economical while still providing important information and instruction. LSP courses provide invaluable instruction and preprofessional experiences in things employers value, like teamwork, communication skills, global literacy, and the ability to work with data. The challenge for students is to recognize that their LSP coursework can serve as valuable career preparation and to pursue the extra counseling that LSP educators are uniquely positioned to provide. Our challenge as LSP educators is to balance helping students prepare for their careers with managing our own workloads. By involving others in creating blog posts and reusing existing information in screencasts, LSP educators can help both themselves and their students.

Appendix 8A

Examen final
Carta de presentación (100 puntos)

- Encuentra un anuncio para un puesto que te interese. Puede ser un trabajo voluntario, una práctica o un trabajo pagado. Busca en www.hacesfalta.org.mx/, www.idealistas.org/, www.monster.es/, u otros portales que conozcas.
- Copia el anuncio y pégalo aquí.

- Escribe en español una carta de presentación de **dos páginas**, solicitando el puesto. En tu carta utiliza ejemplos específicos de estas dos cosas: (1) el trabajo en la comunidad que hiciste para este curso; (2) el trabajo en equipo que hiciste para este curso.

OJO: Sigue todas las reglas sobres las cartas de presentación, menos la que dice que deben ser de una sóla página. Te pueden ser útiles estas guías:

- http://spanishandillinois.blogspot.com/2014/11/cover-letter-as-final-exam-some.html
- http://spanishandillinois.blogspot.com/2013/06/simple-tips-for-academic-cover-letters.html. Presta atención especial al consejo #4.
- www.donempleo.com/carta-presentacion.asp
- www.modelocurriculum.net/como-escribir-la-carta-de-presentacion.html
- www.careercenter.illinois.edu

References

Abbott, Annie. 2009. "Medios sociales para negocios: Cómo crear un perfil profesional en la web." Spanish & Illinois Blog. http://spanishandillinois.blogspot.com/2009/09/medios-sociales-para-negocios-como.html.

———. 2013. "Student Spotlight: Liz (Girten) White." Spanish & Illinois Blog. http://spanishandillinois.blogspot.com/2013/06/student-spotlight-liz-girten-white.html.

———. No date. "Spanish Majors: ¿Cuáles son sus metas?" www.screencast.com/users/AnnieAbbott/folders/Jing/media/8d61ad07-dfa0-4345-8623-28b1349ab6ff.

Abbott, Annie, and Darcy Lear. 2010. "Marketing Business Languages: Teaching Students to Value and Promote Their Coursework." *Global Business Languages* 15: 3–15.

Blake, Robert J. 2013. *Brave New Digital Classroom: Technology and Foreign Language Learning.* Washington, DC: Georgetown University Press.

College Board. 2016. "Cumulative Debt of Bachelor's Degree Recipients by Sector over Time." http://trends.collegeboard.org/student-aid/figures-tables/cumulative-debt-bachelors-recipients-sector-time.

Doyle, Michael Scott, and T. Bruce Fryer. 2015. *Éxito comercial: Prácticas administrativas y contextos culturales,* 6th ed. Boston: Cengage.

"Emprendimiento para principiantes." No date. www.youtube.com/watch?v=5SU_xhlwCuw.

Ferguson, Margaret. 2012. "The Letter of Recommendation as Strange Work." *PMLA* 127, no. 4: 954–62. doi: 10.1632/pmla.2012.127.4.954.

FLN (Flipped Learning Network). 2014. "What Is Flipped Learning?" http://flippedlearning.org/cms/lib07/VA01923112/Centricity/Domain/46/FLIP_handout_FNL_Web.pdf.

Fowler, Geoffrey A. 2013. "An Early Report Card on Massive Open Online Courses." *Wall Street Journal*, October 8. http://online.wsj.com/news/articles/SB10001424052702303759604579093400834738972.

Frederick, Bonnie, Juan Mosqueda, and Sandra García Ángeles. 2000. *Spanish for Veterinarians: A Practical Introduction*. Ames: Iowa State University Press.

Fryer, T. Bruce. 2012. "Languages for Specific Purposes Business Curriculum Creation and Implementation in the United States." *Modern Language Journal* 96, no. s1: 122–39.

Grosse, Christine Uber, and Geoffrey M. Voght. 2012. "The Continuing Evolution of Languages for Specific Purposes in the United States." *Modern Language Journal* 96, no. s1: 190–202.

Jaschik, Scott. 2014. "Pressure on the Provosts: 2014 Survey on Chief Academic Officers." *Inside Higher Ed*. www.insidehighered.com/news/survey/pressure-provosts-2014-survey-chief-academic-officers.

Long, Mary, and Izabel Uscinski. 2012. "The Continuing Evolution of Languages for Specific Purposes Programs in the United States: 1990–2011." *Modern Language Journal* 96, no. s1: 173–89.

Malcolm, Hadley. 2014. "Job Outlook for 2014 Grads Puzzling." *USA Today*, May 19. www.usatoday.com/story/money/personalfinance/2014/05/18/job-outlook-2014-graduates/8809801/.

Massé, Michelle A., and Katie J. Hogan. 2010. *Over Ten Million Served: Gendered Service in Language and Literature Workplaces*. Albany: State University of New York Press.

MLA (Modern Language Association). 2011. "Professional Employment Practices for Non-Tenure-Track Faculty Members: Recommendations and Evaluative Questions." www.mla.org/pdf/clip_stmt_final_may11.pdf.

Richardson, Will. 2009. *Blogs, Wikis, Podcasts, and Other Powerful Web Tools for Classrooms*. Thousand Oaks, CA: Corwin Press.

Rubio, Fernando, and Joshua J. Thoms. 2014. "Hybrid Language Teaching and Learning: Looking Forward." In *Hybrid Language Teaching and Learning: Exploring Theoretical, Pedagogical and Curricular Issues*, edited by Fernando Rubio and Joshua J. Thoms. Boston: Cengage.

Supiano, Beckie. 2013. "Career Centers Stretch to Fill New Roles." *Chronicle of Higher Education*, September 30. http://chronicle.com/article/College-Career-Centers-Stretch/141863/.

UIUC (University of Illinois, Urbana-Champaign). No date. "Release Forms." http://publicaffairs.illinois.edu/resources/release/.

University of Texas at Austin. 2016. "Cultural Interviews." http://culturalinterviews.wikispaces.com/.

Weber, Lauren. 2014. "The Liberal Arts Majors That Pay the Most." *Wall Street Journal*, May 15. http://blogs.wsj.com/atwork/2014/05/15/the-liberal-arts-majors-that-pay-the-most/.

PART III
Exploring Workplace Realities

9 Court Interpretation of an Indigenous Language

The Experiences of an Unexpected LSP Participant

Mary Jill Brody

This chapter describes the experience of becoming and serving as a court interpreter in the United States for an "exotic language," Tojol-ab'al—a Mayan language spoken by about 60,000 people in Chiapas State in Mexico. It is organized as a discussion of a series of questions about interpretation situations and ends with several suggestions about how such work might be facilitated. My professional background is as a linguistic anthropologist; I have worked for my entire academic career on aspects of this language. I am thus an experienced translator, but my focus was never on learning to speak the language. As a linguistic anthropologist, my goal has been to learn about the language and the culture and to translate those for English- and Spanish-speaking academic audiences; a core concept in anthropology is that cultures must be translated, as well as languages (Geertz 1973). I have studied the grammatical structure of the Tojol-ab'al language and the structure of narratives and conversation in it. In the process, I learned to carry out typical everyday conversations of local interest, focusing on such topics as the crops and the weather, the family, and illnesses.

This chapter is also partly about how I became an "unexpected LSP participant" (Long 2013) as a court interpreter for undocumented monolingual Tojol-ab'al speakers (or those with very little Spanish) who find themselves in trouble with the law in the United States. Along the way, I discuss the different types of translation involved in anthropological linguistics versus court interpretation.

My academic experience did very little to prepare me to translate technical US legal concepts and terminology, which in fact have no linguistic or cultural counterpart in Tojol-ab'al. Most Tojol-ab'al people live in small villages, where disputes are handled by local customary law, and most people never even encounter the official Mexican legal system; the confrontation between expectations of Tojol-ab'al customary law and US law is even more striking than the often-dramatic encounters between Mexican customary and civil law as described by Haviland (2001) for a Tzotzil community. For members of indigenous Mexican communities who travel to the United States, the expectations of the rule of law based on customs and practices resist taking into account the supremacy of a system of US county, state, or federal law, resulting in a great deal of miscomprehension when confrontations occur. Kobcek (2008) points out that in cross-cultural legal translation, there is translation between languages and also translation between legal systems, and the translation gaps may be equally wide in each case. Additionally, "the absence of an exact correspondence between legal concepts and categories in different legal systems is one of the greatest difficulties encountered in comparative legal analysis. It is of course to be expected that one will meet rules with different content; but it may be disconcerting to discover that in some foreign law there is not even that system for classifying the rules with which we are familiar" (David and Brierley 1985, 16).

As an indigenous ethnic community, the Tojol-ab'al do not have the depth of transborder history of some other indigenous migrant groups, such as the Mixtecs, who have been crossing borders of Mexican states and the US border for decades (Stephen 2007). The Tojol-ab'al have been much less adventurous, and began making temporary migrations to the United States in large numbers only after the Zapatista uprising in 1994. In the aftermath of that uprising, small communities were suddenly connected to the local centers of Las Margaritas and Comitán by networks of paved roads, electricity, and schools. In addition to facilitating the transporting of local crops to market, the roads fostered out-migration from communities where opportunities for earning were decreased by such economic changes as those brought about by the North American Free Trade Agreement, which itself was the proximate cause of the uprising (Collier 1994). The more Tojol-ab'al people (mostly men) travel to the United States as undocumented workers, the greater the likelihood of their encounter with the US legal system: "The demand for legal translation is on the increase around the world owing to globalization and the increased contact and exchange between peoples and states" (Cao 2007, 1).

In late 2006, I received an e-mail with a sound file from a colleague, John Haviland, who was working with another Mayan language—Tzotzil—as a court interpreter in Maricopa County, Arizona. While he was there, the court brought him a speaker of a language that they hoped he could also interpret. After interviewing this individual, Haviland suspected that the language was Tojol-ab'al, and sent me the sound file. Thus began my sporadic career as an untrained court interpreter, the only individual in the country, to my knowledge, certified in any way to interpret Tojol-ab'al.

Questions

Court interpretation in any language is part of a high-stakes situation for all parties. Court interpretation in an exotic language offers unique challenges that can complicate the situation even further, as shown by the answers given to the four questions considered in the following subsections.

Who Can Interpret "Exotic Languages"?

The first question to consider is, who can interpret "exotic languages"? As Roy (2000, 3) explains, "Interpreting for people who do not speak a common language is a linguistic and social act of communication, and the interpreter's role in this process is an engaged one, directed by knowledge and understanding of the entire communicative situation, including fluency in the languages, competence in appropriate usage within each language, and in managing the cross-cultural flow of talk."

What are the qualifications for an interpreter of a "less commonly spoken language"? More recently, I was recruited by Lionbridge, a private company that, among other specialties, "offers telephonic, onsite and simultaneous interpretation services in over 300 languages—including support for rare languages" (Lionbridge 2016) as a Tojol-ab'al interpreter. In order to qualify for Lionbridge, I submitted my academic résumé, which lists my publications about Tojol-ab'al and the professional presentations I have made about it, along with a list of my previous experiences in interpretation.

Another component of the Lionbridge certification process involves a recorded telephonic interpreting task, where one is asked to interpret increasingly longer and more complex English sentences in a set, short period of time. The sentence prompts are in everyday language, with no legal technical terminology. My question about this part of the certification is, what were the qualifications of the person evaluating my verbal interpreting? How would they know if I were speaking Tojol-ab'al or not, not to mention if my interpretations were on target or not? An experienced interpreter could evaluate apparent fluency versus hesitation, as I struggled with the longer target sentences. A linguist experienced with the languages of the Americas could evaluate whether the phonological inventory I used matched that of Tojol-ab'al by referring to publications about the language. A highly experienced Mayan linguist, like my colleague mentioned above, could make an educated guess given certain core vocabulary items (not used in the Lionbridge stimulus sentences). My best guess is that an experienced interpreter of another indigenous language evaluated my performance to determine if I sounded like I knew what I was doing. In fact, I mostly did not know what I was doing; I just muddled through. I would have evaluated my own interpretation as "poor."

So, who can interpret? Even a legally untrained person like me can qualify in the case of "urgent need" (see below).

How to Establish Mutual Intelligibility?

The second question to consider is, how to establish mutual intelligibility? As we have already seen, it is not a simple matter to determine what language an undocumented indigenous person speaks. I was once sent to Colorado to interpret for a man who was unable to understand Spanish interpreters but who said that he spoke Tojol-ab'al. When I got there and spoke to him in Tojol-ab'al, he replied, in Spanish, that he did not speak English—and he did not, in fact, speak Tojol-ab'al. It is possible that he was a speaker of Tulatulabal, another indigenous language of Mexico, and that the court interpretation services misunderstood. There was no time, obviously, to make further determinations about what indigenous language he spoke, if any. However, it turned out that I was actually able to interpret for this man using the first dialect of Spanish that I learned when I was a young anthropologist in the field for the first time—the Spanish spoken by rural, uneducated, nonnative speakers of Spanish in Mexico, which I call Mayan campesino Spanish. I suspect that some of the same factors that kept the Q'anjobal speakers (discussed below) from understanding the professional Spanish interpreters were also at play in this man's situation of noncomprehension.

The linguistic interview sent to me as a sound file by my colleague represents a meticulous method for determining what the "exotic" language actually is. Another means used by several courts is a telephonic interview. This was actually the follow-up to my experience with Maricopa County, as I explain below. This is highly recommended to avoid the unnecessary expense of transporting the wrong interpreter, an important consideration for the courts.

What Constitutes a (Legal/Real) Conversation (in Tojol-ab'al)?

The third question to consider is, what constitutes a (legal/real) conversation (in Tojol-ab'al)? After I informed the Maricopa County court interpretation service officer and the judge in the case that the language on the sound file was indeed Tojol-ab'al, they arranged for a telephonic interview from the courtroom to determine if the defendant and I would actually be able to communicate. I stood in my university office to swear that I would tell the truth, and everyone in the courtroom heard my voice coming from a speakerphone amplifier. After swearing me in, the judge asked that I speak with the defendant. I greeted him, told him my name, and asked how he was doing. There was a brief pause, and then the young man let loose with a torrent of Tojol-ab'al, trying to tell me all at once everything that had happened to him. He had been incarcerated for eleven months without being able to speak to anyone in his language, so he had a lot to say; this kind of disorientation is common for indigenous people incarcerated in the United States (Haviland 2003). After an interval, during which I mostly asked him to slow down and asked him a few questions about where he was from and the like, the Spanish–English bilingual court interpretation services officer determined that we had had a conversation, and that it was not in Spanish. This evaluation (along with my academic résumé) resulted in a legal document (posted on my website; see Brody 2016), an administrative order stating that I would be allowed to interpret for this case, excerpted as follows:

> Whereas the Superior Court of Arizona in Maricopa County is experiencing an urgent need for qualified English–Tojolabal court interpreter owing to demand for interpretation services in Mexican indigenous languages and lack of availability of current contractors;
>
> Whereas the existing court interpreter vendors do not have qualified and reliable Tojolabal language interpreters;
>
> Due to these circumstances and the urgency in providing interpretation to the trial divisions and other vital court programs, it is necessary to temporarily engage the services of qualified providers.
>
> IT IS ORDERED:
>
> 1. Ms. Mary Jill Brody, a professor at Louisiana State University, be allowed to work as an English–Tojolabal contract court interpreter during the period February 2, 2007, and June 30, 2007.

The interaction that I had with the defendant was hardly a conversation by Tojol-ab'al standards (see Brody 1986), where there is much repetition of words and phrases between interlocutors and repetitions of stories or parts of stories between co-narrators. However, it was apparent to the court translation services officer that there had been a back-and-forth interaction, with satisfaction on the part of the defendant, and I gave my assurance that we understood each other. This interaction and evaluation were sufficient to establish me legally as a "qualified" interpreter.

What Constitutes Good or Adequate Interpretation for Languages That Are Less Commonly Spoken?

The fourth question to consider is, what constitutes good or adequate interpretation for languages that are less commonly spoken? Public Law 95–539, the Court Interpreters Act (effective October 28, 1978), builds on Title VI of the 1964 Civil Rights Act and requires interpretation for those who do not speak English in courts; this is further clarified by the Clinton Executive Order 13166, "Improving Access to Services for Persons with Limited English Proficiency" (Berk-Seligson 2002, 245ff., and reviewer's comments). It seems logical that there should be standards set at the highest levels for court interpreters of any language. The federal government and many states now have exams for court interpreters that are no doubt stricter than those imposed by Lionbridge, and various private organizations train interpreters; several academic programs also offer certificates in interpretation (Berk-Seligson 2002). Professional organizations have developed standards of ethics and best practices for interpretation, such as the National Association of Juridical Interpreters and Translators. However, there remain several kinds of barriers to good interpretation that are exacerbated in situations of less commonly known languages.

The first of these barriers an interpreter encounters is that a broad array of nonlinguistic phenomena that might be called cultural barriers. Even initiating a conversation can involve overcoming unforeseen cultural barriers. An anecdote will serve to exemplify the nature of such cultural barriers. A number of years ago, I volunteered to speak with two Q'anjob'al (a Mayan language and ethnic group in Guatemala) men who were incarcerated in a federal detention center in Louisiana. I do not speak Q'anjob'al, but I suspected that I might be able to communicate with them in Mayan campesino Spanish (see above). When they arrived in the interrogation room, prison jumpsuits rolled up at wrists and cuffs, they looked terrified, with their eyes downcast. Extrapolating from my experience with the Tojol-ab'al, I greeted them with a handshake that involved barely grazing palms, and avoided eye contact. We sat together for a while in silence, as is appropriate among Mayans who do not know each other. Then, with my eyes still on the floor, I said softly in Spanish "We come from very far away."[1] One, then the other, repeated, "We come from very far away." From then on, we were able to communicate in Spanish. My suspicion, borne out by my experience, is that the hearty handshakes, direct eye contact, and rapid speech with multisyllabic words of the professional interpreters had prevented them from even beginning to have an interaction with the Q'anjob'al speakers. As Kobcek (2008, 54) points out, the court interpreter must be an "intercultural expert." In this aspect of court interpretation, my anthropological experience stands me in very good stead.

Another category of barrier to communication is what I would call ethnolinguistic—differing expectations of what is appropriate in a particular situation of communication. In my experience, it has been very difficult to restrict Tojol-ab'al speakers to the strict question/answer format of the courtroom. In fact, the US courtroom presents a format for communication that is quite foreign to Tojol-ab'al speakers. I have found that when Tojol-ab'al speakers are asked a question in the courtroom, even a strict yes/no question, their inclination is to start in with a narrative version of their story about what happened that got them in trouble.[2] This misunderstanding of the rules of discourse in the courtroom is very difficult to overcome (Berk-Seligson 2002; Wadensjö 1998). As a linguistic anthropologist, I am always more interested in the narrative than in a yes/no answer; as an interpreter, I am restricted to the format of interpretation only. At times, I have been asked to explain to the defendant that narrative answers are not appropriate, and that he must confine himself strictly to answering the questions asked.

Berk-Seligson (2002) enumerates the pragmatic errors committed by some court interpreters who are not aware of these ethnolinguistic issues. Again, my anthropological background helps to keep me from making many of these types of errors in interpretation.

Then, of course, there are the strictly linguistic barriers—lack of vocabulary for legal terminology in indigenous languages. Matilla (2012, 1) points out that legal language is notoriously problematic, even for native speakers of national languages, to the extent that "legal language does not qualify as a language in the same way as French, Finnish, or Arabic." Berk-Seligson (2002, 15–17ff.) lists the lexical and grammatical features of "legalese" that contribute to its opaqueness. The language of the law is a language for a specific purpose par excellence. "It is a fact that translating law between any languages is not a straightforward affair" (Cao 2007, 2). The translation of "jury of your peers," for example, involves both cultural and linguistic concepts that are alien to individuals who are familiar only with customary law and have never heard of the practice of trial by jury, not to mention the issue of who would be their "peers"—I have used the circumlocution "a group of people from here who will decide if you are guilty or not guilty."

It is unrealistic to expect to be able to engage in strict interpretation; direct equivalences for terms and concepts do not exist (Matilla 2012). In fact, "given the complexity and difficulty of legal translation, one may wonder whether law is translatable and whether true equivalence can be achieved in legal translation" (Cao 2007, 32). The greater the difference between the languages (and cultures) involved, the more difficult the task. For translation of legal terms into a language lacking similar concepts, circumlocution is necessary, and it takes extra time, both to devise and to perform.

De Groot (1992, 21ff.) points out that the crucial issue to be taken into consideration when translating legal concepts is the fact that "the language of the law is very much a system-bound language, i.e., a language related to a specific legal system. Translators of legal terminology are obliged therefore to practice comparative law." I would argue that interpreters from indigenous languages are asked to perform this same task, with the added challenge of a greater distance between legal systems than that presupposed by de Groot, who references legal communication in the European Union. The challenge is how to meet both the legal requirements and the interpretation needs of defendants, whether they are speakers of an indigenous language or uneducated speakers of a well-known language like Spanish, while avoiding the role of advocate and maintaining the role of an engaged but disinterested interpreter.

All these challenging levels of translation and interpretation end up taking time. I have heard complaints on the part of various court personnel that interpretation takes too much time and that using interpreters is too costly (see Santos 2014). Additionally, police officers sometimes find it unfair that extra attention is granted certain individuals whom they view as criminals; I have heard some claim that it would be more efficient just to deport them.

Suggestions for Solutions

After having engaged in about two cases a year over seven years, I still consider myself very much a novice court interpreter. However, I have learned a great deal about the responsibilities of the interpreter to be neutral, as well as the pitfalls that await the unwary interpreter. I have taken time when in the field in Chiapas to work with a sophisticated bilingual Tojol-ab'al/Spanish speaker, one who has seen episodes of the television program *La Ley y El Orden* (*Law and Order*) dubbed into Spanish on Mexican television, and who thus has gained at least some limited understanding of the US court system. She has helped me to translate the basic set of rights in a culturally appropriate manner and has marveled with me how monolingual Tojol-ab'al speakers could possibly be Mirandized. My experience has led me to offer some suggestions for how to enhance the success of court interpretation of "exotic languages."

Take the Time

My first suggestion is to build in time for the interpreter to spend with the subject ahead of court to establish common ground; to explain rules, rights, protocol; and to develop shared understandings of legal terms. This goes somewhat beyond the usual interview with the attorney ahead of the court appearance. As an anthropologist, I have learned that one key to conducting successful interviews is to give the respondent time to process questions and answer them in his or her own terms; the pressures of the courtroom do not offer this kind of time. The time involved and the range of topics covered—as mentioned above, it is difficult to impossible to keep Tojol-ab'al defendants on topic because they want to tell their whole story from the beginning at each opportunity—risks threatening the injunction for the court interpreter's impartiality. However, the goal is not to become the defendant's advocate; that is the role of the attorney. This being understood, I do find that having time to let the defendant tell me his or her story lessens his or her compulsion to retell it in the courtroom, where it is usually inappropriate.

This precourt discussion should also include a description to the subject of the roles and rules involved in the courtroom. It has often been difficult for me as an interpreter to make Tojol-ab'al speakers understand that my role is merely one of interpretation, that the lawyer is their advocate, and that it is the judge who is asking them questions, not me (Berk-Seligson 2002; Roy 2000; Wadensjö 1998). Also during this initial period, every effort should be made to explain to the interpreter all the charges against the defendant, and any other topics that are anticipated to come up in the court hearing. Knowing about these topics ahead of time allows the interpreter to prepare necessary translations or, more often, circumlocutions. Of course it is impossible to promise no surprises in the courtroom. However, to the extent that they can be reduced, more time will be saved.

How Court Officials Can Help

Judges, lawyers, and other court personnel will ultimately be better served the more they know about the needs of interpreters of "exotic languages," and how they can help. It seems that it must fall to the interpreter to provide this guidance (Wadensjö 1998). Supposedly, the interpreter is simply a tool to allow for communication (however, for a dialogic approach to court interpretation, see Wadensjö 1998). However, for interpretation from exotic languages, the interpreter's role unfortunately sometimes comes to the fore. Being present in the courtroom via audio or teleconferencing may only serve to further spotlight rather than background the role of the interpreter. Remote interpretation can be more economical for the court, but it can also be very confusing for the defendant.

Legal language is specialized technical language. Lawyers and judges can be encouraged to make the effort to explain legal terms in everyday language and to speak slowly in short sequences to facilitate consecutive interpretation. This might sound simple, but it is a difficult practice to sustain for those accustomed to a quicker pace.

Finally, I have learned that my own role as interpreter is not that of a partisan cultural broker or representative but one of informed and neutral linguistic and cultural interpreter.

Conclusion

Legal language is complex and heterogeneous. Even a basic understanding of the law is not mutual when Mexican defendants from rural ethnic backgrounds who speak an indigenous language are confronted with county, state, or federal US law in a courtroom situation. It becomes part of the duty of the court interpreter to translate across legal systems, languages, and cultures so as to successfully convey the undertakings of the court. Legal interpretation is high-stakes translation; the outcomes of legal proceedings have serious consequences for the defendant's life. This merits taking the greatest possible care to ensure good interpretation, as illustrated by this chapter's brief analysis of dealing with an "exotic" language such as Tojol-ab'al.

Notes

1. The use of first person plural is considered polite in many Mayan languages.
2. A reviewer pointed out that many subjects, even English speakers, respond to court questions with narratives.

References

Berk-Seligson, Susan. 2002. *The Bilingual Courtroom: Court Interpreters in the Judicial Process, with a New Chapter*. Chicago: University of Chicago Press. (Orig. pub. 1990).

Brody, Mary Jill. 1986. "Repetition as a Rhetorical and Conversational Device in Tojolab'al (Mayan)." *International Journal of American Linguistics* 52, no. 3: 255–74.

———. 2016. "Tojolabal Maya Court Language Translation Service." www.tojolabal.org.

Cao, Deborah. 2007. *Translating Law*. Clevedon, UK: Multilingual Matters.

Collier, George, with Elizabeth Lowery Quaratiello. 1994. *Basta! Land and the Zapatista Rebellion in Chiapas*. Oakland: Food First.

David, René, and John Brierley. 1985. *Major Legal Systems in the World Today*. London: Stevens.

de Groot, G.-R. 1992. "Recht, Rechtssprache und Rechtssystem: Betrachtungen über die Problematik der Übersetzung juristischer Texte." In *Terminologie et Traduction*; quoted by Kobcek (2008, 56–57).

Geertz, Clifford. 1973. "Thick Description: Toward an Interpretive Theory of Culture." In *The Interpretation of Cultures: Selected Essays*, edited by Clifford Geertz. New York: Basic Books.

Haviland, John B. 2001. "La invención de la costumbre: El diálogo entre el derecho zinacanteco y el ladino durante seis décadas." In *Costumbres, Leyes, y Movimiento Indio en Oaxaca y Chiapas*, edited by Lourdes de León. Mexico City: CIESAS/Porrúa.

———. 2003. "Ideologies of Language: Some Reflections on Language and US Law." *American Anthropologist* 105, no. 4: 764–74.

Kobcek, Alenka. 2008. "The Challenges of Intercultural Legal Communication." *International Journal of Euro-Mediterranean Studies* 1, no. 1: 53–71.

Lionbridge. 2016. "Lionbridge Interpreter Services." www.lionbridge.com/solutions/interpreter-services/.

Long, Sheri Spane. 2013. "The Unexpected Spanish for Specific Purposes Professor: A Tale of Two Institutions." In *Scholarship and Teaching on Languages for Specific Purposes*, edited by Lourdes Sánchez-López. Birmingham: University of Alabama UAB Digital Collections. http://contentdm.mhsl.uab.edu/cdm/compoundobject/collection/faculty/id/161/rec/19.

Matilla, Heikki E. S. 2012. *Comparative Legal Linguistics*. Farnham, UK: Ashgate.

Roy, Cynthia B. 2000. *Interpreting as a Discourse Process*. New York: Oxford University Press.

Santos, Fernando. 2014. "As the Demand for Court Interpreters Climbs, State Budget Conflicts Grow as Well." *New York Times*, June 14. www.nytimes.com/2014/06/15/us/as-the-demand-for-court-interpreters-climbs-state-budget-conflicts-grow-as-well.html.

Stephen, Lynn. 2007. *Transborder Lives: Indigenous Oaxacans in Mexico, California, and Oregon*. Durham, NC: Duke University Press.

Wadensjö, Cecilia. 1998. *Interpreting as Interaction*. London: Longman.

10 | Señor Google and Spanish Workplace Information Practices

Information Literacy in a Multilingual World

Alison Hicks

What does the term "information literacy" mean to you? If you work within higher education, perhaps your eyes are glazing over as an image of a citation guide comes to mind. If you last entered a library when card catalogues were in existence, perhaps the question is bringing back long-repressed memories of the tedious hours you spent at the microfilm machine. Either way, it is unlikely that you are making the connection between information literacy and the shiny new, paperless workplaces of today. Yet, I posit that just like the library—and even, possibly, like language learning—information literacy has an image problem. Rather than focusing on the grammar of information use—teaching students the nuts and bolts of arcane citation rules or the mechanics of how to navigate the periodicals room—information literacy should be understood as a practice that helps to connect learners with the broader realities of today's globalized information societies. In effect, though traditional, academic information literacy still predominates within higher education today, a number of librarians are starting to think more holistically about the role of information and the scope of information literacy education. As the knowledge economy continues to grow, it is clear that the workplace forms one particular area where information literacy is both essential yet underdeveloped within higher education.

In this chapter, I, as a librarian, seek to explore what information literacy looks like within the globalized, multilingual environments that language learners enter upon graduation and how we can scaffold these realities in the classroom. I start by introducing the concept of workplace information literacy as well as presenting an overview of the most current research and thinking on the topic. I then explore results from twelve semistructured interviews that I carried out with Spanish-speaking working professionals in Argentina, Chile, and the United States. Encompassing a variety of professions, these interviews were designed to provide a snapshot of both bilingual and Spanish-language information practice in the workplace as well as to serve as teaching and learning resources for the classroom. I finish by examining some of the ways that workplace information is starting to be introduced in the classroom at the University of Colorado, Boulder. Throughout this chapter, I aim to situate the concept of workplace information literacy within the goals of world language learning in order to start a much broader conversation about the possibilities and the potential of workplace information literacy within the classroom.

Workplace Information Environments

Traditionally, information literacy has been treated as a purely academic process. Arising in the 1970s, the concept of information literacy was originally conceived as a way to teach students how to navigate the physical library as well as how to introduce students to the mechanics of research. Inspired by the work of Skinner (1953), who understood learning to center on a change in external behavior, information literacy was seen as a functional, transferable skill or a set of fixed steps that needed to be followed when engaged in library research (Eisenberg and Berkowitz 1990). Even the rise of online information, and the move to house books in off-site facilities, did little to change the idea that information literacy was both strategic and generic, ideas that were later enshrined in a number of national standards (e.g., the *Information Literacy Competency Standards for Higher Education*; ACRL 2000). Yet, as information started to play an ever more important role within modern society, a number of librarians started to question this narrow conception of information literacy. Reflecting the shift from a behaviorist to a constructivist understanding of learning, librarians began to reconceptualize information literacy as a learning process (Limberg and Alexandersson 2010) or as a habit of mind (Addison and Meyers 2013) that is achieved through the creation of mental models (Talja, Tuominen, and Savolainen 2005, 83). Accordingly, instead of focusing on behaviors that could be judged by national standards, information literacy began to be framed as the development of an awareness of one's own process of using information to learn (Bruce 2008). The focus on reflection and process took a holistic approach to learning and emphasized the affective nature of research and inquiry (Kuhlthau 2004). These ideas have had an enormous influence in the field; yet, in focusing on individual experience, information literacy was still positioned as decontextualized and generic (Sundin 2008, 24). It would not be until social constructivist theorists came along that information literacy would start to move beyond its academic antecedents to engage with the idea that information literacy is both situated and social, arising out of a community's understanding of competent practice (Talja and Lloyd 2010, xii). In other words, seen through a social constructivist lens, information literacy is contextual and dynamic rather than static and linear, emerging from and specific to a setting. These understandings served to both broaden the scope of research and practice and to open the door to workplace information literacy.

Workplace information literacy arose in the late 1990s from the recognition that information environments were getting ever more complicated (Bruce 1999). Originally conceived as a process that professionals "go through to seek and use information to complete their work," workplace information literacy research swiftly took a different turn, to academic information literacy, when early researchers found that workplace information practices were neither linear nor always well planned (Cheuk 2000, 178). The breach within academic information literacy was further widened when researchers discovered that information work rarely involved a sole individual, but was instead driven by a number of collective needs and catalysts. It was not until the 2000s, however, that these ideas were developed through the publication of a number of studies by Lloyd (2004, 2009) of firefighter and emergency service worker information practices. By expanding research beyond typical white-collar professions, Lloyd demonstrated that information literacy is dependent on social (people) and corporeal, or embodied, knowledge as well as the more commonly assumed and recognizable textual information modalities. In addition, by demonstrating how firefighter activities were mediated by a situated reconciliation of practices, she provided further evidence that information literacy is context dependent rather than generic and transferable between settings. These ideas led her to reconfigure information literacy on the basis of processes of becoming and knowing within a specific setting, or the development of ways of understanding within an environment (Lloyd 2007, 182). They have also been crucial to the evolution of workplace information literacy.

Since Lloyd first started exploring the concept of workplace information literacy, the topic has grown in importance, and a number of reviews have been published that examine the state of the field (Inskip 2014; Williams, Cooper, and Wavell 2014). One of the most accessible reports on the topic was done by Project Information Literacy, which is a national study of young adults and their research habits (Head 2012). Centering on the information experiences of students after they graduate, this report explored perceptions of the role of information literacy in the workplace as well as challenges that both graduates and employers faced. The report uncovered a wealth of detail about what happens to students after they graduate and enter the workplace. One of the most interesting findings from this report, however, was that though students tended to be explicitly hired for their information and technology competencies, many employers were dissatisfied with how students performed when they got into the workplace. For many employers, this was linked to the realization that students tended to rely exclusively on digital sources rather than engaging holistically with the multitude of paper and social sources (e.g., knowing who to call) that exist within the workplace information environment. For other employers, they were frustrated with students' inability to draw patterns and make connections across their work. Students, too, found it hard to adjust. The workplace was far more ambiguous as well as faster paced than college, and though they perceived that some information strategies transferred across contexts, entering the workplace formed a steep learning curve.

Accordingly, though this literature review provides a brief overview of the topic, it is clear that the definition and the ability to describe workplace information literacy is continuing to develop. Most important for this study, however, is the idea that information literacy should not be seen as generic or universal. Instead, recent scholarship demonstrates that information literacy arises from the needs and the requirements of a community, an idea that raises a number of important questions about the nature of information literacy education. On one hand, these issues force us to question our assumptions that information literacy skills will transfer unproblematically to new contexts. On the other hand, they also mean that we must think carefully about what these ideas mean within a field such as world languages, where graduates have no clear career path. Although this chapter cannot hope to answer either of these issues definitively, this literature review demonstrates both the need and the rationale for research that begins to explore these complex questions.

Spanish-Speaking Workplaces

Having reviewed the relevant literature in the field, the chapter now explores what information literacy looks like in Spanish-language environments. Recognizing that the use of Spanish is neither standardized nor homogenous, however, this investigation aims to serve as a snapshot rather than a model of information usage.

Research Objectives

This research project arose from a recognition that though Spanish is becoming more common in the workplace in the United States, and though students were increasingly traveling abroad to do internships in Spanish-speaking countries, there had been little examination of how bilingual or Spanish-speaking professionals worked with information in their everyday jobs. Accordingly, this research was driven by two important questions:

- How are bilingual or Spanish information environments constituted in workplace settings? What are the similarities and differences between these environments?
- How is information literacy developed within these settings?

Together, these research questions aimed to explore the complexities of today's information environments by examining what the information environments looked like in workplaces that were characterized by languages other than English as well as how interviewees developed an understanding of these spaces.

Research Design

Research was carried out in two phases. The first half of the research focused on the information environments of bilingual professionals in Colorado. Colorado was chosen because the state has experienced a 40 percent growth in its number of Latino residents since 2000 (US Census Bureau 2011). Currently home to the eighth-largest Latino population in the United States, about 500,000 people out of the 1 million self-identified Latino residents are Spanish speakers (MLA 2013). This means that there is an increased need for Spanish-language graduates in a variety of information professions. Four interviews were carried out in the spring and summer of 2013. Recruited through personal contacts using a purposive sampling technique to ensure that a wide range of professions was included, interviewees included an immigration lawyer (whose clients are 90 percent Spanish speaking), a Spanish newspaper journalist/editor, a Spanish/English interpreter, and a Spanish-language instructor (non-tenure-track) in higher education. (See table 10.1.)

Table 10.1 Coloradan Interviewees

Profession	First Language	Second Language	Years in the Profession
Immigration lawyer	Native English speaker (United States)	Lived and studied in Spanish-speaking countries	3
Spanish journalist	Native Spanish speaker (Venezuela)	Lived and worked in the United States for more than 10 years	14
Interpreter (Spanish/English)	Native Spanish speaker (Mexico)	Lived and worked in the United States for more than 20 years	15
Spanish teacher (higher education)	Native English speaker (United States)	Lived and studied in Spanish-speaking countries	8

Table 10.2 Latin American Interviewees

Profession	Country	Years in the Profession
Architect	Argentina	25
Engineer	Argentina	6
Journalist	Argentina	12
Lawyer	Argentina	10
Translator	Chile	8
Teacher (high school)	Chile	18
Editor	Chile	5
Graphic designer	Chile	24

The second half of the research focused on the information environments of native Spanish-speaking settings. Argentina and Chile were chosen as settings for this research due to the author's personal contacts and experiences in the Southern Cone region. Eight interviewees (four in each country) were recruited using a similar purposive sampling technique, and they were scheduled in the spring and summer of 2013. In Argentina, interviews were carried out with a journalist, a lawyer, an architect and an engineer. In Chile, interviews were carried out with a translator, a graphic designer, a teacher, and an editor. (See table 10.2.)

Interviews were semistructured (see appendix 10A for a list of questions) and were carried out in Spanish in Argentina and Chile and in English in Colorado, although the Coloradan participants often engaged in code-switching. Carried out in-person at a location of the interviewee's choosing, interviews lasted between 25 and 55 minutes and were audio recorded using the author's laptop before being transcribed and translated into English when necessary. The Coloradan interviewees were offered a $10 Amazon gift card for their time. Because, at the time, Amazon was unavailable in Argentina and Chile, these participants were offered the equivalent of $10 iTunes gift cards for their time. Interview data were coded twice by the author—once to establish core themes and a second time to further develop these themes. Before the interview started, interviewees were asked to sign a consent form indicating that they agreed to be interviewed and that they agreed to the recording of the data to be made available in the classroom.

Results and Findings

The interviews demonstrated a number of interesting findings about information practices in the workplace. Given that the results of the bilingual interviews have been analyzed more completely elsewhere and were mostly carried out in English, this section focuses on findings from the Latin American interviews. And because the focus of this chapter is on classroom practice, this section gives only an overview of the key findings. (For more detail about the study and its findings, see Hicks 2014.)

One of the major findings relates to the richness and variety of information practices in the workplace. Although the professions whose members were interviewed may not be typical information professions (e.g., jobs that are related to the collection, preservation, or dissemination of information, such as a museum curator), information was entwined throughout the interviewee's typical workday. Thus, common information practices that interviewees mentioned included tasks as broad as researching house fittings and looking for standards and communication protocols to reviewing textbooks and looking up the biography of an artist for a magazine article assignment. Furthermore, probing revealed that information practices were not just limited to searching for information or researching topics. Instead, information work tended to include a variety of information management tasks; for example, storing and cataloging data that are used in their field. The variety of information tasks also meant that respondents engaged with an eclectic and surprising number of sources. Digital or online textual sources were frequently cited as the most important information used in the workplace, although interviewees further mentioned that they used videos, social media, and blogs, depending on the information task. Interviewees also commented on how much they rely on Wikipedia and Google. This finding is especially compelling given the tendency of librarians and members of teaching faculties to look down on or to ban the use of these tools in the classroom. Perhaps the most intriguing finding, however, was the realization that interviewees frequently rely on social sources—or people, friends, and colleagues—to help resolve daily information needs. This can involve groups of people; the Argentine engineer, for example, relies heavily on both a support team in the United States and a software team in Europe for assistance. It can also involve specific individuals, as in the case of the Argentine architect, who mostly relies on her business partner and local contacts. These findings are particularly interesting given that most information literacy instruction tends to focus on the use of textual rather than social sources of information.

Another useful finding from these interviews relates to the idea that interviewees overwhelmingly demonstrated the importance of paying greater attention to information literacy. Although interviewees, unsurprisingly, did not use the phrase "information literacy," their responses demonstrated that an ability to manage information is of vital importance within the workplace (e.g., finding and maintaining lists of contacts). In addition, interviewees' answers frequently demonstrated that they had encountered a number of information literacy challenges in the workplace, which additional or better training could have helped to mediate. Thus, interviewees frequently talked about their feelings of being overwhelmed, either by the flows of information or by their own inefficient information management practices. Others demonstrated an uncritical reliance on common tools like Google; the Argentine engineer, for example, revealed that he often equated the quality of articles with their ranking in Google. In this respect, though these professionals have developed admirable coping strategies for dealing with information problems (e.g., working out elaborate file structures or preservation techniques) over the years, it is clear that there is always room for improvement. The need for information literacy was also seen in interviewees' responses to questions about their perceptions of new and recently hired employees. Just as in the findings of Project Information Literacy, the interviewees often saw that students entered the workplace with impressive technological skills (e.g., being able to create a Web page). At the same time, they swiftly found that they often had little sense of how to employ these skills critically within new environments or the daily information practices in the workplace (e.g., how to keep up with developments in the field). Thus, the Argentine architect bemoaned the students' lack of attention to the importance of making personal contacts, while the Chilean translator found that students often failed to evaluate information that they found on the internet.

Responses from all three sets of interviews thereby demonstrate the importance of information and information literacy within the workplace. At the same time, one of the benefits of studying three different countries is that interviewees also revealed a number of differences between common workplace information practices in Argentina, Chile, and the United States. One of the major departures was related to the context or the varying environmental conditions of each region and its subsequent effect on information practices. In Chile, the teacher talked about how she still used many textual resources because the internet connection was not always very stable. Similarly, the high price of books in Chile affected the graphic designer's information habits because he had to wait until he visited Argentina for a conference in order to stock up on the most recent publications. And these differences were not limited to offline resources. The United States–based translator, for example, perceived that it was much harder to find Spanish resources through English Google, which meant that she had adopted a variety of adaptive strategies to find the information that she needed.

Another interesting difference revolved around the use of social media. For Argentine and Chilean respondents, social media tended to be used as a tool to maintain private relationships rather than to engage in professional activity. Thus, the Argentine lawyer found that the idea of using social media to search for colleagues online was strange, while the Chilean editor used LinkedIn to catch up with old friends from his university rather than to make new professional connections. This was in direct contrast to the United States, where professionals felt obliged to use social media to contact colleagues and make connections in the field, even though a couple expressed discomfort doing so. There were similar differences related to professional networks. In Colorado, for instance, interviewees regularly relied on national professional associations and networks, possibly linked to the lack of local professional associations that focused on Spanish-language topics and issues. In Argentina, however, interviewees asserted that, though they were members of professional associations, they rarely attended events or engaged with other members because they preferred to rely on personal contexts and introductions. A couple of interviewees in Chile mentioned that there was no professional association within the country with which they could be affiliated. These differences can probably be related to the centralized nature of professions within much of Latin America (e.g., the architect community in Argentina is much smaller than in the United States, as well as being centered in Buenos Aires) as well as the more interpersonal and socially structured nature of the cultures studied.

Spanish-Speaking Classrooms

Together, these themes provide a tiny snapshot of workplace information practice for a project that aimed to explore what workplace information literacy looks like in fields that a Spanish major may enter upon graduation. This means that though these interviews are interesting in themselves, they were originally recorded in order to structure educational needs. Information literacy instruction plays an important role within current librarian professional practice and at the University of Colorado, Boulder. As the Romance language librarian, this focus means that I am integrated into the undergraduate curriculum, providing research instruction in both of the writing courses that the department offers, SPAN 3000 (Advanced Spanish-Language Skills, a fifth-semester, high-intermediate/advanced course) and SPAN 3010 (Advanced Rhetoric and Composition, a course that is taken after the sixth semester of language study). Forming a neat pairing, these courses allow me to introduce research and inquiry concepts into the first course, and then to revise and reinforce these concepts in the second course. An added bonus is that the graduate students who teach SPAN 3000 gain an additional research refresher that tends to help them in their own work. But as the instructor of SPAN 3010 and I worked together, we grew increasingly dissatisfied with the structure of the advanced class. As SPAN 3010 is taken toward the end of the undergraduate degree program, it became apparent that a focus on academic information literacy practices was increasingly anachronous; not only would most students be leaving academia but many of the pay-walled resources that they were using would be unavailable after graduation. At the same time, both the instructor and I realized the importance of real-world Spanish and information abilities. These ideas formed the nucleus of this project.

When I started thinking about how to integrate these concepts into a writing course, I was influenced by the concept of personal learning environments (PLEs). These are defined as "the tools, communities and services that constitute the individual educational platforms learners use to direct their own learning and pursue educational goals" (ELI 2009), and thus they form a way for learners to reflect and think about the objects and sources that contribute to their personal learning goals, whether these are formal or informal or digital or analog. Typically represented visually (for examples, see *EdTechPost* n.d.), the benefit of the PLE is that it respects the idea that the way that people learn and think about information is very personal, yet it also creates a structuring framework to organize and think about the tools and sources of information that one uses to participate within the information environment of a community. This means that, despite the frequent focus on technology, PLEs are not just a set of applications (ELI 2009, 1). Instead, the PLE represents a new approach to learning, which is driven by personal interest and in light of community practices—a space for the learner to create, explore, and communicate (Dalsgaard 2006, 2). Within the context of this project, these ideas are represented by the fact that each professional has adapted his or her own strategies for dealing and working with information in the workplace (see figure 10.1). Thus, by listening to the interviews and thinking about the information environments that the professionals describe, students would get a sense of how professionals approach information in the workplace. In turn, by thinking about their own learning environments and then comparing the two, students would be able to reflect on their own practices and decide whether they want to change or develop aspects of their own PLEs before they arrive in the workplace. This is a holistic and critical approach to workplace information literacy that scaffolds the broad, open information environments of today while providing a student-centered approach to learning that focuses on self-regulation and participation.

Since this research was carried out, concepts of workplace information literacy have been integrated into SPAN 3010. Centering on a close understanding of the interviews that were carried out with professionals, the instructor and I dedicate class time to introducing students to the concept of a PLE before leading a discussion about the purpose and importance of reflecting on one's information

Señor Google and Spanish Workplace Information | **179**

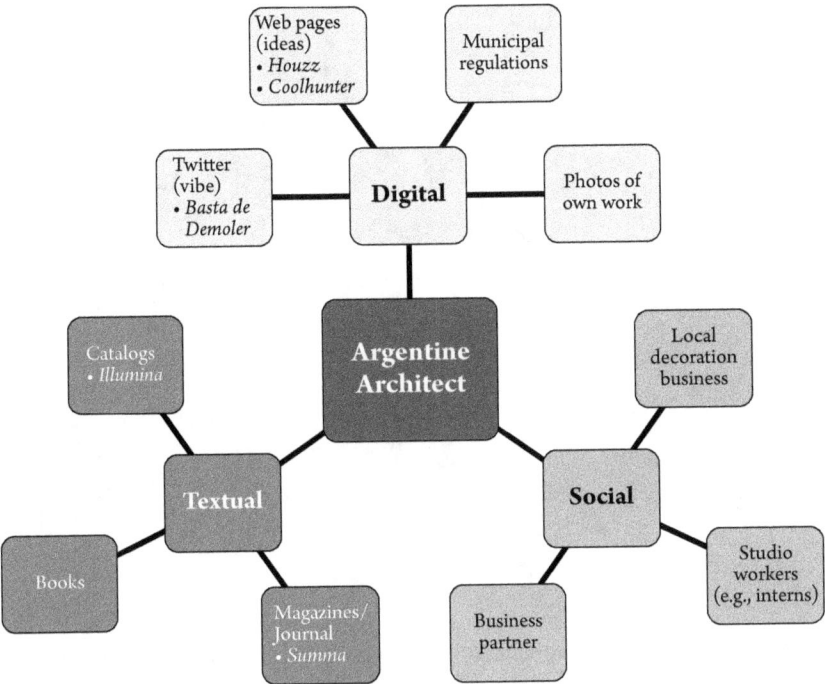

Figure 10.1 Visual Representation of the Argentine Architect's Personal Learning Environment

environments. This discussion is supplemented by images of PLEs that we had pulled from the Web. The class then listens to two of the interviews (the Argentine journalist and the bilingual journalist), paying careful attention to the sources that the interviewees used, the reasons why they use them, and how they evaluate information in the workplace. A discussion ensues about the differences between the two professionals as well as student practices. For homework, students draw their own PLE (see figures 10.2 and 10.3). Although this lesson plan has been introduced into only one class so far, initial analysis of the PLE homework drawings shows that students engage productively with the assignment, reflecting widely on their uses of information for school and for leisure. Analysis of these diagrams is still ongoing, but one of the most noticeable themes that has emerged relates to the stark differences between academic and leisure practices. Within their personal lives, students indicate that they rely on a number of social sources—for example, friends, parents, classmates, and acquaintances (in person and through social media). Similarly, students demonstrate that they use a wide variety of multimedia sources in their personal life, including Khan

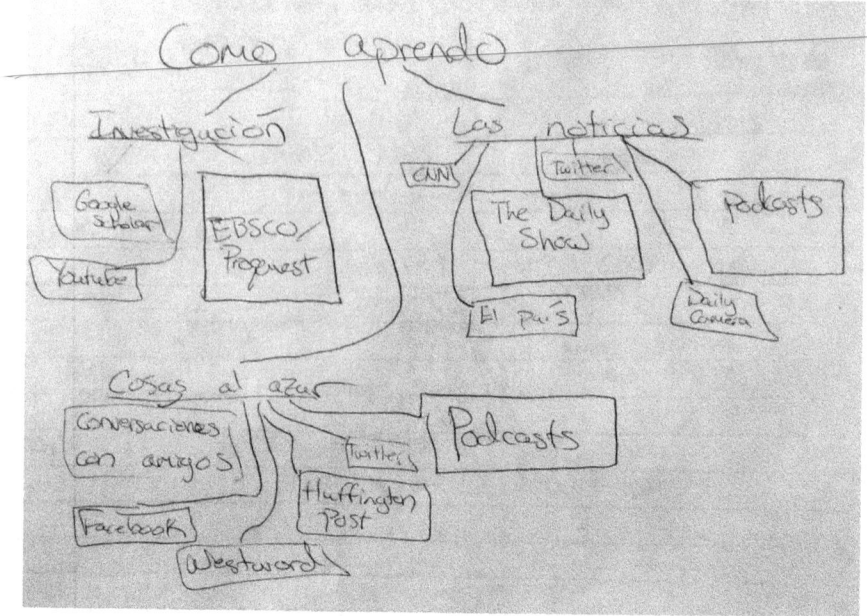

Figure 10.2 Visual Representations of Student A's Personal Learning Environment

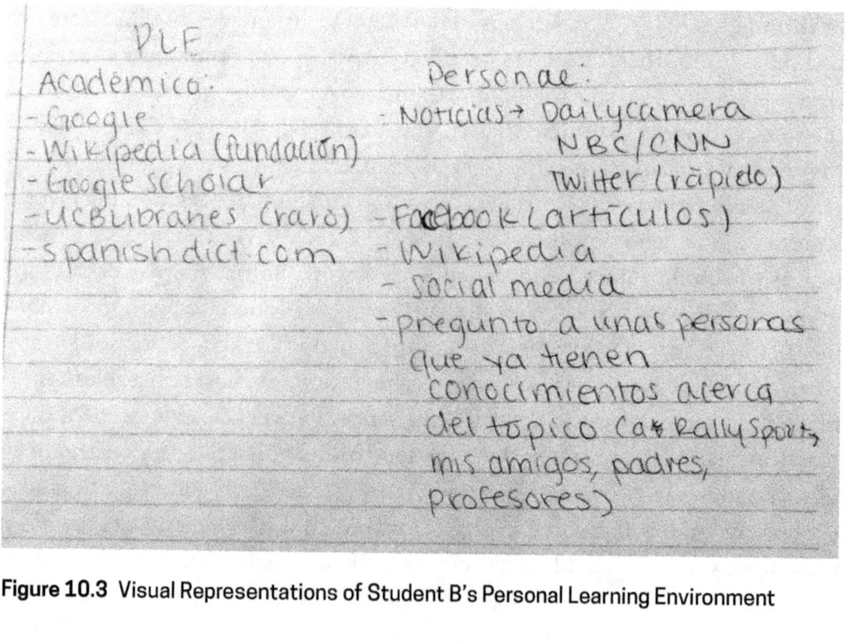

Figure 10.3 Visual Representations of Student B's Personal Learning Environment

Academy videos, TV news, NPR segments, podcasts, cell phone apps, and events. In contrast, students indicate that the sources they use for academic research are almost entirely textual. Although the academic environment is very different from the workplace, this rigid separation of sources provides evidence that students associate textual sources with "serious" work. This may further help to demonstrate why, as Project Information Literacy points out, students find it hard to go beyond the use of Web sources in the workplace. The reliance on social sources is also particularly interesting, given the extensive use of these sources in the workplace, and suggests that further bridging work may be needed to help students make connections between their leisure and workplace information practices.

This course marks just the beginning of what I expect to be a fruitful partnership with SPAN 3010, and in the future, I hope that these interviews can be adapted for other professional Spanish classes. I further plan to release these interviews under a Creative Commons license so they can be adopted outside the University of Colorado, Boulder. Initial analysis of student PLE diagrams also suggests other fruitful areas of research. One idea would be to engage in deeper reflection about the differences between Spanish, bilingual, and personal learning environments. This could also involve activities that are inspired by Kramsch's (1993, 228) research into activities that teach students about the boundaries between cultures, for example:

- What differences do you see between your learning environment and the one that you heard about in the interview?
- Thinking about these differences, have you identified any area of your own PLE that you would like to improve—for example, information management, note-taking tools, and doing research in Spanish?
- Imagine you have to teach a class of Costa Rican students how to do research in the US workplace. Knowing what you do about the differences between Spanish and English research, what would you focus on?

Future engagement with this topic could include asking students to interview their own bilingual or native speakers in a profession of their choice, either in person or via online video conferencing services.

Conclusion

In this chapter, I set out to explore the concept of workplace information literacy as well as what this might look like and how it might be integrated into the classroom. The analysis of existing research on workplace information literacy demonstrates the growing importance of this topic as well as the idea that information literacy cannot be confined to academic representations and understandings. The results from twelve interviews that were carried out with Spanish-speaking and bilingual (English/Spanish) professionals demonstrate the timeliness of this topic because answers reveal that professionals engage in a variety of information activities and that they need to develop advanced competencies with a wide range of digital, physical, and social information sources in the workplace. Finally, in providing an example of how workplace information literacy can be integrated into the curriculum, this chapter has demonstrated the feasibility of this approach and has opened up the conversation about how to proceed. In highlighting how librarians' engagement in the changing world of information practices neatly complements world language educators' strengths, this chapter demonstrates the need for librarians and these educators to collaborate and further explore this topic.

This chapter describes one librarian's attempt to integrate workplace information literacy into the world language curriculum, and I hope it will contribute to the start of a productive conversation on this topic. At the same time, many questions remain to be answered. One key problem that did not form the focus of this chapter, but which should be raised as part of future conversation, is, first, whether it is possible to really prepare students for the workplace, and, second, whether this is a role that higher education should undertake. As I have considered in more detail elsewhere, the question of whether education that is centered on the workplace undermines the goals of a liberal arts education by focusing on graduate employability rather than intellectual agility is a tricky one, though I believe that the use of reflective PLE pedagogy goes some way toward mitigating these concerns (Hicks 2015). Similarly, we must also raise the larger question of transfer; if we see information literacy as a situated and social practice, then it is important that we consider what and how student learning can be transferred from an academic to a workplace setting. Most students will find that access to library resources will disappear after graduation, whereas this study, as well as findings from Project Information Literacy, demonstrates that typical academic research is neither directly transferrable to the workplace nor always valued. We must also be wary of assuming that immediacy and access to information mean that students are inherently more able to wrangle these new digital landscapes; though students may be more accustomed to online searching, for example, numerous studies indicate that they may lack the critical thinking that must go hand in hand with these skills. These questions are complex, and they tie in with a number of conversations that are being held on campus today. Most important, however, is the fact that these ideas demonstrate the need to move beyond stereotypes; just as language educators teach more than grammar, librarian educators focus on more than books and play an active role in engaging with students as they are learning within information societies today. Just like language learning, information literacy cannot be reduced to the comprehension of a set of codes. Instead, it forms a rich sociocultural practice that helps to engage learners with dynamic information environments, both in the workplace and beyond.

Appendix 10A: Interview Questions (Also Translated into Spanish)

What is your job title/industry?

How long have you worked in this position? In the field?

What is your highest educational qualification?

What training did you get?

Can you tell me about a typical job/process when you may have to look for information?

> **RQ1. How is the information environment constituted for novices and experienced people in the field?**
> - What sources of information do you use/feel are important in your job?
>   - Prompt: Physical, textual, social, online, colleagues/peers/supervisor
>   - Prompt: Has this changed?
>   - Prompt: What technologies do you use? Physical objects? Web pages?
>   - Prompt: How do you know what is good? Reliable? How do you evaluate?
>   - Prompt: How do you know where to search/know exists?
>   - Prompt: If search is ongoing, how do you keep up?
>   - Prompt: Where do you ask for help?
>   - Prompt: Is there anything you still want to know/learn?
>   - Prompt: Is this different from research in English/Spanish?
>
> **RQ2. What types of information are considered important by novices and experienced people in learning about their practices and profession?**
> - How do you seek information about your job?
> - How do you seek information about your profession?

- How do you keep up? Learn?
- How has this changed since you started your job?
- What information competencies do employers need and expect from graduates?
- Do you think new graduates are prepared for this job? If not, why not?

RQ3. How is this information experienced?

- What challenges did you face during this transition from college/school to the workplace?
- What information competencies, learned and developed in college/school, did you use for solving information problems in the workplace?
- What personal characteristics do you think are necessary to be able to succeed?
- What adaptive strategies did you develop to gain an edge in the workplace?
    - Prompt: Training, mentoring, supervisor, social media, online community, coworker, formal versus informal
- Would any of this be different in a Spanish/English-speaking country?

References

ACRL (Association of College and Research Libraries). 2000. *Information Literacy Competency Standards for Higher Education*. Chicago: American Library Association. www.ala.org/acrl/sites/ala.org/files/content/standards/standards.pdf.

Addison, Colleen, and Eric Meyers. 2013. "Perspectives on Information Literacy: A Framework for Conceptual Understanding." *Information Research* 18, no. 3: 1–14. www.informationr.net/ir/18-3/colis/paperC27.html.

Bruce, Christine. 1999. "Workplace Experiences of Information Literacy." *International Journal of Information Management* 19, no. 1: 33–47.

———. 2008. *Informed Learning*. Chicago: Association of College and Research Libraries.

Cheuk, Bonnie. 2000. "Exploring Information Literacy in the Workplace: A Process Approach." In *Information Literacy around the World: Advances in Programs and Research*, edited by Christine Bruce, Phillip Candy, and Helmut Klaus. Wagga Wagga, Australia: Centre for Information Studies at Charles Sturt University.

Dalsgaard, Christian. 2006. "Social Software: E-learning beyond Learning Management Systems." *European Journal of Open, Distance, and E-Learning*. www.eurodl.org/materials/contrib/2006/Christian_Dalsgaard.htm.

EdTechPost. No date. "PLE Diagrams." http://edtechpost.wikispaces.com/PLE+Diagrams.

Eisenberg, Mike, and Robert Berkowitz. 1990. *Information Problem-Solving: The Big Six Skills Approach to Library & Information Skills Instruction*. Norwood, NJ: Ablex.

ELI (Educause Learning Initiative). 2009. *Seven Things You Should Know about Personal Learning Environments*. http://net.educause.edu/ir/library/pdf/ELI7049.pdf.

Head, Alison. 2012. *Learning Curve: How College Graduates Solve Information Problems Once They Join the Workplace*. Project Information Literacy Research Report. http://projectinfolit.org/images/pdfs/pil_fall2012_workplacestudy_fullreport_revised.pdf.

Hicks, Alison. 2014. "Bilingual Workplaces: Integrating Cultural Approaches to Information Literacy into Foreign Language Educational Practices." *Journal of Information Literacy* 8, no. 1: 21–41. doi:10.11645/8.1.1865.

———. 2015. "Drinking on the Job: Integrating Workplace Information Literacy into the Curriculum." *LOEX Quarterly* 41, no. 4: 9–15.

Inskip, Charles. 2014. "Information Literacy Is for Life, Not Just for a Good Degree: A Literature Review." http://www.cilip.org.uk/sites/default/files/documents/IL%20in%20the%20workplace%20literature%20review%20Dr%2C%20C%20Inskip%20June%202014.%20doc.pdf.

Kramsch, Claire. 1993. *Context and Culture in Language Teaching*. Oxford: Oxford University Press.

Kuhlthau, Carol. 2004. *Seeking Meaning: A Process Approach to Library and Information Services*. Westport, CT: Libraries Unlimited.

Limberg, Louise, and Mikael Alexandersson. 2010. "Learning and Information Seeking." In *Encyclopedia of Library and Information Sciences*, edited by Marcia Bates and Mary Niles Maack. Boca Raton, FL: CRC Press.

Lloyd, Annemaree. 2004. "Working (in) Formation: Conceptualizing Information Literacy in the Workplace." In *Lifelong Learning: Whose Responsibility and What Is Your Contribution? Proceedings of the 3rd International Lifelong Learning Conference, Yeppoon, Queensland, Australia, 13–16 June 2004*, edited by Patrick Danaher. Rockhampton: Central Queensland University Press. http://library-resources.cqu.edu.au:8888/access/detail.php?pid=cqu:1415.

———. 2007. "Learning to Put Out the Red Stuff: Becoming Information Literate through Discursive Practice." *Library Quarterly* 77, no. 2: 181–98.

———. 2009. "Informing Practice: Information Experiences of Ambulance Officers in Training and On-Road Practice." *Journal of Documentation* 65, no. 3: 396–419.

MLA (Modern Language Association). 2013. "Language Enrollment Database." www.mla.org/flsurvey_search.

Skinner, B. F. 1953. *Science and Human Behavior*. New York: Macmillan.

Sundin, Olof. 2008. "Negotiations on Information Seeking Expertise: A Study of Web-Based Tutorials for Information Literacy." *Journal of Documentation* 64, no. 1: 24–44. doi: 10.1108/00220410810844141.

Talja, Sanna, and Annemaree Lloyd. 2010. "Integrating Theories of Learning, Literacies and Information Practices." In *Practising Information Literacy: Bringing Theories of Learning, Practice and Information Literacy Together*, edited by Annemaree Lloyd and Sanna Talja. Wagga Wagga, Australia: Centre for Information Studies.

Talja, Sanna, Kimmo Tuominen, and Reijo Savolainen. 2005. "'Isms' in Information Science: Constructivism, Collectivism and Constructionism." *Journal of Documentation* 61, no. 1: 79–101. doi: 10.1108/00220410510578023.

US Census Bureau. 2011. "State Characteristics: Population by Race and Hispanic Origin." http://factfinder2.census.gov.

Williams, Dorothy, Katie Cooper, and Caroline Wavell. 2014. "Information Literacy in the Workplace." www.researchinfonet.org/wp-content/uploads/2014/01/Workplace-IL-annotated-bibliography.pdf.

Conclusion

LSP Studies and the Future of Higher Education

Mary K. Long

In the introduction to this volume, I situated the work presented here within discussions that call for changes in how languages other than English are taught in the United States, and I noted that "the interdisciplinary field of languages for specific purposes (LSP) studies provides many of the student-centered, multidisciplinary curricular design and research elements that have been proposed in these discussions." Now, at the close of the volume, it is worthwhile to consider the contents within the broader frame of the changes faced by all of higher education.

In a recent article, Jessica Hullinger (2015) succinctly summarized concerns about and predictions for higher education. Concerns center on the nature of what students learn and how well that prepares them with the effective communication, critical thinking, and decision-making skills needed for professional and personal success: "In one survey, 60% of employers complained that job applicants lack interpersonal and communication skills. They can pass a calculus exam, but they can't identify or solve problems on the job, or negotiate, or lead a meeting." Citing another survey of 318 companies carried out by the American Association of Colleges and Universities in 2013, Hullinger notes that "93% of employers cared more about 'critical thinking, communication, and problem-solving skills' than an undergraduate's concentration. They need hires who can take on multiple responsibilities, which requires flexibility and a plethora of skills." She goes on to note that "for the college students of tomorrow, these soft skills, obtained through hands-on experiences, will be the yardstick for learning," and she quotes Richard Miller, president of Olin College of Engineering (known for the success of its experiential-based curriculum): "'We need to stop worrying about trying to make them experts in very narrow fields.... Instead, let's focus on teaching them the process of learning itself.'"

In October 2015 the American Association of Colleges and Universities published *Faculty Leadership for Integrative Liberal Learning* (Ferren and Paris 2015), which articulates a set of principles and practices to guide integrative liberal learning for today's students. These overlapping principles reflect a more holistic concept of undergraduate education that focuses on student empowerment and self-development; intentionally integrated learning opportunities and experiences; and greater clarity and transparency of learning outcomes for students, faculty, and other stakeholders.

Just as was the case with the new directions for language teaching, LSP studies is also on the cutting edge of the multidisciplinary, integrated learning experiences and meaningful assessment measures that are being mapped out for the future of undergraduate education in general. The survey presented in chapter 1 of this book "revealed a rich diversity of interests, topics, and potential disciplinary approaches that reflect the complexities of the contemporary global context, which seems to simultaneously demand research that furthers theoretical knowledge while also mapping out best practices for applying this knowledge to human interactions." The other chapters in the book give clear and useful examples of best practices sustained by theoretical knowledge from a number of disciplines. Taken as a whole, the chapters also demonstrate certain continuities that can inform both future LSP and general educational research, curriculum development, and pedagogical practice.

Each chapter demonstrates the importance of connecting interdisciplinary academic knowledge to real-world contexts. The importance of making such connections is multifaceted. The last two chapters portray approaches to understanding how academic knowledge informs and is complemented by an understanding of how individuals continue to acquire new knowledge in daily life, whether through personalized learning systems in workplace information practices or through the multiple levels of knowledge that must be communicated about language, culture, and the law—as well as cultural and courtroom communication practices, in the case of court interpretation.

This book's other chapters demonstrate the motivational value of connecting the classroom to the real world. This can be achieved in the classroom by thoughtfully making changes to traditional materials, such as the verb paradigm charts that present question-and-answer structures together as they would be used in conversation, or by introducing life-guiding concepts such as leadership through cultural scenarios. Another dynamic avenue for connecting classroom learning to the real world comes through engagement with professionals in community organizations, internships, and service learning, supported by guidance in reflective practices from the instructor. As noted by the authors of several chapters, students were more engaged in the learning process and were more satisfied with their learning outcomes when they were "able to actually use all the Spanish they had learned in real-life situation," as Risner and her colleagues explain in chapter 2. Furthermore, as Risner and her colleagues note, students gained a sense of confidence in their future prospects for a "bilingual life" and the ability to "compete for future jobs." The higher levels of motivation and engagement derived from an awareness of the real-world uses of their language skills also lead students to achieve greater language proficiency and cross-cultural competence. And their consequent satisfaction and confidence inspire students to continue to study languages and to seek out further interdisciplinary connections—that is, to become lifelong learners.

The chapters of this book also provide multiple examples of ways to empower students with the responsibility for their own learning through an open dialogue between instructors and students about course goals and envisioned outcomes. Because of LSP courses' more dialogical interaction between instructor and student, as well as the focus on learning processes rather than simple information transfer, these courses demonstrate underlying principles that facilitate the tailoring of courses to the specific learning goals and needs of unique student populations, including English-as-a-second language students of engineering, heritage learners of Spanish, and Air Force cadets studying French, German, or Spanish.

All the chapter authors note the satisfaction that they derive as instructors from the success of their students and the rewarding nature of a more dialogic relationship. They also note the added efforts required to perform roles outside the classroom, whether to establish community relationships, provide individualized student career counseling, or develop materials targeted to the needs of unique student groups. We hope that the educational success stories presented in this volume will not only inspire other instructors to develop similar courses and programs but also help government and school administrators at all levels to recognize the value of the instructors' dedication and added efforts, and consequently will provide the necessary administrative and economic support. Given adequate status and support, LSP studies will grow in breadth and depth, strengthening its essential role in meeting the educational needs of the twenty-first century.

References

Ferren, Ann S., and David C. Paris. 2015. *Faculty Leadership for Integrative Liberal Learning* American Association of Colleges and Universities. http://secure.aacu.org/store/detail.aspx?id=FACLEAD.

Hullinger, Jessica. 2015. "This Is the Future of College." *FastCompany*, May 18. www.fastcompany.com/3046299/the-new-rules-of-work/this-is-the-future-of-college.

Contributors

Annie Abbott is an associate professor and academic professional at the University of Illinois, Urbana-Champaign, and director of undergraduate studies in the Department of Spanish and Portuguese. Her teaching and research focus on community service learning, social entrepreneurship, and business Spanish, with a focus on advocacy and civic engagement. She is author of *Comunidades: Más allá del aula* and *Día a día—De lo personal a lo profesional*.

El-Hussein Aly is an associate professor of applied linguistics at Helwan University and director of the Language Department in the School of Continuing Education of the American University in Cairo. He has directed programs and curriculum development in Arabic, English for specific purposes, and translation. His research focuses on sociocultural learning, including learners' roles and responsibilities in the learning process, instructors' cognition of their role, and the effect of group work on learning.

Anthony Becker is an assistant professor in the English Department at Colorado State University. He has been teaching in the TEFL/TESL (Teaching English as a Foreign/Second Language) program there since 2012. He received a PhD in applied linguistics from Northern Arizona University. Aside from work dealing with language for specific purposes, his other research and teaching interests include second language assessment, second language writing, and computer applications in applied linguistics.

Cristin Bleess received a master's degree in Spanish-language teaching. At Castle View High School in Castle Rock, Colorado, she led the development of the Spanish for Leadership program and was the world language coordinator for the Douglas County School District. She has taught in Texas, Minnesota, and

Mexico, and was a Fulbright exchange teacher in Colombia. Currently, she is with the Peace Corps in Albania, training secondary English teachers.

Mary Jill Brody is the Doris Z. Stone Professor of Latin American Studies in the Department of Geography and Anthropology at Louisiana State University. She received her doctorate in anthropology from Washington University. Her research career has been devoted to the study of the structure and use of the Mayan language Tojol-ab'al. This expertise led to her being asked to interpret in court for undocumented monolingual Tojol-ab'al speakers in the United States.

LeAnn Derby has been an officer in the US Air Force for twenty-eight years. She teaches French at the US Air Force Academy and is director of faculty development in the Department of Foreign Languages. Her research includes formative and summative student assessment design, statistical analysis, immersion and cultural program assessment, student leadership development, and program evaluation.

Janet Graham is an adjunct professor of international business at Baker University and a global business instructor at the Center for Advanced Professional Studies, a profession-based learning program in the Blue Valley School District in Overland Park, Kansas, that has spread to twenty-two school districts nationwide. Her World Language and Leadership course was recently recognized as an outstanding community-engaged learning experience by the Global Engagement Initiative of the American Council on the Teaching of Foreign Languages.

Alison Hicks is an assistant professor and the Romance languages librarian at the University of Colorado, Boulder. She worked as a librarian in Buenos Aires before receiving her master's degree in information science from the University of Texas, Austin. Her research interests center on transition and information literacy practices within intercultural settings, and her work has been published in *Portal*, the *Journal of Information Literacy*, and *Communications in Information Literacy*.

Carmen King de Ramírez is an assistant professor of Spanish at the University of Arizona and a nationally certified medical interpreter. Previously, she designed and taught curriculum for the Spanish for the Professions Minor/Certificate Program at Arizona State University–Phoenix. She has published on the subjects of service learning, culture for the professions, heritage learners, and medical interpretation, and she has directed community internships in international settings.

Barbara A. Lafford is a professor of Spanish linguistics and heads the Faculty of Languages and Cultures in the College of Letters and Sciences at Arizona State University. She has published extensively on a wide variety of topics and edited the 2012 focus issue on languages for specific purposes for the *Modern Language Journal*. With Carmen King, she cohosted the Third International Symposium on Languages for Specific Purposes / Centers for International Business Education and Research Business Language Conference in 2016.

Mary K. Long is senior instructor and director of the Spanish for the Professions major in the Department of Spanish and Portuguese at the University of Colorado, Boulder. She publishes in the area of languages for specific purposes as well as Mexican literature and culture. She is coeditor of two volumes: *Teaching Gender through Latin American, Latino, and Iberian Texts and Cultures* (Sense Publishing, 2015); and *Mexico Reading the United States* (Vanderbilt University Press, 2009).

Jean W. LeLoup is professor of Spanish in the Department of Foreign Languages at the US Air Force Academy and professor emerita of Spanish at the State University of New York College at Cortland. She is cofounder and comoderator of FLTEACH, the Foreign Language Teaching Forum's discussion list. Her current areas of research are the integration of culture and leadership in the language curriculum and language immersion in the classroom.

Tatiana Nekrasova-Beker is an assistant professor of applied linguistics and TEFL/TESL (Teaching English as a Foreign/Second Language) at Colorado State University, where she is currently teaching graduate courses in the TEFL/TESL program. Her research interests include usage-based approaches to second language acquisition, the role of formulaic language in fluency and syntactic development, project-based methods in second language instruction, and corpus-based analyses of texts on English for specific purposes.

Robert A. Quinn is the author of numerous articles, a grants recipient, a department chair, and an evaluator for the Fund for the Improvement of Postsecondary Education as well as a consultant for publishers and an outside evaluator for university language departments. He has been *Hispania*'s associate editor for technology and associate editor for methodology and a professor of Spanish at the US Military Academy at West Point. He currently interprets for physicians, attorneys, and federal courts.

James Rasmussen is an associate professor of German in the Department of Foreign Languages at the US Air Force Academy. His current areas of research include the integration of leadership development and literary study in the advanced foreign language classroom as well as the intersections of literature and philosophy in the German-speaking regions of Europe.

Mary Risner is associate director of the Center for Latin American Studies at the University of Florida, where she develops and manages initiatives that integrate world languages and area studies across the K-16 curriculum. She has a doctorate in curriculum and instruction specializing in educational technology, and her educational background is also in marketing, Latin American studies, and language teaching.

Ismênia Sales de Souza is an associate professor of Portuguese and Spanish in the Department of Foreign Languages at the US Air Force Academy, director of research for the Department of Foreign Languages, coach of character and leadership at the US Air Force Academy, and the Rocky Mountain states' representative for the American Association of Teachers of Portuguese. Her areas of research are nineteenth-century peninsular literature, Latin America literature, language acquisition, and comparative literature.

Lourdes Sánchez-López is associate professor of Spanish and founding director of the Spanish for Specific Purposes Certificate Program at the University of Alabama at Birmingham. She directed the First International Symposium on Languages for Specific Purposes in 2012 and edited the volume *Scholarship and Teaching on Languages for Specific Purposes* (UAB Digital Collections, 2013). She is coauthor of two textbooks, *El mundo hispanohablante contemporáneo: Historia, política, sociedades y cultura* (Routledge, 2016); and *Pueblos: Intermediate Spanish in Cultural Contexts* (Cengage, 2007).

Melissa Swarr is an assistant principal in the Donegal School District in Lancaster County, Pennsylvania, and a former Spanish teacher. She has a master of arts degree in Spanish and also received a master's degree in educational administration. After teaching postsecondary introductory Spanish for health care, she realized that specialized coursework is more successful as an advanced secondary course and developed a curriculum for this level.

Index

Letters f and t following the page number indicate figures and tables.

academic purposes, as research domain, 19*t*
Academic Words List (AWL), 109, 111
ACTFL. *See* American Council on the Teaching of Foreign Languages (ACTFL)
adult instruction, 89
advocacy videos, in business language education, 41*t*
Air Force Academy, 74–84, 80*t*, 81*f*, 83*f*
alienation, 55
alumni, in career counseling, 148
American Association of Colleges and Universities, 187–88
American Council on the Teaching of Foreign Languages (ACTFL), 39, 40, 42, 73
American Institute for Foreign Trade, 2
andragogy, 89
Apprentice, The (television program), 43
Arabic for specific purposes (ASP): advising in, 138; courses, 132*t*; defining, 131–32; evaluation in, 137–38; feedback in, 139; information elicitation in, 136–37; instructor roles in, 134*t*, 135–38, 140–41; learner roles in, 134–35, 135*t*, 138–39, 140–41; literature gap in, 129; material provision in, 137; needs assessment in, 137; needs identification in, 133–34, 135–36, 139; research questions with, 132
Argentina, 176–77
ASP. *See* Arabic for specific purposes (ASP)
assessment, 22*t*, 23*t*
AWL. *See* Academic Words List (AWL)

blogs, 145–48
Bloom's Taxonomy, 91
business: etiquette, 43; models for education in, 40–41, 41*t*; as research domain, 19*t*; in secondary education, 38–39; Spanish for, 38–39
business terminology, 37

CALL. *See* computer-assisted language learning (CALL)
CAPS. *See* Center for Advanced Professional Studies (CAPS)
career counseling: alumni in, 148; blogs in, 145–48; campus career service center in, 143; curated content in, 144–45; growing need for, 143–44; as invisible workload, 144; screencasts in, 148–52
career service center, 143

CBI. *See* content-based instruction (CBI)
Center for Advanced Professional Studies (CAPS), 47–50, 49
Center for International Business Education and Research (CIBER), 15, 32n4, 39, 40, 43
Chile, 176–77
CIBER. *See* Center for International Business Education and Research (CIBER)
Civil Rights Act of 1964, 162
collaboration, in project-based learning, 102, 108, 117–18
communication strategies, 22*t*
community engagement, as research domain, 19*t*
Complete Lexical Tutor, 109
computer-assisted language learning (CALL), 14
conference presentations, 150–51
conferences, state foreign language, 39
conjugation, in verb charts, 93, 94*t*, 95*t*
constructivism, 170–71
content-based instruction (CBI), 101–2
content instructors, collaboration with, 108
conversational paradigm: considerations in, 88; input/output processing paradigm in, 91–92; processing paradigms in, 92–97, 92*t*, 94*t*, 95*t*; research implications, 97–98; verb forms in, 88–89; verb paradigm in, 89–91
conversational structures, 20*t*, 21*t*
copresentation, in business language education, 41*t*
course assessment, 23*t*
course development, 23*t*
court interpretation, 157–66
Court Interpreters Act, 161–62
cover letters, 150
cultural competence: leadership and, 74–75; as pedagogical issue, 22*t*; US Air Force Academy and, 74–84, 80*t*, 81*f*, 83*f*

cultural etiquette, 43
cultural perspectives, 20*t*, 22*t*, 24*t*
cultural scenarios, 84–85
culture, as research domain, 19*t*
curriculum(a): appropriateness of, 55; career service centers and, 143; changes for contemporary workplace, 37; course development and, 46; current state of LSP, 38–39; as English for specific purposes, criteria for, 130–31; heritage-learner considerations with, 55–56; as lacking in business language courses, 38–39; LSP research and development of, 14; in Network of Business Language Educators, 41*t*; Spanish for health care, 44–47; Spanish for leadership, 41–44; standards and, 88; student-centered, 4; World Language and Business Leadership, 47–50

Department of Foreign Languages (DFF) (US Air Force Academy), 74–84, 80*t*, 81*f*, 83*f*
diplomacy, as research domain, 19*t*
discipline-specific language, in project-based learning, 109–11, 111*t*
Doyle, Mike, 9n5

EAP. *See* English for academic purposes (EAP)
engineering course, project-based learning in, 106–17, 107*f*, 111*t*–113*t*, 115*t*
English for academic purposes (EAP), 14
English for specific purposes (ESP), 2, 14, 32n1, 130–31
ESP. *See* English for specific purposes (ESP)
etiquette, 43
Executive Order 13166, 162
exhibit booths, in business language education, 41*t*
exotic languages, 159–60
extracurricular activities, 138

Five Cs of the National Standards for Foreign Language Education in the United States, 40, 88
formal aspects, 20, 21t

genre-specific features, 20t, 22t
globalization, 37, 169
goals, professional, of heritage learners, 59–60, 59t
Google, 175, 176
grammar, with heritage learners, 62t

health care: question/answer techniques in, 87–88; as research domain, 19t; Spanish for, 44–47
heritage learners (HLs): alienation of, 55; cultural skills with, 60–61; linguistic skills with, 60–61; literature review on, 56–57; mentorship with, 63–65; as pedagogical issue, 22t; in professional community internships, 55; professional goals of, 59–60, 59t; professionalism with, 63t; professional preparation with, 61–67, 62t, 63t; research methodology with, 57; service learning and, 55, 57; vocabulary in, 61, 62t
heritage learners (HLs):
hybrid language learning, 149

identity formation, in LSP interns, 22t
information literacy: globalization and, 169; Google and, 175, 176; importance of, 176; meanings of, 169; origin of concept, 170; personal learning environments and, 178–81, 179f, 180f; in Project Information Literacy, 171–72, 181, 182; social constructivism and, 170–71; social media and, 176–77; as social practice, 182; and Spanish-speaking classrooms, 177–81, 179f, 180f; and Spanish-speaking workplaces, 172–77, 173t, 174t;

stereotypes and, 182–83; workplace information environments and, 170–72
input/output processing paradigm, 91–92
interconnectedness, of economies, 37
intercultural competence: leadership and, 74–75; as pedagogical issue, 22t; US Air Force Academy and, 74–84, 80t, 81f, 83f
international development, as research domain, 19t
interns, identity formation in, 22t
internships, 55, 57, 59t, 60t
interpretation, as research domain, 19t
interview, in project-based learning, 121–23
interview questions, 183

job listings, 14–15
journalism, as research domain, 19t

K-12 initiatives, 40
KeyWords Extractor, 109

language, formal aspects of, 20, 21t
language production, 20–21
language selection, 20t, 21t
languages for specific purposes (LSP), 1–4; increase in interest in, 13; job listings in, 14–15; in secondary education, current state of, 38–39
law, as research domain, 19t
leadership: development, 74–75; intercultural competence and, 74–75; Spanish for, 41–44, 74; studies, 73–74; US Air Force Academy and, 74–84, 80t, 81f, 83f; in World Language and Business Leadership, 47–50
legal language, 157–66
letters of recommendation, 143
Lexical Frequency Profile, 109
LinkedIn, 175

Lionbridge certification, 159–60
LSP. *See* languages for specific purposes (LSP)

materials development, 23*t*
Maxwell, John C., 43
media, as research domain, 19*t*
medicine. *See* health care
mentorship, with heritage learners, 63–65
Miller, Richard, 187
MLA. *See* Modern Language Association (MLA)
Modern Language Association (MLA), 1, 9n7, 14
morphology, 20, 21*t*
mutual intelligibility, with exotic languages, 160

Nation, Paul, 110
needs analysis (NA), 104–6, 105*t*, 120–21
Network of Business Language Educators (NOBLE), 40, 50, 51
newsletter, in business language education, 41*t*

orthography, with heritage learners, 62*t*

PCI. *See* professional community internships (PCI)
personal learning environments (PLEs), 178–81, 179*f*, 180*f*
phonetics, 20, 21*t*
phonology, 20, 21*t*
Pinterest, 144–45
planning graphic, in project-based learning, 118
PLEs. *See* personal learning environments (PLEs)
pragmatics, 20*t*, 21*t*
processing paradigms, 92–97, 92*t*, 94*t*, 95*t*

professional community internships (PCI), 55, 57, 59*t*, 60*t*
professional goals, of heritage learners, 59–60, 59*t*
professionalism, with heritage learners, 63*t*
professional preparation, with heritage learners, 61–67, 62*t*, 63*t*
professional presentations, structure of, 20*t*, 21*t*
program assessment, 23*t*
programmatic issues, 22–23, 23*t*
project-based learning: assessment of, 116–17; collaboration in, 102, 108, 117–18; content-based instruction and, 101–2; discipline-specific language analysis in, 109–11, 111*t*; diverse needs in, 118–19; in engineering course, 106–17, 107*f*, 111*t*–113*t*, 115*t*; interview in, 121–23; L2 learning and, 102; needs analysis in, 104–6, 105*t*, 120–21; overview of, 101–4; planning graphic in, 118; preparation in, 108–14, 111*t*–113*t*; project diary in, 118; scaffolding in, 115–16; student support in, 114–16, 115*t*; success factors in, 103–4; target language use in, 106–7, 107*f*; task analysis in, 111–14, 112*t*–113*t*
project diary, in project-based learning, 118
Project Information Literacy, 171–72, 181, 182
pronouns, in verb charts, 93, 94*t*

Q'anjob'al, 162
question/answer techniques: in medicine, 87–88; verb forms in, 88–89

registers, 20*t*
research: areas with student benefits, 25, 28–29; domain areas, 18, 18*t*, 28;

obstacles, 26–27, 29–30; preparedness, 25; production, areas affecting, 25–27, 29; research on, 16–27, 19t–24t; topics for focus of, 18–24, 20t–24t
restricted language, 129–30
Richardson, Will, 149

scaffolding, in project-based learning, 115–16
Scholarship and Teaching on Languages for Specific Purposes, 2, 14
screencasts, 148–52
secondary education: current state of LSP curricula in, 38–39; K-12 initiatives in, 40; three models in, 40–41, 41t
selection, language, 20t, 21t
semantics, 20, 21t
service learning (SL): heritage learners and, 55, 57; as research domain, 19t, 23t
social constructivism, 170–71
social media: in business language education, 41t; career counseling and, 145; information literacy and, 176–77
social networks, 22t
social work, as research domain, 19t
SPAN 3010, 177–78
Spanish: for business, 38–39; for health care, 44–47; for leadership, 41–44, 74
Spanish-speaking classrooms, 177–81, 179f, 180f
Spanish-speaking workplaces, 172–77, 173t, 174t
Standards for Foreign Language Learning, 103
state foreign language conferences, 39
stereotypes, 182–83
synergogy, 89
syntax, 20, 21t

target language use (TLU), 106–7, 107f
task analysis, in project-based learning, 111–14, 112t–113t
Thunderbird School of Global Management, 2
TLU. *See* target language use (TLU)
Tojol-ab'al, 157–58, 160–61, 162–63
tourism, as research domain, 19t
translation, as research domain, 19t
21 Indispensable Qualities in a Leader (Maxwell), 43

United Kingdom, 2
US Air Force Academy, 74–84, 80t, 81f, 83f

verb chart, 89–90, 92–97, 92t, 94t, 95t
verb forms, in question/answer techniques, 88–89
verb paradigms, 89–91
vocabulary, 20, 21t, 61, 62t

webinars, in business language education, 41t
Web Vocabprofile, 109–10
Wikipedia, 175
workplace information environments, 170–72
workshops, in business language education, 41t
World Language and Business Leadership, 47–50

YouTube, 145

www.ingramcontent.com/pod-product-compliance
Lightning Source LLC
Chambersburg PA
CBHW052100300426
44117CB00013B/2212